Time & Necessity

STUDIES IN
ARISTOTLE'S THEORY OF MODALITY

═══

JAAKKO HINTIKKA

OXFORD
AT THE CLARENDON PRESS

Oxford University Press, Ely House, London W. 1

GLASGOW NEW YORK TORONTO MELBOURNE WELLINGTON
CAPE TOWN IBADAN NAIROBI DAR ES SALAAM LUSAKA ADDIS ABABA
DELHI BOMBAY CALCUTTA MADRAS KARACHI LAHORE DACCA
KUALA LUMPUR SINGAPORE HONG KONG TOKYO

ISBN 0 19 824365 0

First published 1973
Reprinted 1975

Printed in Great Britain by litho by The Anchor Press Ltd
and bound by Wm Brendon & Son Ltd
both of Tiptree, Essex

PREFACE

MOST of the chapters of this book have appeared earlier as separate papers over the years. The earliest material included here was first published in 1957. These papers are reprinted together because they deal with closely related subjects and because the arguments presented in them seem to illuminate and reinforce each other. In order to bring this out, I have added a number of new cross-references.

The main subjects discussed here are, first, Aristotle's theory of modal notions (necessity and possibility), and, secondly, those Aristotelian doctrines and assumptions that we must understand in order to appreciate his ways with modal notions. This second class of topics includes Aristotle's implicit no less than his explicit assumptions concerning ambiguity, time, and infinity. These subjects are accordingly dealt with in their respective chapters below. Discussing them will sometimes lead us further afield than is strictly necessary for the purpose of making sense of Aristotle's theory of modality. The intrinsic interest of the subjects under scrutiny nevertheless seems to justify these excursions.

Although the different chapters appearing below seem to go together very well, I am fully aware that they do not come close to exhausting the over-all subject of this book. There are in fact several well-defined special topics falling under my general theme that are not taken up here. For instance, only selected aspects of Aristotle's modal syllogistic are discussed. Nor is Aristotle's own discussion of time in the *Physics* analysed in any detail. Likewise Aristotle's highly interesting distinctions between different levels of potentiality or possibility are not dealt with here.

More importantly, there are central aspects of the entire structure of Aristotle's modal notions that remain to be brought into the open and discussed systematically. For instance, the influence of what I have called Aristotle's conceptual teleology— that is, the preferred role of such goal-directed notions as *telos* in his conceptual practice—is not discussed here, although it is conspicuous in much of what he says about necessity, chance, and change. I have made a stab at this group of problems in my earlier paper 'Päämäärä, sattuma ja välttämättömyys', *Ajatus*, 26 (1964), 61–81, but I do not feel ready to present my tentative conclusions to English-speaking scholars.

Most importantly, I am tantalized by the new ideas—I should like to think, insights—I have gained in the very process of putting together this book. It seems to me that what is established here gives us useful clues for understanding several further problems: how Aristotle's different discussions of modal notions and of the problems to which they give rise hang together; what his main difficulties were; what the different ways out are that he tried to take; and what connects this theory of modality in the narrow sense with such further topics as the important distinction between *kinesis* and *energeia* and his use of modal notions in his philosophical and scientific argumentation in certain crucial passages of the *Nicomachean Ethics*, the *Physics*, and the *Metaphysics*. Unfortunately, however, I cannot hope to do full justice to these new ideas in this book without waiting another fifteen years for it. For this reason, I have forgone the temptation to extend my discussion to them on this occasion. An interested reader may nevertheless want to pay special attention to Aristotle's difficulties in trying to disentangle himself from determinism, analysed below in Chapters VIII and IX. They already offer some indications as to what the 'dialectic' of Aristotle's modal notions was, it seems to me. Thus this book is, I hope, a stepping-stone to further studies rather than the last word on its subject.

Of its several chapters, Chapter I is a revised and expanded version of a paper which appeared under the same title in *Inquiry*, 2 (1959), 137–51. In its present form it also incorporates most of my note, 'Different Kinds of Equivocation in Aristotle', *Journal of the History of Philosophy*, 9 (1971), 368–72.

Chapter II is a retouched reprint of a paper with the same title which originally appeared in *Inquiry*, 3 (1960), 17–28, and which was subsequently reprinted (without changes) in *Aristotle: Modern Studies in Philosophy*, ed. by Julius M. E. Moravcsik (Doubleday Anchor Books, Garden City, N.Y., 1967), pp. 34–50.

Chapter III first appeared in *Acta Philosophica Fennica*, 14 (1962), 5–22. It has been revised and expanded for republication.

Chapter IV was published under the title 'Time, Truth, and Knowledge in Ancient Greek Philosophy' in the *American Philosophical Quarterly*, 4 (1967), 1–14. In addition to small changes, a new section and a half have been added to it here.

Chapter V covers much of the same ground as my first paper on Aristotle, 'Necessity, Universality, and Time in Aristotle', *Ajatus*, 20 (1957), 65–90. It has been so thoroughly rewritten, however, that only a few lines of the original paper survive. The new version also incorporates most of my short paper, 'A. O. Lovejoy on Plenitude in Aristotle', *Ajatus*, 29 (1967), 5–11. The original paper has in the meanwhile been reprinted as Bobbs-Merrill Reprints in Philosophy, no. 106.

Chapter VI originally appeared in the *Philosophical Review*, 75 (1966), 197–212. It is reprinted here virtually intact.

Chapter VII is a greatly expanded version of my note, 'An Aristotelian Dilemma', *Ajatus*, 22 (1959), 87–92.

Chapter VIII first appeared in the *Philosophical Review*, 73 (1964), 461–92. I have corrected a few small mistakes and added some supplementary material. A German translation of the original paper is scheduled for publication in *Logik und Erkenntnistheorie des Aristoteles*, ed. by Fritz-Peter Hager (Wissenschaftliche Buchgesellschaft, Darmstadt).

Chapter IX first appeared in the *American Philosophical Quarterly*, 1 (1964), 101–14. I have tried to clarify the argument of this paper by adding new material. I have also added a discussion of Aristotle's own argument for the conclusion of the 'Master Argument'.

To the Editors of the *American Philosophical Quarterly*, the *Philosophical Review*, and the *Journal of the History of Philosophy*, I am grateful for permission to reprint the papers mentioned above that first appeared in these journals. I am indebted also to the publishers, Universitetsforlaget, Oslo, for permission to reproduce material from *Inquiry*, and Societas Philosophica Fennica for permission to reprint the papers from *Acta Philosophica Fennica* and *Ajatus*.

I shall follow the usual conventions in discussing Aristotle and in referring to his works (by the page, column, and line of the Bekker edition). In translations from Aristotle, I have used Clarendon Aristotle Series translations, whenever available, and otherwise preferred the Oxford translation (*The Works of Aristotle*, translated under the editorship of Sir David Ross, Clarendon Press, Oxford). However, occasionally Loeb Classical Library (W. Heinemann Ltd. and Harvard University Press) translations are used instead, and frequently small changes are made without explicit notice. Whenever other translations are used, the translator is mentioned.

In a volume of this sort, intellectual debts are likely to be more numerous and varied than one can acknowledge in a preface. I must in any case say that I have learned a great deal from G. E. L. Owen and Julius M. E. Moravcsik, although both of them will quickly disown many of my conclusions. On the somewhat more mundane—although perhaps no less important— level of actual editing, I am very happy to have enjoyed the help of Mr. Unto Remes and Mr. Simo Knuuttila, extending far beyond the call of duty. This help was made possible by the Academy of Finland through *Valtion humanistinen toimikunta*. I am also indebted to the same body for most of my other research opportunities since 1970. Last but not least, I am indebted to the Clarendon Press both for accepting this volume for publication and for waiting patiently for its completion.

JAAKKO HINTIKKA

April 1972

CONTENTS

I. Aristotle and the Ambiguity of Ambiguity   1

II. Aristotle's Different Possibilities   27

III. On the Interpretation of *De Interpretatione* 12–13   41

IV. Time, Truth, and Knowledge in Aristotle and Other Greek Philosophers   62

V. Aristotle on the Realization of Possibilities in Time   93

VI. Aristotelian Infinity   114

VII. On Aristotle's Modal Syllogistic   135

VIII. The Once and Future Sea Fight: Aristotle's Discussion of Future Contingents in *De Interpretatione* 9   147

IX. Aristotle and the 'Master Argument' of Diodorus   179

Index of Texts   215

General Index   221

I

ARISTOTLE AND THE AMBIGUITY
OF AMBIGUITY

1. *General remarks on Aristotle's terminology*

IT would not be a simple enterprise—and probably not a very profitable one, either—to try to classify philosophers as being easy or difficult to understand. There is more than one way of making one's point clear, and there is likewise more than one reason why a philosopher's works may be difficult to understand. A philosopher may have a beautifully supple style and yet give rise to considerable difficulties of interpretation. David Hume is probably the best example of this. In spite of lucidity and persuasiveness in almost every individual passage of his works, it is often very difficult to see exactly what he is assuming in his reasoning, precisely what his words mean, and just how his several arguments are related to each other. Hume is very conscious of the demands of polished and clear style, but he is much less concerned with the consistency of his terminology or even with the consistency of his assumptions.

In all these respects, Aristotle is one of the most striking contrasts to Hume that one can find among major philosophers. Of course, one does not expect to find an elegant style in writings that are, as Aristotle's surviving works mostly are, sets of lecture notes or drafts for treatises rather than finished works of literature. But even so, understanding his writings is notoriously difficult. There are passages that have exercised scholars for centuries and are still extremely difficult to understand fully. The famous passage on the immortality of a certain part of the human soul in *De Anima* III 5. 430ª22 ff. will do as an example.

This does not mean, however, that Aristotle is not a rewarding thinker to study. In fact, the contrary seems to be the case. Aristotle's writings may be prima facie extremely difficult to understand, but if one can find clues to his meaning, one can often go quite far by their means. One reason is that Aristotle is normally sensitive to the precise sense of a word. He typically chooses his terms with an eye to the argument he is carrying on, and he usually keeps in mind what he has said earlier and what he will go on to say later. For this reason, one can often tell quite a lot about his meaning just by observing carefully the terms he uses and by comparing them with his words elsewhere. Thus a considerable part of what I am going to say concerning his doctrines in this work will be based on a detailed analysis of his actual formulations.

A word of warning is in order here, however. When I say that Aristotle was careful with his words I do not mean that his terminology is systematic or even consistent. Aristotle had some amount of technical terminology. For instance, in some cases he made distinctions between the meanings of terms that were apparently more or less interchangeable in the ordinary usage of his time. (The way he uses the notion of homonymy is, as we shall see later in this chapter, a good example of the way he sharpens the ordinary usage.) But he is not always consistent even in his more technical terminology. In general, he seems to rely more on the connotations of words as he found them than on the explicit introduction of technical terms.

When I said that Aristotle is sensitive to the sense of his words, I had in mind the fact that he usually seems to have some good prima-facie reason for choosing the way he expresses himself. And this reason is usually not a mere desire to be persuasive; still more seldom, if ever, is it a quest for elegance. Aristotle's ways with his terms are often firmly grounded in his logical insights and in his philosophical doctrines; and for this reason a thorough logical and philosophical analysis of the issues he is discussing may sometimes throw more light on the very meaning of his actual words than the most acute philological exegesis. To put the same point in a slightly different way, in any particular discussion of a specific problem Aristotle's terminology is likely to be tailored rather carefully to the problem and to the ideas by means of which he is trying to solve it. For this reason, it is important to observe his terminology and phraseology rather closely. For example, if in some particular discussion he makes use of several words with apparently similar meanings, we are well advised to look out for differences between their respective meanings. (We shall follow this strategy in our examination of *De Interpretatione* 12–13 in Chapter III.) Similarities of phraseology should be examined for possible cross-references to other parts of the same discussion or to other discussions of similar problems elsewhere. (Examples will be found, e.g. in Chapters II and VIII.) And there are still other ways in which an examination of Aristotle's actual wording can be useful for the understanding of his doctrines.

All this is not contradicted by the fact that Aristotle does not always carry over the distinctions he makes and the phraseology he adapts to his needs to the other parts of his works. He is far from having a consistent terminology. He is perfectly happy with a distinction as long as he needs it, but he may be equally happy to give it up as soon as he does not need it any longer. He may also express one and the same distinction in a different way in different works. (If I am right, the equivalence of the accidental homonymy which is mentioned in the *Nicomachean Ethics* with the plain homonymy of most of his other works, which I shall comment on later in this chapter, is a case in point.) It looks as if some of the later Aristotelians of antiquity had elevated this practice of Aristotle's to the status of a principle as against the Stoics who insisted on a uniform terminology.

Combined with Aristotle's conspicuous conciseness, this terminological informality creates problems for a reader of Aristotle. It is one of the presuppositions of the present study, however, that these problems are not always insoluble and that they are often extremely interesting.

2. *The role of ambiguity in Aristotle's arguments*

If it is useful in general to keep an eye on Aristotle's terminology, it is doubly useful in the case of those concepts that are among his most important tools. For reasons we cannot discuss here, a considerable part of Aristotle's philosophical activity consists of what we would find very difficult not to call conceptual analysis. Typically, he starts his discussion of a given problem by surveying the opinions that others have had on it. Among these 'others' there are both his predecessors and the ordinary people of his time. (G. E. L. Owen has shown very nicely that for Aristotle *endoxa* or generally held opinions were among the 'phenomena' that were to be 'saved', if they stood up to critical scrutiny.[1]) In addition to the opinions of others, Aristotle's data usually comprise some obvious truths concerning the subject-matter at hand and perhaps also some empirical observations concerning it. From these data Aristotle tries to extract the principles of his own view by means of comparison and criticism. Often the survey of the opinions of others and of the obvious truths gives rise to problems or *aporiai* which are of conceptual nature. Sometimes Aristotle tries to reconcile the different views. Sometimes he arrives at his own views by rejecting certain views and by accepting others.

It is interesting to observe that Aristotle's professed reliance on the views of others as sources of his own doctrines extends to cases where he is in reality proposing something quite new. It has given rise to the charge, which is not entirely unjustified, that he is projecting his own problems and sometimes even his own views on to his predecessors. The reason for this is not, I think, a desire to buttress his own opinions by reading them back into the works of others. The main reason for Aristotle's peculiar relation to his predecessors is rather his method of arriving, or at least trying to arrive, at his own views through the examination of the 'facts of the case' which included the opinions of others. In Chapter V below we shall have a glimpse of the assumptions on which this practice was based.

Whether Aristotle's arguments are designed to be constructive or destructive, they are typically logical and dialectical rather than factual. And the conceptual device that he most often uses in these arguments is to point out ambiguities or, more generally, to point out that certain words and phrases are used in more than one way. Such writings as *Metaphysics Δ* bear witness to his highly developed sensitivity to differences of meaning and of sense. Aristotle's criticisms of the Platonists frequently turn on allegations of ambiguities and his defence of his own science of 'being as being'—that is, metaphysics—likewise turns heavily on the distinction between different kinds of difference in meaning.

It may thus be expected that an examination of Aristotle's notion of ambiguity will be useful for all serious study of his

---

1 'Τιθέναι τὰ φαινόμενα', in Suzanne Mansion, ed., *Aristote et les problèmes de méthode. Communications présentées au Symposium Aristotelicum tenu à Louvain du 24 août au 1ᵉʳ septembre 1960* (Publications Universitaires, Louvain, 1961), pp. 83–103.

philosophy. Recent discussion seems to bear out this expectation. Two highly important contemporary studies of the development and structure of Aristotle's metaphysics, Owen's and Patzig's,[2] depend heavily for their conclusions on what the authors claim to have found concerning the variants of Aristotle's concept of ambiguity. The importance of these studies is measured by the fact that they both suggest important qualifications and even modifications to the magnificent portrait of the development of Aristotle's metaphysics that was painted several decades ago by Werner Jaeger.

The labours of Owen and Patzig notwithstanding, there seems to be room for further dissection of Aristotle's concept of ambiguity. We shall find such an analysis very useful indeed in our study of the variants of Aristotle's concept of possibility. Perhaps it is not too bold to suggest that a close reading of the text in this respect may also contribute something to the great discussion of Aristotle's development that Jaeger (and Thomas Case) started. In this book we shall set our sights lower, however, and concentrate to begin with on what we actually find in the text concerning ambiguity.

3. *Two types of ambiguity*

Let us start from an actual example of a passage in which Aristotle makes use of the notion of ambiguity. A celebrated instance is his defence of the study of 'being as being' (i.e. metaphysics) in *Metaphysics* Γ 2.

There are many senses in which a thing may be said to 'be' (τὸ δὲ ὂν λέγεται μὲν πολλαχῶς), but all that 'is' is related to one central point (πρὸς ἕν), one definite kind of thing (μίαν τινὰ φύσιν), and is not said to be by a mere ambiguity (καὶ οὐχ ὁμωνύμως). Everything which is healthy is related to health, one thing in the sense that it preserves health, another in the sense that it produces it, another in the sense that it is a symptom of health, another because it is capable of it. . . . As, then, there is one science which deals with all healthy things, the same applies in other cases also. . . . It is clear then that

² G. E. L. Owen, 'Logic and Metaphysics in Some Earlier Works of Aristotle', in I. Düring and G. E. L. Owen, eds., *Aristotle and Plato in the Mid-Fourth Century* (Almqvist and Wiksell, Gothenburg, 1960), pp. 163–90; Günther Patzig, 'Theologie und Ontologie in der Metaphysik des Aristoteles', *Kant-Studien*, 52 (1961), 185–205.

it is the work of one science to study the things that are, *qua* being. (Sir David Ross in the Oxford translation of the works of Aristotle, *Met. Γ* 2. 1003ᵃ 33–ᵇ16)

These passages show that the Aristotelian notion of ambiguity is not as unambiguous as one perhaps hopes. We see Aristotle distinguishing two different kinds of multiplicity of meaning: on one hand what I shall call the *multiplicity of applications* (expressed by λέγεται πολλαχῶς) and on the other hand what Sir David calls mere ambiguity but what I shall call *homonymy*. The latter term is chosen because it is already used by Aristotle. My usage will violate the current distinction between homonymy and ambiguity, according to which 'homonyms are formally indistinguishable present descendants of dissimilar older forms, while an ambiguous word is single in origin and multiple only in usage'. However, the violation is smaller than first appears. As observed by W. V. Quine (to whom the last quotation is due), the only thing that distinguishes ambiguity and homonymy (in the customary sense of the word) is etymology, which we may here simply disregard.

In view of the importance of the notion of ambiguity for Aristotle's thought, it is worth while examining the varieties of this notion in some detail. I shall try to show that Aristotle normally distinguishes homonymous applications of a word from multiple ones and that he uses such terms as τὰ ὁμώνυμα and τὰ πολλαχῶς λεγόμενα for this purpose. I shall also argue that a number of other idioms are used by Aristotle to express multiplicity of applications as distinguished from homonymy. Furthermore, I shall offer a few comments on the nature of the distinction. In the following chapter the results of this study will be used to analyse the varieties of the Stagirite's notion of possibility.

4. *Multiplicity of applications wider than homonymy*

There are many passages that show explicitly that for Aristotle multiplicity of applications is a broader notion than homonymy. The following passages are cases in point:

We have pointed out elsewhere that 'potency' and the word 'can' have several senses (λέγεται πολλαχῶς). Of these we may neglect all the potencies that are so called by homonymy. (*Met. Θ* 1. 1046ᵃ4–7)

Since the science of the philosopher treats of being *qua* being universally and not in respect of a part of it, and being has many senses and is not used in one only (τὸ δ' ὂν πολλαχῶς καὶ οὐ καθ' ἕνα λέγεται τρόπον), it follows that if the word is used homonymously and in virtue of nothing in common to its various uses, being does not fall under one science (for the meanings of a homonymous term do not form one genus); but if the word is used in virtue of something in common (εἰ δὲ κατά τι κοινόν), being will fall under one science. The term seems to be used in the way we have mentioned, like 'medical' and 'healthy'. For each of these also we use in many senses (πολλαχῶς λέγομεν). (*Met.* K 3. 1060^b31 ff.)

Now every term which possesses a variety of meanings (λέγεται πολλαχῶς) includes those various meanings either owing to a mere coincidence of language (ὁμωνύμως), or owing to a real order of derivation in the different things to which it is applied. (*De Gen. et Corr.* I 6. 322^b29 ff.)

The following passage clearly also pertains to the same distinction, although the phrase πολλαχῶς λέγεται does not occur:

... essence will belong, just as 'what a thing is', primarily and in the simple sense to substance, and in a secondary way to the other categories also ... For it must be either by a homonymy that we say these *are*, or by adding to and taking away from the meaning of 'are' (in the way in which that which is not known may be said to be known), the truth being that we use the word neither homonymously nor in the same sense, but just as we apply the word 'medical' by virtue of a *reference* to one and the same thing (πρὸς τὸ αὐτὸ μὲν καὶ ἕν), not meaning one and the same thing, nor yet homonymously; for a patient and an operation and an instrument are called medical neither by homonymy nor with a single meaning (καθ' ἕν), but with reference to a common end (πρὸς ἕν). (*Met.* Z 4. 1030^a29 ff.)

5. *Homonymy equals accidental homonymy*

We shall have occasion to return to these passages later. Here I shall only note that in all of them τὰ πολλαχῶς λεγόμενα appears as a class wider than τὰ ὁμώνυμα. This is supported by many other passages. (Cf. sections 9–10 of the present chapter.) And there is not, to the best of my knowledge, a single good counter-instance in the Aristotelian corpus. A few passages may seem to suggest a different relation between τὰ ὁμώνυμα and τὰ πολλαχῶς λεγόμενα. But on closer examination they turn out to be compatible with what has been said here. A case in point is *Eth. Nic.* I 6. 1096^b26 ff.

where Aristotle refers to as accidental homonyms (τὰ ἀπὸ τύχης ὁμώνυμα) terms that he elsewhere calls homonyms *simpliciter*. Does this mean that Aristotle has two senses of homonymy, a wider and a narrower? Most likely it is only an indication of the origin of Aristotle's terminology. Literally, τὰ ὁμώνυμα are things that share the same name; and this seems to have been a widespread usage in antiquity. Used in this way, the term does not say anything about whether or not the things share anything more than the name. In fact, τὰ ὁμώνυμα was generally used as a synonym for τὰ συνώνυμα; and Aristotle himself occasionally uses the two words interchangeably.[3]

In his more technical terminology, however, Aristotle distinguished between homonyms and synonyms. Both a pair of homonyms and a pair of synonyms share a term (ὄνομα). However, homonyms share it completely as a matter of chance; they share it but do not share anything else. In short, by τὰ ὁμώνυμα Aristotle *meant* τὰ ἀπὸ τύχης ὁμώνυμα, This explains why the latter expression is used for the former in *Eth. Nic.* I 6. 1096ᵇ26. It also explains another passage in which Aristotle refers to as 'total homonymy' what obviously is his usual notion of homonymy.[4]

6. *An explanation of Aristotle's choice of terms*

A comparison between the literal meanings of the terms ὁμώνυμος and πολλαχῶς λέγεται shows why it is idiomatically natural that the former should express a stronger notion than the latter. ῾Ομωνυμία suggests to Aristotle that two things share a name, an ὄνομα, and nothing else, that the name has a totally different meaning in the two applications. In contrast, πολλαχῶς λέγεται ordinarily means 'said in many ways'.[5] This makes the term very

---

[3] Homonymy in the sense of sharing a term: *De Gen. et Corr.* I 10. 328ᵇ21; *Met. A* 9. 990ᵇ6; *Met. Z* 9. 1034ᵃ22–3, ᵇ1; *Met. M* 4. 1079ᵃ2 and *Met. M* 10. 1086ᵇ27. (*Phys.* VII 3. 245ᵇ16, *De Part. An.* I 3. 643ᵇ7 and II 2. 647ᵇ18 may also be cases in point.)

[4] See *Eth. Eud.* VII 2. 1236ᵃ17 and ᵇ25. The synonymy of 'accidental homonymy' and plain 'homonymy' in Aristotle had already been pointed out by Alexander; see *In Aristotelis Metaphysica Commentaria*, ed. M. Hayduck (Berlin, 1891), p. 241, line 26.

[5] Since most of the distinctions in *Met. Δ* are formulated by Aristotle in terms of πολλαχῶς λέγεται rather than in terms of homonymy, a reader should be extremely cautious and not assume without other evidence that his distinctions amount to pointing out genuine ambiguities.

apt to express any diversity of applications, whether it be due to a real difference in meaning, to different relations to one and the same basic meaning, or just to a difference in context.

7. *Homonymy* v. *synonymy*

Aristotle explains his sense of homonymy (together with that of the contrary notion of synonymy) in the beginning of the *Categories*. According to these explanations, two things are synonymous if both the same name (i.e. term) and the same definition (λόγος) are applicable to them. They are homonymous if they share only the name, the definitions (λόγοι) being different in the two cases. (In these definitions, λόγος should perhaps be understood as an explanatory phrase or an account of the meaning of the name rather than as a definition.) I have already pointed out that Aristotle sometimes violates his own definition of homonymy. Similarly, he violates the definition of synonymy at least once by calling a pair of objects synonyms although, according to his own considered judgement, they share only the name but not the definition.[6]

These violations are little more than occasional reversions to looser usage. But in another respect Aristotle violates the definitions of homonymy and synonymy given in *Categories* 1 almost systematically. In so far as the definitions are concerned, only *things* can be called homonymous or synonymous, not *words*. And two things can be called synonymous only if the *same* term is applied to them. Both these limitations are transgressed by Aristotle. A word is said to be homonymous in *De Gen. et Corr.* I 6. 322ᵇ29 ff.;[7] and similar uses of the notion of synonymy are found in *Top.* VIII 13. 162ᵇ37, *Soph. El.* 5. 167ᵃ24 and in *Rhet.* III 2. 1404ᵇ37–1405ᵃ2. In many other passages, too, Aristotle is obviously interested exclusively in the word and not in the things to which it is applied. In fact, he sometimes seems to express synonymy and homonymy by such phrases as ἓν σημαίνειν and πολλὰ σημαίνειν (or πλείω σημαίνειν), respectively. In the sequel, we shall take the same liberty as Aristotle and talk about synonymy (homonymy) in connection both with certain terms and with the entities to which they are applied.

---

[6] See *Met. A* 6. 987ᵇ10; cf. 9. 990ᵇ6, 991ᵃ6, and *Met. I* 10. 1059ᵃ13.
[7] Cf. also *Top.* V 2. 129ᵇ30 ff.

8. *Homonymy v. synonymy not really a dichotomy*

Observing that the explanations given in *Categories* 1 are not entirely representative of Aristotle's usage helps us to dispose of a difficulty to which these explanations give rise. I am arguing that Aristotle has two notions of ambiguity, of which that expressed by πολλαχῶς λέγεται is wider than homonymy. From the explanations of *Categories* 1 it may nevertheless appear that there is no room for a notion wider than homonymy. Each pair of things that share a name either also share the definition or do not share it. Hence the distinction seems to constitute a dichotomy. However, Aristotle goes on to define a third notion, viz. that of paronymy. This notion has often been taken by commentators to be somehow intermediate between homonymy and synonymy.[8] But such an interpretation is not justified by the text of the *Categories* alone, for there paronymy appears as a notion incomparable with synonymy and homonymy: things are defined to be synonyms or homonyms in so far as they share the *same* name, whereas two things are paronyms when they are called by different names (terms) of which one is nevertheless derived (grammatically) from the other. However, this objection to conceiving of paronyms as an intermediate class can be discounted by observing that Aristotle himself frequently uses his notion of synonymy in connection with two *different* terms which share a definition (i.e. terms that are synonymous in the customary modern sense of the word).[9] It is perhaps significant that Aristotle does not often contrast the terms 'homonymous' and 'synonymous'. Most of these contrasts occur in the *Topics* and even in the *Topics* synonymy is contrasted not only to homonymy but also to paronymy.[10]

9. *Partial and complete discrepancy of definitions*

The passages quoted in section 2 suggest a division that is more sophisticated than the explanations given in *Categories* 1 and more representative of what Aristotle actually does. Broadly speaking,

---

[8] See, e.g., Simplicius, *In Aristotelis Categorias Commentarium*, ed. by C. Kalbfleisch (Berlin, 1907), p. 37, lines 3–4: 'Paronyms are somehow between homonyms and synonyms, sharing in both and being deficient of both.'

[9] Cases in point are found in *Top.* VIII 13. 162b37, *Soph. El.* 5. 167a24, *Met.* Γ 4. 1006b18 and *Rhet.* III 2. 1405a1 ff.   [10] *Top.* II 2. 109b4–6.

the view that emerges from the quotations seems to be this : the distinction between homonymy (complete difference of definitions) and synonymy (identity of definitions) is not a dichotomy because definitions may be partially identical, partially different. Those applications of a term in which the λόγοι are (completely) identical are synonymous (the expressions καθ' ἕν and ἓν σημαίνειν are also sometimes used by Aristotle) ; in those applications where the definitions are partly (or totally) different the term is 'said in many ways', πολλαχῶς λέγεται. On different occasions Aristotle gives different accounts of the members of this intermediate class between synonyms and homonyms. Sometimes they are said to have definitions that are different but still related to one central point (sc. to be πρὸς ἓν λεγόμενα; cf. the quotation given in section 3) ; sometimes their definitions are said to be derivable from each other by adding to and taking away.[11] In *Eth. Nic.* I 6. 1096ᵇ26 ff. the different non-homonymous senses of the term 'good' are said to be connected either by all being derivable from one kind of good (i.e. being ἀφ' ἑνός) or by all contributing to one kind of good or else by analogy. Sometimes the intermediate cases are simply said to have something in common. We also have paronymous terms which are derived from each other by some grammatical process. Obviously, then, there are several kinds of intermediate cases between synonymy and homonymy, not all of which are listed by Aristotle in any particular passage. It does not seem possible to give a general description that would cover all of them.

10. *Instances of* τὰ πολλαχῶς λεγόμενα

We can find many examples to illustrate these points and to confirm my claim that τὰ πολλαχῶς λεγόμενα really include all the intermediate cases. In *Met. Γ* 2. 1004ᵃ22 ff. Aristotle is discussing the different opposites of one (or same) :

. . . since there are many senses (πολλαχῶς . . . λέγεται) in which a thing may be said to be one, these terms also will have many senses, but yet it belongs to one science to know them all; for a term belongs to different sciences not if it has different senses (πολλαχῶς), but if it has different senses [sc. is not καθ' ἕν], *and* its definitions (λόγοι) cannot be referred to one central meaning [sc. are not πρὸς ἕν].

[11] *Met. Z* 4. 1030ᵃ29, quoted in section 4.

This criterion for all the different applications of a term to fall within one and the same science which is employed here is the one used by Aristotle in *Met. K* 3. 1060ᵇ31 ff. (quoted above in section 4). Again: '. . . all that is is said to "be" in virtue of something single and common, though the term has many meanings (πολλαχῶς λεγόμενον) . . .' (*Met. K* 3. 1061ᵇ11–12).

The discussion in *Met. Γ* 4 is also relevant here. There are plenty of passages where πολλαχῶς λεγόμενα or one of its cognates is used to indicate a multiplicity of applications different from homonymy; in them the different applications of the expression in question can be distinguished from each other by introducing a further qualification, or can be derived in some other way from one and the same basic use.[12] We may also note that the contradictory of πολλαχῶς is sometimes expressed by Aristotle as ἁπλῶς[13] —a word which almost by definition (*Top.* II 11. 115ᵇ29 ff.) indicates the absence of qualifications. In *Met. Γ* 2 (cf. section 3 above) the uses of 'being' and 'one' in the different categories are said to refer all to the same starting-point, thus showing that the different applications are not homonymous. For this reason, the following instances of πολλαχῶς or πολλαχῶς λέγεται stop short of homonymy: *Phys.* I 2. 185ᵃ21 and ᵇ6; *Met. A* 9. 992ᵇ19; *Met. Z* 1. 1028ᵃ10; *Met. N* 2. 1089ᵃ7 and 16.

The obvious parity of πολλαχῶς λέγεται with such expressions as πλεοναχῶς λέγεται (and the interrogative ποσαχῶς λέγεται) suggests that the latter ones are applicable in the same situations as the first one. Aristotle's usage shows that this expectation is justified. I have not found a trace of difference between the cases in which the three terms are applied, and often they are used obviously interchangeably.[14]

A special comment should perhaps be made on a puzzling passage in *Met. E* 2: 'But since what is, when spoken of *haplōs*, has a multiplicity of uses (λέγεται πολλαχῶς) . . .' (1026ᵃ33–4; Aristotle goes on to list the same senses of being he mentions in *Met. Δ* 7). The combination of ἁπλῶς λέγεται and πολλαχῶς λέγεται comes close to being a contradiction in terms here.

[12] *Phys.* I 7. 190ᵃ31; *Phys.* V 4. 227ᵇ3; *De Part. An.* II 2. 648ᵃ36, 649ᵇ6; *Met. Γ* 2. 1005ᵃ7; *Met. Δ* 11. 1019ᵃ5; *Met. Z* 1. 1028ᵃ31; *Eth. Nic.* V 9. 1136ᵇ29.

[13] E.g. *Phys.* I 3. 186ᵃ24; cf. *De Part. An.* II 2. 648ᵇ11.

[14] In op. cit., pp. 220–1 Simplicius also ascribes to Aristotle the view that πλεοναχῶς λέγεται applies to intermediate cases of ἀφ' ἑνός and πρὸς ἕν rather than to cases of homonymy and synonymy.

It is perhaps not very difficult to see what Aristotle has in mind, however. In *Met. E* 1. 1025ᵇ10 he has contrasted the various departmental sciences with a science that would study what is ἁπλῶς or ᾗ ὄν. The use of ἁπλῶς at 1026ᵃ33 likewise seems to indicate that Aristotle is distinguishing the whole class of 'things that are' that he is studying from the fields of the various departmental sciences. Hence in the passage at hand ἁπλῶς λέγεται rules out the uses of 'is' peculiar to the different specialized sciences, while πολλαχῶς λέγεται refers to the different uses of 'is' in the different categories. Hence everything is in order here from my point of view. (It will also be seen that this explanation squares with my observation below in section 12 that πολλαχῶς λέγεται and ἁπλῶς λέγεται sometimes merely refer to a division and to the lack of one, respectively, within the field of application of a term.)

11. *A further difficulty*

This does not yet remove all our difficulties. The explanation of homonymy in terms of the λόγος does not always work. Often Aristotle indicates that the *logos*, the explanatory phrase used to express a thing's essence, may itself be ambiguous.[15] The definitions given in *Categories* 1 therefore do not take us very far. Now it might be suggested that for Aristotle every term had exactly one proper definition, and that the notion of homonymy is to be defined with respect to this unique definition proper rather than to any arbitrary accounts people may give of its meaning. This may very well be so. However, the explanations Aristotle gives as to how correct definitions are to be found do not help us here very much. Apparently they did not always help Aristotle himself very much, either. For instance, he is not consistent in classifying analogical and metaphorical uses of a word. In *Top.* VI 2. 140ᵃ6–8 metaphorical expressions are distinguished from the homonymous ones, whereas in *Met.* Θ 1. 1046ᵃ6 certain metaphorical uses of a term turn out to be homonymous (by comparing this passage with *Met.* Δ 12. 1019ᵇ33). In *Eth. Nic.* I 6. 1096ᵇ26 ff. analogically connected things appear (as we have seen) as a subclass of τὰ πολλαχῶς λεγόμενα rather than of τὰ ὁμώνυμα. In *Met.* Θ 6. 1048ᵃ35 ff. it is said that actuality and

¹⁵ See, e.g., *Top.* I 15. 107ᵇ6 ff.; *Top.* V 2. 129ᵇ30–32; *Phys.* VII 4. 248ᵇ17.

potentiality are both analogical notions; and Aristotle never worries about them in the way he is always wary of homonymy. In contrast, it appears from *Phys.* VII 4. 249ª23–5 that analogical uses of a word may very well be homonymous.

The paramount fact is that some of Aristotle's favourite examples violate his own principles. It simply is not true that all the pairs of things he calls homonymous have literally nothing in common except the term. For instance, Aristotle says repeatedly that a dead hand and a living hand, a dead eye and a living eye, etc., are homonyms.[16] The reason why he says this is clear enough. He wants to define 'hand' or 'eye' in terms of the function of the organ in question. For this reason, the definition does not apply to a dead hand or a dead eye. But from this it does not follow that the definition of a dead hand or eye will have nothing in common with that of a living organ. It is difficult to see how it could avoid having part of the definition in common; a dead hand presumably has to be defined by reference to the living hand it used to be.

Similarly, in *Met. A* 9. 991ª5–8, Aristotle seems to imply that a particular man and a statue (clearly one representing a man) can only be called 'men' by homonymy. Now it seems impossible to define a statue of a man without using the term 'man' or its definition in the process. Hence there ought to be something in common with the two applications of 'man'; and hence they ought to be classified as an instance of τὰ πολλαχῶς λεγόμενα rather than as an instance of τὰ ὁμώνυμα according to the latter of Aristotle's explanations.

The similarity of this example with Aristotle's own paradigm of homonymy (*Cat.* 1ª2; ζῷον applied to a man and to a picture) suggests that even the latter should be classified among τὰ πολλαχῶς λεγόμενα if we were following Aristotle's instruction literally. It is possible, of course, that the Stagirite is playing here with the well-known ambiguity of the Greek word ζῷον. But this strikes me as far too simple-minded a point to be made by Aristotle, who had already in the Περὶ ἰδεῶν presented a highly sophisticated argument concerning essentially the same picture-paradigm situation.[17]

---

[16] *Meteor.* IV 12. 390ª13; *De An.* II 1. 412ᵇ22; *De Part. An.* I 1. 640ᵇ36; *De Gen. An.* I 19. 726ᵇ24; II 1. 734ᵇ25; II 1. 735ª8; *Met. Z* 10. 1035ᵇ25; *Pol.* I 1. 1253ª20–5.

[17] See *The Works of Aristotle, Translated under the Editorship of Sir David Ross* (Clarendon Press, Oxford, 1938–52), vol. 12 (Select Fragments), pp. 127–8.

It is also difficult to believe that Aristotle should not have recognized any connection between the different applications of ξένος discussed in *Rhet.* III 11. 1412ᵇ11 ff. One more instance of homonyms that certainly have something in common—if only by way of contrast—occurs in *Phys.* III 3. 202ᵃ27–8. The instance of homonymy ('unknown is known') that is given by Aristotle in the last quotation of section 4 is also likely to be of this nature (meaning—perhaps: 'unknown is known to be unknown'). Cf. also *Eth. Nic.* V 1. 1129ᵃ26 ff.; a comparison with 1130ᵃ32 ff. suggests that the 'homonyms' mentioned there are by no means unconnected.

12. *Terms with several meanings v. terms covering different cases*

We have to realize that the distinction between homonyms and terms that merely have different applications often amounts to something rather different from a distinction between complete and partial discrepancy of definitions. Sometimes it amounts to a difference between genuinely ambiguous terms on the one hand and on the other terms whose field of application falls into different parts for some non-logical reason. These non-logical reasons are illustrated by the fact that the applications of a term are apparently for Aristotle instances of τὰ πολλαχῶς λεγόμενα as soon as they fail to fall within 'one and the same species'. This is shown by *Eth. Eud.* VII 2. 1236ᵇ24 ff. where the contradictory of what is obviously πολλαχῶς λεγόμενον is referred to as falling under one species.[18] This point probably also underlies Aristotle's view that attributes that are found within more than one species are defective in that they cannot be part of the essence of anything: 'Now specifically distinct animals cannot present in their essence a common undifferentiated element, but any apparently common element must really be differentiated.' (*De Part. An.* I 3. 643ᵃ1 ff.)

Another way of putting essentially the same point is to say that Aristotle is likely to speak of homonyms when he is stressing what we would call a conceptual (logical) disparity of two applications of the same term, and of τὰ πολλαχῶς λεγόμενα when he is dealing with some other kind of disparity of applications. From this point of view, we can understand why Aristotle should call

---

[18] Cf. also *Eth. Eud.* VII 2. 1236ᵃ16 ff.

a dead hand and a living hand homonymous; he was calling attention to what for him was a *conceptual* (logical) difference between two kinds of application of the word hand. Conversely, it is now understood why Aristotle uses the phrase πολλαχῶς λέγεται or one of the subordinate locutions διχῶς λέγεται, τριχῶς λέγεται, etc., in many passages where he is not concerned with ambiguity of a term at all in the modern sense of the word. (Cf. section 6 above and for διχῶς also section 15 below.)

An especially clear-cut case in point is found in *An. Pr.* I 17. 37ᵃ16. Since the Stagirite is there in the midst of a logical discussion we may reasonably expect him to be rather careful with his terms. He says that the expression

(1) it is not possible that no *A* is *B*

is used in two ways (διχῶς λέγεται); it may mean either

(2) some *A* is necessarily *B*

or

(3) some *A* is necessarily not *B*.

Why is this so? From Aristotle's definition of possibility (rather, of contingency; see section 4 of the next chapter) it follows that the unnegated part of (1) or

(4) it is possible that no *A* is *B*

is really a conjunction of two propositions, viz.

(5) it is not necessary for any *A* to be *B*

and

(6) it is not impossible for any *A* to be *B*.

The negation of (4), i.e. (1), consists therefore of two parts in the sense of being a disjunction of two propositions. These propositions are, of course, the negations of (5) and (6). But these negations are nothing but (2) and (3) respectively. Hence Aristotle's point here is simply that (1) has two applications *in the sense of being the disjunction of the two propositions* (2) *and* (3), either of which can make (1) true. Obviously, there is no semblance of ambiguity here, in spite of Aristotle's use of the phrase διχῶς λέγεται. Rather, what we have here is an unambiguous expression which covers two different cases. Such an expression is comparable with a term whose field of application falls into two parts for some reason different from ambiguity.

Another instance in which διχῶς λέγεται does not refer to

ambiguity occurs in *De Int.* 10. 19^b20. Aristotle's point there is
that the copula 'is' may be used to form two kinds of affirmative
and negative propositions. As far as I can see, it is not so much
as suggested that any single sentence could have both kinds of
propositions as its meaning.

An objection suggests itself here. Many terms that we would
never call ambiguous cover more than one case in the sense of
having a non-continuous field of application. For instance, most
of our general terms apply to more than one individual. Is this
not a very poor reason for trying to assimilate them to ambiguous
terms? Whether the reason is poor or not, it is Aristotle's. It is, in
effect, one of the reasons he gives (in *Soph. El.* 1. 165ᵃ11 ff.) for
studying sophistical refutations. These are due to the fact,
Aristotle says, that words and phrases often stand for more than
one thing (πλείω σημαίνειν). And this is in turn inevitable,
according to Aristotle, because the number of words and phrases
is finite while that of things is infinite. His reason has therefore
nothing to do with the meanings of terms; it pertains solely to the
multiplicity of things to which the terms apply.

13. *A guess at the sources of the distinction*

In fact, Aristotle sometimes seems to assimilate terms whose field
extends over more than one species even to homonymous terms.
There is a passage[19] that suggests that for Aristotle the field of
application of a non-homonymous term must be continuous:
'Now some things have no extremities at all; and the extremities
of others differ specifically and are homonymous; how should,
e.g., the end of a line and the end of walking touch or come to be
one?' This passage also suggests that terms that admit difference
of species, i.e. terms whose field of application falls into specifically different parts, are homonymous. This suggestion is supported by *Phys.* VII 4. 249ᵃ3–8 and 21–5. The interpretation of
Phys. VII 4 is a very difficult matter; nevertheless I do not see
how passages like the following can be understood without the
assumption that Aristotle thinks that specific differences within
the field of application of a term make it homonymous:

So we have now to consider how motion is differentiated; and this
discussion serves to show that genus is not a unity but contains a

[19] *Phys.* V 4. 228ᵃ24 ff.

plurality latent in it and distinct from it, and that in the case of homonymous terms sometimes the different senses are far removed from one another while sometimes there is a certain likeness between them, and sometimes again they are nearly related either generically or analogically, with the result that they seem not to be homonymous though they really are.

My interpretation is supported by such passages as the following (I shall modify the Oxford translation slightly):

Evidently, then, there cannot be Forms such as some maintain, for then one man [sc. the sensible individual] would be perishable and another [sc. the ideal man] imperishable. Yet the Forms are said to be the same in species with the individuals and not merely to be homonymous with them; but things which differ in kind are farther apart than those which differ in species. (*Met.* I 10. 1059ª10 ff.)

Here we can perhaps have a glimpse at the sources of Aristotle's distinction between homonyms and terms that merely have different applications. Classifying terms that merely have different cases with genuinely ambiguous terms easily leads to difficulties. For instance, it is obvious that the different things that are good do not fall within any single species. Nevertheless, Aristotle held that they are all connected with each other. There seem to have been two incompatible tendencies influencing Aristotle's treatment of ambiguity. On one hand, he was suspicious of every division within the field of application of a term and tended to classify terms whose fields admitted a difference in species with homonymous terms. On the other hand, Aristotle seems to have considered homonyms—one is tempted to say, puns—as fairly typical instances of ambiguity. However, such words as 'being', 'one', 'good', etc., readily give rise to conflicts between these tendencies. Another source of trouble is the doctrine of categories. In his early writings Aristotle clearly thought of terms that are used in more than one category as homonymous.[20] One reason for doing so is clear; if terms whose applications fall within different species are for this reason homonymous, the same holds *a fortiori* for terms whose applications fall into different categories. Yet Aristotle later came to think of some such terms not as homonymous but merely as possessing a multiplicity of applications. He emphatically re-

[20] See, e.g., *Top.* I 15. 107ª3–12.

jected the idea that such terms are mere homonyms, as witnessed by the passages quoted above in sections 3 and 4 from *Met. Γ* 2 and *Met. Z* 4, respectively.

The intermediate class of non-homonymous τὰ πολλαχῶς λεγόμενα serves to cater for the difficult cases. It is to be expected that the terms that earlier were assimilated by Aristotle to homonyms merely because they covered different cases are now relegated to the terms 'said in many ways'. The passages quoted earlier in this section may therefore be taken to support my claim that in his most mature writings Aristotle classified terms with several cases as having different applications, i.e. as typical instances of τὰ πολλαχῶς λεγόμενα. It is probably not an accident that most of these passages are from works that are known to be early (*Physics* VII) or betray an early preoccupation (criticism of Plato in *Met. I* 10).

Gradually Aristotle seems to have attached more and more importance to the class of τὰ πολλαχῶς λεγόμενα, included more and more terms in it, and distinguished it more clearly from the homonyms. The primacy of substance over the other categories enabled Aristotle to connect the different uses of terms that are applied in several categories with each other; thus they, too, could be classified as τὰ πολλαχῶς λεγόμενα as distinguished from homonyms. Other types of systematically ambiguous terms followed suit.

14. *Homonymy in the* Topics

This view of the relation between τὰ πολλαχῶς λεγόμενα and τὰ ὁμώνυμα in Aristotle squares with the fact that the two are not distinguished as sharply from each other in the *Topics* and the *Sophistici Elenchi* as in some other writings of Aristotle's. For it is generally agreed that these works (of which the second seems to be merely the final chapter of the first) are among the earliest in the Aristotelian corpus. It must be pointed out, nevertheless, that even in these we find a distinction between homonymy and multiplicity of applications. In the *Sophistici Elenchi* ὁμωνυμία occurs as a particular type of ambiguity, viz. as the ambiguity of a term. It is distinguished from ἀμφιβολία, i.e. from the ambiguity of a phrase, as well as from other fallacies that turn on the misuse of language. In contrast, πολλαχῶς λέγεται is used as a wider

term which applies to all these fallacies.²¹ Also in *Soph. El.* 6.
168ᵃ25 homonymy is represented as one of the many types of
ambiguity that turn on double meaning (τὸ διττόν), while in *Soph.
El.* 19. 177ᵃ11–25 the terms διττόν and πολλαχῶς (διχῶς) λεγόμενον
are applied without perceptible difference.

In the *Topics* the distinction between homonymy and multiplicity of applications is more blurred. But even there we find an
unmistakable distinction. In *Top.* II 3. 110ᵇ16 ff. Aristotle discussed instances of τὰ πολλαχῶς λεγόμενα which are explicitly
said not to be cases of homonymy.

It may also be pointed out that in the *Topics* Aristotle perhaps
had a good reason for disregarding the distinction between the
different kinds of ambiguity. What he was interested in there was
the technique of actual argumentation. Now in a disputation it
may be quite as disastrous to fail to keep track of the different
applications of a term as to fail to distinguish the different
meanings of a homonymous term. This may have been one
reason why Aristotle was not happy with terms that cover several
different cases, and why he tended to treat them on a par with
homonymous terms. In other words, the reason why Aristotle
discussed the multiplicities of application of different words and
phrases is not likely to be that they possess several irreconcilable
meanings. Rather, he does it to gain as much clarity as possible
concerning the matter in hand:

The reason why the term you use, or the whole expression signifying
the property, should not bear more than one meaning is this, that an
expression bearing more than one meaning makes the object described
obscure . . . (*Top.* V 2. 129ᵇ35 ff.)

It is useful to have examined the number of meanings of a term . . . for
clearness' sake (for a man is more likely to know what it is he asserts,
if it has been made clear to him how many meanings it may have) . . .
(*Top.* I 18. 108ᵃ18 ff.)

It is characteristic of Aristotle that even when he realizes that
a term may have several applications without any logical harm
resulting therefrom, he still feels uncomfortable:

We must first distinguish the senses in which we use the words 'ungenerated' and 'generated', 'destructible' and 'indestructible'. These
have many meanings (πολλαχῶς . . . λεγόμενον), and though it may

---

²¹ See *Soph. El.* 7. 169ᵃ22 ff.

make no difference to the argument, yet some confusion of mind must result from treating as uniform in its use a word which has several distinct applications (πολλαχῶς). (*De Caelo* I 11. 280ᵇ1 ff.)

In the same vein, Aristotle says in *Soph. El.* 17. 176ᵃ4 ff. that one must not give a single answer to an ambiguous question even when the answer is the same no matter in what sense the question is taken. This may be contrasted with Aristotle's insistence in the *Prior Analytics* that one cannot ever obtain a false conclusion from true premisses. In the *Sophistici Elenchi* Aristotle is therefore requiring much more than what is necessary for the purpose of obtaining true conclusions.

Because Aristotle's purpose in the *Topics* thus tends to confuse the difference between homonymy and multiplicity of applications, one must try to avoid relying on this particular work of Aristotle's in elucidating the distinction. Similarly, the obviously early date of this work ought to make one wary about generalizing from what one finds there.

15. *Focal meaning, amphiboly, and paronymy*

This is not yet all that can be said here, however, and perhaps we should not emphasize too much the *ad hoc* purposes of the *Topics*, either. G. E. L. Owen has even expressed the view that in the *Topics* Aristotle was running together the notion of homonymy and the kind of multiplicity of uses he expresses by πολλαχῶς λέγεται, especially the important πρὸς ἕν ambiguity which Owen labels 'focal meaning'.[22] There are in fact a number of things to be said for this opinion, although really instructive evidence is hard to come by.

Some light is perhaps shed on the matter by one of the passages already mentioned. In *Top.* II 3. 110ᵇ16 ff. Aristotle mentions in so many words an equivocation which is a case of τὰ πολλαχῶς λεγόμενα but not of homonymy. Owen explains this apparent counter-example to his claim by saying that Aristotle is here dealing with the equivocation of a phrase and not a single word. This is likely to be correct, although Owen does not discuss in detail what really makes this case different from homonymy.

---

[22] See G. E. L. Owen, 'Aristotle on the Snares of Ontology', in R. Bambrough, ed., *New Essays on Plato and Aristotle* (Routledge and Kegan Paul, London, 1965), pp. 69–95.

(One may, e.g., ask whether the real reason for the difference is perhaps the fact that the expression in question is propositional rather than predicative, which makes it impossible to speak here of homonymous, i.e. equally named, objects, rather than the mere difference between simple and complex expressions.) However, this passage is in several respects extremely interesting. One striking thing about it is its similarity with the famous passage in *Met. Γ* 2 in which Aristotle argues that 'to be' is 'said in many ways', and yet is not homonymous and that everything that is can therefore be subjected to one science:

Topics	*Metaphysics*
Take, for instance, the statement the science of many things is one. (*Top.* II 3. 110ᵇ17, modified Loeb Library translation)	Not only in the case of things which have one common notion does the investigation belong to one science, but also in the case in which they are related to one common nature. (*Met. Γ* 2. 1003ᵇ12–14)
Here the things in question may be the end or means to an end (τοῦ τέλους καὶ τοῦ πρὸς τὸ τέλος): e.g. medicine is the science producing health and of diet. (*Top.* II 3. 110ᵇ38–111ᵃ2)	... there is one science which deals with all the healthy things, [and] the same applies in other cases also. [For] everything which is healthy is related to health, one thing in the sense that it preserves health, another in the sense that it produces it, another in the sense that it is a symptom of health, another because it is capable of it. (*Met. Γ* 2. 1003ᵇ11–13, 1003ᵃ34–ᵇ1)

No matter what we can say of Aristotle's terminology, it is obvious that what he is doing in *Met. Γ* 1–2 is to give a positive answer to a special case of the question he is discussing in *Top.* II 3 as an example of a non-homonymous phrase that is πολλαχῶς λεγόμενον. Moreover, in the part of the *Topics* passage that was quoted above Aristotle also gives in one of the senses of the question a positive answer to it.

One should not overlook, of course, that in *Met. Γ* 1–2 and in *Top.* II 3 Aristotle is dealing with the equivocation of entirely different expressions. In the former the possible ambiguity of the question whether the different 'beings' are subject to the same science is not raised, and in the latter the multiplicity of uses of 'being' is not considered. Nevertheless Aristotle's awareness of the widely different kinds of ways in which the science of different things can be one, which he exhibits in *Top*. II 3, may very well be indicative of the line of thought that later led him to the idea of a non-homonymous focal meaning of 'being' put forward in *Met. Γ* 1–2. In fact, the examples used in the two passages are similar: 'medical' occurs as an example of focal meaning in *Met. Γ* 1–2; 'medicine' is used as an example in *Top*. II 3. At least *sub specie aeternitatis* we can thus almost say that all Aristotle had to do in order to move from the view taken in the *Topics* passage to the view he takes in *Met. Γ* 1–2 is to appeal to a special case of 'the science of many things', viz. to the science of the many different things that can be said to be—the same stratagem he applies in the *Topics* to the question at large.

From this point of view, Aristotle's later device was not so much a 'sophisticated variant on the idea of homonymy' (as Owen claims) as a sophisticated variant on the idea of amphiboly or the equivocity of a complex phrase. In fact, it seems to me that the questions that Owen's article provokes concerning the relation of amphiboly to non-homonymous multiplicity of uses (of single words) in Aristotle are very important and perhaps occasion some additions to the remarks in sections 13–14 above on the development of Aristotle's views.

It is obvious that in a certain sense the idea of focal meaning presupposed the assimilation of the equivocity of single words to those of longer phrases. We may recall that the possibility of a non-homonymous multiplicity of uses is explained by Aristotle as turning on 'adding to and subtracting qualifications' (*Met. Z* 4. 1030ᵃ32–3). Now, one cannot subtract qualifications from a single word nor add to it and still keep it single. What Aristotle presumably has in mind is therefore the definition or explanatory formula that can be used to express the meaning of a term. It is true, admittedly, that there are things one can do to a single word along these lines: one can add different suffixes and prefixes to it in accordance with grammatical rules. This is in fact precisely what goes into Aristotle's notion of paronymy (*Cat*. 1. 1ᵃ12–15). The notion does not carry anyone very far, however, and hence the consideration of the explanatory *logoi* is necessary for Aristotle's idea of 'adding to and taking away' to be workable. It is probably no accident that several examples of the 'unused' materials for the idea of focal meaning that Owen finds in the

Topics have to do with the different grammatical forms of one and the same word, just as in the case of paronymy.

Thus the development of the idea of a focal meaning is apt to lead to an emphasis on longer explanatory formulas and their variants in connection with discussions of equivocity. Such non-homonymous multiplicities of uses as focal meaning are probably as much and more heirs to the idea of amphiboly as modifications of the idea of homonymy (or of the idea of paronymy). The device of focal meaning owes its genesis as much to the breakdown of the homonymy–amphiboly distinction as to the breakdown of the synonymy–homonymy dichotomy. Owen's own remarks and notes contain in fact evidence to show how easy it was for Aristotle to go from a word to its definition (or explanatory formula) and back: 'it makes no difference which one says' (p. 73; cf. Owen's note 2). Further evidence is also forthcoming. For instance, from *An. Pr.* I 35 it appears that what the syllogistic variables stand for in Aristotle is not always a single word, but might be a longer *logos*. This seems to be viewed by Aristotle as an unimportant accident of language.

There does not seem to be much of a difference between what one can say of a single word and what one can say of a complex phrase in the parts of the *Topics* we have been considering, either. In 110^{b}16 ff. Aristotle does not *say*, or in any other way emphasize, that he is dealing with the equivocity of a phrase as contrasted with that of a single word: he simply mentions a case of non-homonymous multiplicity of uses as an illustration of the *topoi* he is there discussing. In *Top.* I 15. 107^{b}6 ff. a *logos* is said to be homonymous, not amphibolous, as we might expect. Owen suggests that this is due to the fact that the ambiguity in question turns on that of the single word *symmetrōs*. There is not much evidence one way or the other, but even if Owen is right, the passage nevertheless illustrates the fact that the difference between homonymy and amphiboly was not very great for Aristotle.

The insignificance of the difference is also indicated by the fact that the word 'amphiboly' is often used by Aristotle for purposes other than the marking of the equivocity of a phrase. For instance, in *Poetics* 25. 1461^{a}26 amphiboly is attributed to a single word. The relative insignificance of the ideas of amphiboly and paronymy in Aristotle's mature writings perhaps also becomes natural in this way.

Thus Owen's remarks seem to me to add up to a point different from what he himself primarily emphasizes. What they bring out, it seems to me, is the role of the concept of amphiboly in the formation of Aristotle's idea of a non-homonymous multiplicity of uses.

16. *Further expressions for multiplicity of applications as distinguished from homonymy*

The only thing that remains is to ascertain that Aristotle uses certain other expressions in the same way as πολλαχῶς λέγεται. I am not interested here in the whole range of terms employed by Aristotle; I shall confine my remarks to those terms that will figure in the sequel.

In many passages where Aristotle uses διχῶς λέγεται, the different senses in question can be distinguished and sometimes are actually distinguished from each other by a further qualifying epithet. Thus, in *Phys.* I 8. 191ᵇ1 ff., the phrase 'a doctor does something' is said to have two uses (διχῶς λέγεται), apparently because a doctor may do something *qua* a doctor or *qua* something else. In *Phys.* VI 2. 233ᵃ24 it is said that a continuum can be infinite in two ways (διχῶς λέγεται), either with respect to division or with respect to extremities.[23] We may note that in many of these cases Aristotle goes on using one and the same term although he has pointed out that it is used in different ways. Similarly, a construction with διχῶς is often used by Aristotle when an attribute has two applications in that a thing may have this attribute either actually or potentially; see *De Anima* III 6. 430ᵇ7, *Met. Γ* 5. 1009ᵃ32, and *Eth. Nic.* VII 3. 1146ᵇ32. It is perfectly clear that such a duality of applications does not make the attribute itself ambiguous. In *Phys.* II 2. 194ᵃ12, nature is said to be twofold, applying both to form and to matter. But it is very soon seen that the two uses of φύσις are not unrelated; in 194ᵃ16 Aristotle speaks of two natures, and goes on to discuss whether the form or the matter of a thing is more properly its nature—something he could not do if nature were homonymous.

I am not saying that the meaning of διχῶς λέγεται has escaped

---

[23] Similar uses of διχῶς λέγεται or of the plain διχῶς are to be found in *An. Post.* I 2. 71ᵇ33; *Soph. El.* 18. 176ᵇ32; *De Gen. et Corr.* I 7. 324ᵃ26 ff.; *Met. Δ* 23. 1023ᵃ27; *Eth. Nic.* VII 11. 1152ᵇ27, *Pol.* I 6. 1255ᵃ4.

the translators. Although the usage is not uniform, the Oxford translators sometimes render διχῶς λέγεται without speaking of meaning or ambiguity at all.[24]

These examples show that διχῶς λέγεται is used by Aristotle in the same situations as πολλαχῶς λέγεται; i.e. that it was not confined to cases of homonymy. This appears to be the case also with the phrase κατὰ δύο τρόπους λέγεται, as is indeed suggested by its literal synonymy with διχῶς λέγεται. The phrase is used by Aristotle in *Met. Δ* 8. 1017ᵇ23 to distinguish two uses of substance. In *Met. H* 1. 1042ᵃ29 it turns out that their difference is that of actuality and potentiality; hence we have a case of multiplicity of applications rather than of homonymy. In *Met. Δ* 14. 1020ᵇ14, the phrase is used to distinguish two senses of quality, one of which is said to be more appropriate than the other. This comparability shows again that we are not dealing with homonymy. Further confirmation is found in the passage from *Met. K* 3. 1060ᵇ31 ff. which was quoted above in section 2. For if κατὰ δύο τρόπους λέγεται expresses duality of applications rather than homonymy, one is bound to expect that the phrase οὐ καθ᾽ ἕνα λέγεται τρόπον which occurs in the passage in question will be tantamount to πολλαχῶς λέγεται. This is obviously the case.

---

[24] Cases in point are *De Int.* 10. 19ᵇ21, *De Caelo* I 11. 280ᵇ13, *Met. Δ* 3. 1014ᵃ16–17; *Met. Z* 4. 1029ᵇ30.

II

ARISTOTLE'S DIFFERENT POSSIBILITIES

1. *The interrelations of modal notions in Aristotle*

THE results of my examination of the varieties of ambiguity in Aristotle (see Chapter I above), can be used to analyse his notion of possibility. This notion is closely connected with the other modal notions, notably with those of necessity and impossibility. Since these notions are somewhat more perspicuous than that of possibility, it is advisable to start from them.

Aristotle knew that the contradictory (negation) of 'it is necessary that *p*' is not 'it is necessary that not *p*' but rather 'it is not necessary that *p*' (*De Int.* 12. 22ª3 ff.). The last two phrases are not contradictories, either, for they can very well be true together (*De Int.* 13. 22ᵇ1 ff.), the latter being wider in application than the former. By parity of form, 'it is not necessary that not *p*' is wider in application than 'it is necessary that *p*'.

These relations are conveniently summed up in the following diagram (which is not used by the Stagirite):

(i)
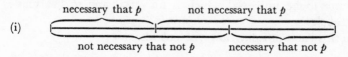

According to Aristotle, 'impossible' behaves like 'necessary' (*De Int.* 12. 22ª7 ff.). We can therefore illustrate it by means of a diagram similar to (i). In fact, the diagram will be virtually the same as the one for 'necessary', for 'the proposition "it is impossible" is equivalent, when used with a contrary subject, to the proposition "it is necessary" '. (See *De Int.* 13. 22ᵇ5.) In other words, 'impossible that *p*' is equivalent to 'necessary that not *p*', 'impossible that not *p*' equivalent to 'necessary that *p*', etc. We can therefore complete the diagram (i) as follows:

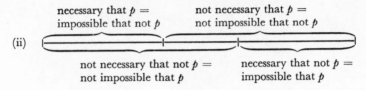

(ii)

2. *The two notions of possibility*

The problem is to fit the notion of possibility into the schema (ii). In this respect, Aristotle was led by two incompatible impulses. On the one hand, he was naturally tempted to say that 'possible' and 'impossible' are contradictories: something is possible if and only if it is not impossible. (See, e.g., *De Int.* 13. 22ª16–18, 32–8.) On this view, we get the following diagram:

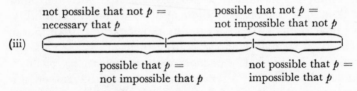

(iii)

But this temptation is not the only one. In ordinary discourse, saying that something is possible often serves to indicate that it is *not* necessary. Aristotle catches this implication. For him, 'if a thing may be, it may also not be' (*De Int.* 13. 22ᵇ20; see also 22ª14 ff.). Essentially the same point is elaborated in the *Topics* II 6. 112ᵇ1 ff. There Aristotle says that 'if a necessary event has been asserted to occur usually, clearly the speaker has denied an attribute to be universal which is universal and so has made a mistake'.

On this view, our diagram will look like this:

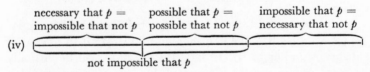

(iv)

It is seen that (iii) and (iv) differ in that in (iii) the range of possibility comprises everything that is necessary, while in (iv) possibility and necessity are incompatible.

It appears from the *De Interpretatione* that Aristotle did not immediately see that the assumptions underlying (iii) and (iv) are incompatible. Not surprisingly he ran into difficulties which he discusses in a not entirely clear way in *De Int.* 13. 22ᵇ11–23ᵃ7 (although I suspect that the confusion of the usual translations of this passage is not altogether Aristotle's fault). This passage will be commented on in the next chapter. Suffice it therefore to say here only that in the end Aristotle perceived clearly enough that the gist of the difficulty lies in the relation of possibility to necessity (*De Int.* 13. 22ᵇ29 ff.). He is led to distinguish two senses of 'possible' one of which satisfies (iii) and the other (iv). (*De Int.* 13. 23ᵃ7–27.) However, Aristotle does not make any terminological distinction between the two. In so far as the distinction is vital, I shall call the notion of possibility that satisfies (iii) 'possibility proper' and the notion that satisfies (iv) 'contingency'.

3. *Homonymy* v. *multiplicity of applications*

Now we can see why the distinction between a diversity of applications and homonymy is absolutely vital for this chapter. We have found a clear-cut case of homonymy: the notions of contingency and of possibility proper have different logical properties. They cannot be covered by a single term 'possibility' unless it is borne in mind that this word has different meanings on different occasions. Their relation is therefore one of homonymy (cf. section 12 of Chapter I above).

But in addition to this duality of 'contingency' and 'possibility proper' there is a different kind of distinction. One of these two logically different notions, viz. possibility proper, covers *two kinds of cases*. When one says that p is possible (in the sense of possibility proper), one sometimes could also say that p is contingent and sometimes that p is necessary. This does not mean, of course, that the term 'possible' is ambiguous; it merely means that its field of application falls into two parts. It was for Aristotle therefore a typical case of multiplicity of applications as distinguished from homonymy (cf. section 12 of Chapter I). The following diagram makes the situation clear:

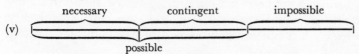

$$(v)$$

The distinction between the different applications of 'possibility proper' loomed large for Aristotle because he tended to

emphasize the distinction between necessity and contingency.
Thus Aristotle argues in *Met. I* 10 that the perishable and the
imperishable are different in kind (εἶδος and γένος). In Chapter
V below I shall argue that the distinction between contingency
and necessity is equivalent for Aristotle to that between what is
perishable and imperishable. The field of application of 'possibility proper' therefore falls into two parts which are different in
kind. We have already seen in sections 12 and 14 of Chapter I
that Aristotle viewed situations of this kind with suspicion,
although he grudgingly admitted that no logical harm need
result. This is probably one of the reasons why Aristotle in the
Prior Analytics preferred the notion of contingency to that of
possibility proper.

4. *Aristotle's definition of contingency*

According to the results of my examination of the ambiguities of
Aristotelian ambiguity, we may expect that the Stagirite usually
refers to the distinction between possibility proper and contingency by means of ὁμωνυμία and that he always refers to the
distinction between the different cases of possibility proper (i.e.
between necessity and contingency) by means of some other
locution, e.g. διχῶς λέγεται, κατὰ δύο τρόπους λέγεται, or πολλαχῶς
λέγεται. An examination of the text will bear out this expectation
as far as the first, the second, and the fourth expressions are concerned. Similarly, the third locution is, we shall find, used by
Aristotle in distinguishing two kinds of cases of contingency (see
section 6 below).

In Aristotle's discussion of the notion of possibility, the key
passage is in *An. Pr.* I 13. 32ᵃ18–21. It is referred to by Aristotle
repeatedly as the definition of possibility (e.g. *An. Pr.* I 14.
33ᵇ23; 15. 33ᵇ28; 15. 34ᵇ27; 17. 37ᵃ27–8).[1] The 'definition' is
clear enough (I shall not discuss here why Aristotle thinks of it as
a definition):[2] 'I use the terms "possibly" and "the possible" of
that which is not necessary but, being assumed, results in nothing
impossible.' This is clearly the notion I have called contingency.
However, it is not the only variant of possibility, for Aristotle

---

[1] In Chapter V (section 12) it will be suggested that this 'definition' looms
large in Aristotle's conceptual horizon also in *Met. Θ*.

[2] Some further remarks on this subject will be offered in Chapter IX, section 5.

continues: τὸ γὰρ ἀναγκαῖον ὁμωνύμως ἐνδέχεσθαι λέγομεν. That is, to say of the necessary that it is possible is to use the term 'possible' homonymously. This explanation obviously serves to motivate the qualification 'which is not necessary' in Aristotle's definition. The use of the word ὁμωνύμως shows that he knows that he is making a choice between two incompatible meanings of ἐνδέχεσθαι (to be possible). The second meaning, under which even necessary things are called possible, is the notion of possibility that satisfies (iii), which I have called possibility proper.

We have thus reached two important conclusions: (*a*) the main notion of possibility employed by Aristotle in the *Prior Analytics* is what I have called contingency; (*b*) Aristotle is aware of the existence of the other notion (possibility proper) which is different from contingency to the degree that the same term can be applied to them only homonymously.

These results are confirmed by other passages. A glance at (iv) shows that contingency is symmetrical with respect to negation: *p* is contingent if and only if not-*p* is also contingent. They are, therefore, convertible to each other. Aristotle makes the same observation and applies it to syllogistic premisses in *An. Pr.* I 13. 32ᵃ29 ff. This shows that his 'possibility as defined' agrees with my 'contingency'. Essentially the same point is made in *An. Pr.* I 17. 37ᵃ22 ff.

Aristotle's awareness of the ambiguity of possibility is also demonstrated by the development of his syllogistic. He frequently points out that the conclusion of a certain syllogism is valid only if one does not understand possibility in the sense defined (i.e. in the sense of contingency) but in a sense in which it is the contradictory of impossibility (e.g. *An. Pr.* I 15. 33ᵇ30–3; 34ᵇ27–32; 16. 35ᵇ32–4; 17. 36ᵇ33–4; 20. 39ᵃ11–13).

5. *An analysis of* An. Pr. *I 13. 32ᵃ21–9*

The fact that Aristotle was aware of the different logical properties of contingency as distinguished from possibility proper seems to me to be in agreement with what he writes immediately after the passages I have quoted (*An. Pr.* I 13. 32ᵃ21–9). This passage has been censured by the recent commentators in spite of the fact that it occurs in all the manuscripts as well as in the translation of the Syrian Georgius and is recognized by Alexander and by

Philoponus (Sir David Ross, *Aristotle's Prior and Posterior Analytics* (Clarendon Press, Oxford, 1949), p. 327, and Sir David Ross and L. Minio-Paluello, *Aristotelis Analytica Priora et Posteriora* (Clarendon Press, Oxford), 1964, ad loc.). However, it seems to me that the passage can be understood as it stands if due allowance is made for Aristotle's conspicuous conciseness. I shall offer a paraphrase of the passage, enclosing explanatory additions as well as my own comments in brackets. The superscripts refer to further comments.

Aristotle has just explained his sense of ἐνδεχόμενον (possible) and distinguished it from the homonymous notion of possibility proper. He goes on:

ὅτι δὲ τοῦτ' ἔστι τὸ ἐνδεχόμενον, φανερὸν ἔκ τε τῶν ἀποφάσεων καὶ τῶν καταφάσεων τῶν ἀντικειμένων· τὸ γὰρ οὐκ ἐνδέχεται ὑπάρχειν καὶ ἀδύνατον ὑπάρχειν καὶ ἀνάγκη μὴ ὑπάρχειν ἤτοι ταὐτά ἐστιν ἢ ἀκολουθεῖ ἀλλήλοις, ὥστε καὶ τὰ ἀντικείμενα, τὸ ἐνδέχεται ὑπάρχειν καὶ οὐκ ἀδύνατον ὑπάρχειν καὶ οὐκ ἀνάγκη μὴ ὑπάρχειν, ἤτοι ταὐτὰ ἔσται ἢ ἀκολουθοῦντα ἀλλήλοις· κατὰ παντὸς γὰρ ἡ φάσις ἢ ἡ ἀπόφασις. ἔσται ἄρα τὸ ἐνδεχόμενον οὐκ ἀναγκαῖον καὶ τὸ μὴ ἀναγκαῖον ἐνδεχόμενον.

That this [= Aristotle's definition] is the meaning of 'possible' is obvious from the opposing affirmations and denials.[1] For [in the other sense of 'possible'] 'it is not possible to apply', 'it is impossible to apply', and 'it is necessary not to apply' are either the same or go together with[2] each other.[3] Consequently their contradictories[4] 'it is possible to apply', 'it is not impossible to apply', and 'it is not necessary not to apply' are the same or go together with each other. For either the affirmation or the negation always applies.[5] [This is not correct, however, for we mean by possibility something more than the absence of impossibility.[6]] That which is necessary will therefore not be possible, and that which is not necessary [nor impossible][7] will be possible.

Further comments:

(1) This elliptic sentence poses two questions:

(a) What are these affirmations and denials affirmations and denials *of*?

(b) What kind of opposition is Aristotle here referring to?

As regards (a), the sequel shows that Aristotle is not dealing with affirmations and denials of possibility in the sense (of contingency) just defined. It turns out (cf. (3) below) that the affirmations and denials pertain to the other sense of possibility (possibility proper). Since Aristotle is obviously trying to justify his own definition, it may be concluded that he is here starting a *reductio ad absurdum* argument.

As regards (*b*), a comparison with the occurrences of ἀντι-κείμενος later in the passage (cf. (4)) suggests that this word—which is Aristotle's vaguest and most general term for opposition of any kind—here refers to contradictory opposition. The alternative would be to understand the sentence as referring to the opposition between the two kinds of possibility; this would suit my interpretation quite as well as the other reading.

(2) In the next chapter it will be argued that ἀκολουθεῖν does not always express in Aristotle's logical writings logical following but typically some sort of weaker 'going together with' not much stronger than compatibility. Here the difference between the different readings is not crucial. (But cf. comment (5) below.)

(3) This is exactly what we get by accepting the other sense of ἐνδεχόμενον, i.e. by not excluding necessity from the range of possibility: 'not possible that *p*' will be equivalent to 'impossible that *p*' which is (cf. diagram (ii)) tantamount to 'necessarily not *p*'.

(4) The following sentence shows that these contradictories are the ἀντικείμενα referred to here.

(5) This sentence seems to explain Aristotle's step from the original possibility-statements to their negations on the weaker assumption that the several alternative statements merely 'go together'. Although the validity of Aristotle's argument is in this case dubious (if two assertions are logically compatible, it does not follow that their contradictories are), his purpose can perhaps be understood on this interpretation, too.

(6) It has already been pointed out above (in section 2) that Aristotle took this view. See especially the reference to the *Topics*, loc. cit. It appears from the expression φανερόν at 32ª21 that Aristotle thought of this point as being perfectly obvious; so obvious, indeed, that he neglected to make it explicit here.

(7) The second part of the last sentence seems strange. The addition I have indicated is a most tempting way of making the passage correct. It is very likely, however, that the passage is Aristotle's as it stands. He knew that his notion of possibility (i.e. contingency) is symmetrical with respect to negation in the sense

that best appears from diagram (iv). He may have thought that this symmetry justifies the transition from 'what is necessary is not possible' to 'what is not necessary is possible'. This leads to a reading of 'not necessary' as an elliptic form of 'not necessary either way', i.e. 'neither necessary nor impossible'. In the sequel, we shall find more indications that this was Aristotle's reading; see section 7 below as well as section 4 of Ch. III.

Here I shall only point out that my interpretation is supported by what we find in the *De Interpretatione*. If it is true that 'not necessary' sometimes does duty for 'neither necessary nor impossible', it may be expected that 'not necessarily not', i.e. 'not impossible', will sometimes mean 'neither impossible nor necessary'. When this is so, 'not impossible' will entail (in fact, it will be equivalent to) 'not necessary'. And this is exactly what we find in *De Int.* 13. 22^{b}14–16, where Aristotle infers 'not necessary' from 'not impossible'. This inference is very difficult to explain otherwise. The inference is based on the sequence of implications (equivalences?) set up by Aristotle in *De Int.* 13. 22^{a}16 ff., where again μὴ ἀδύνατον εἶναι entails μὴ ἀναγκαῖον εἶναι.

The excision of the passage under discussion, as suggested by A. Becker (*Die aristotelische Theorie der Möglichkeitsschlüsse* (Junker und Dünnhaupt, Berlin, 1933), pp. 11–13) is therefore totally unnecessary. The suggestion betrays Becker's failure to see what Aristotle is doing here and to notice that the terminology of the passage exhibits genuinely Aristotelian peculiarities.

6. *A subdivision of contingency*

Having made these distinctions, Aristotle goes on to say (in *An. Pr.* I 13. 32^{b}5 ff.) that possibility has two applications (the expression he uses is κατὰ δύο τρόπους λέγεται). On one hand, it is used to describe what generally happens but falls short of being necessary; on the other hand it is used to describe the indeterminate, that which can be 'thus or not thus' without the prevalence of either alternative. Now the distinction plainly has nothing to do with the difference between possibility proper and contingency. Neither of the two uses distinguished by Aristotle covers what happens necessarily. What we have here is therefore a *subdivision of contingency*. Aristotle's use of the expression κατὰ δύο τρόπους λέγεται suggests that he is not distinguishing two meanings of ἐνδεχόμενον but rather two kinds of cases to which it can be applied (cf. section 16 of Chapter I). This is verified by his remarks on the conversion of statements of contingency. He says that in both cases the possible premiss can be converted into its opposite premiss, i.e. '*p* is contingent' into 'not-*p* is contingent'. This is trivial in the case of a *p* that is contingent because it is 'indeterminate'. But Aristotle also holds that the conversion applies to contingency in the sense of that which 'generally happens'. This may seem mistaken: if *p* happens generally but not necessarily, we certainly cannot infer that not-*p* happens generally. What Aristotle means is that even in this case not-*p* is neither necessary nor impossible and hence contingent in the sense of his definition. If 'what happens generally but not necessarily' were one of several *meanings* of 'contingent', Aristotle would not be able to say that 'contingent' always converts with its opposite. What he means is that in each of the different cases that fall under the term 'contingent' we have a conversion to the opposite of some case—not necessarily of the same case—covered by the term.[3] Hence, he is not dealing with different meanings of ἐνδεχόμενον, but only with different applications of the term. 'Contingent' is not homonymous although it covers different kinds of cases.

7. *An analysis of* An. Pr. *I 3. 25ᵃ37–ᵇ19.*

Some of the passages I have just discussed are referred to by Aristotle earlier in the *Prior Analytics* in connection with the conversion of problematic (possible) premisses (*An. Pr.* I 3. 25ᵃ37–ᵇ19). We are now in a position to understand the context of these references.

In *An. Pr.* I 3. 25ᵇ18–19 Aristotle refers to his later discussions of the conversion of problematic premisses. All the remarks on this subject later in the *Prior Analytics* pertain to contingent premisses. This suggests that the notion Aristotle has in mind in 25ᵇ18–19 is his 'possibility as defined' or contingency. This is confirmed by the way Aristotle explains the notion of possibility

---

[3] Aristotle's awareness of the fact that a case of a concept may be converted into another case of the same concept is also shown by his remarks on τὸ εἰκός in *Rhet.* II 23.1402ᵃ9 ff.

that he is dealing with here: 'But if anything is said to be possible because it is the general rule and natural . . .' (*An. Pr.* I 3. 25ᵇ14 ff.). This recalls one of the different cases of contingency discussed in *An. Pr.* I 13. 32ᵇ4 ff. (see above, section 6). And when Aristotle says that this 'is the strict sense we assign to possible' (Ross's translation), he is obviously anticipating his definition of contingency in 32ᵃ18–20.

I conclude, therefore, that in *An. Pr.* I 3. 25ᵇ14–18 Aristotle is thinking of contingency rather than possibility proper. Now the passage that was just quoted shows that this variant of possibility is contrasted to the one employed in the immediately preceding passage (*An. Pr.* I 3. 25ᵇ7–14). We may, therefore, expect that this latter notion of possibility is what I have called possibility proper. Aristotle's examples show that this is in fact the case. In one of his examples the term 'man' necessarily does not apply to any horse, while in another the term 'white' does not necessarily apply to any coat. This shows that the meaning of possibility that is used here covers cases of necessity as well as cases of contingency. (The examples are both negative in form because he is discussing the conversion of negative premisses.)

Although the testimony of Aristotle's examples thus unambiguously shows that in 25ᵇ7–14 he is discussing possibility proper, one may still be puzzled by his own explanation of the variant of possibility he is using: 'Whatever is said to be possible because it is necessary or because it is not necessary admits of conversion like other negative statements . . .' For what one would expect here is 'neither necessary nor impossible' instead of 'not necessary'. Some commentators have tried to emend the passage by inserting the negative particle μή so as to make it read 'not necessarily not', although there is no real support for such an insertion in the manuscripts (see Ross, op. cit.). Moreover, this insertion has the disadvantage of making the clause 'because it is necessary' superfluous. In any case, the emendation is quite unnecessary, for we have already found independent reasons for suspecting that Aristotle sometimes uses 'not necessary' (τὸ μὴ ἀναγκαῖον) and, by analogy, 'not necessarily' (μὴ ἐξ ἀνάγκης) as elliptic expressions for 'neither necessary nor impossible' and 'neither necessarily nor impossibly', respectively, as was pointed out above in section 5, comment (7). This suspicion is now confirmed by the fact that the same explanation works here: on my reading the quoted passage says just what one is entitled to expect.

Here one may ask whether my reading is contradicted by the fact that in his second example Aristotle says that it is not necessary that 'white' applies to any coat (τὸ δὲ οὐκ ἀνάγκη ὑπάρχειν). If Aristotle were consistently using the elliptic mode of expression, should he not use double negative οὐκ ἀνάγκη μὴ ὑπάρχειν, since he is here dealing with negative premisses? To this it may be answered that 'neither necessary nor impossible' is symmetrical with respect to negation, so that no extra μή is needed even if the elliptic mode of expression is used. Besides, one of Bekker's manuscripts as well as Philoponus do have the missing μή (see Ross, op. cit.), so that Aristotle may very well have been even pedantically consistent in his usage.

We may conclude that in his treatment of the conversion of negative problematic premisses Aristotle first discusses premisses in which the notion of 'possibility proper' is used and then those in which the notion of contingency is used. In contrast, both these notions are lumped together in Aristotle's discussion of the conversion of positive problematic premisses (25ᵃ37–25ᵇ2). He indicates this as follows: ... ἐπειδὴ πολλαχῶς λέγεται τὸ ἐνδέχεσθαι (καὶ γὰρ τὸ ἀναγκαῖον καὶ τὸ μὴ ἀναγκαῖον καὶ τὸ δυνατὸν ἐνδέχεσθαι λέγομεν) ... Here the words πολλαχῶς λέγεται suggest that he is not exclusively concerned with the different meanings of ἐνδεχόμενον. In fact, it has been pointed out by Ross that the three cases listed in the parenthetical clause cannot possibly be as many different *meanings* of ἐνδεχόμενον. However, it seems to me that it cannot be said, either, that they are just three different cases to which the notion of possibility can be applied. The first two are clear; we have encountered τὸ ἀναγκαῖον and τὸ μὴ ἀναγκαῖον before as the two cases covered by the notion of possibility proper. The recurrence for the fourth time of the elliptic expression τὸ μὴ ἀναγκαῖον (or of one of its variants) where one expects 'neither necessary nor impossible' gives further support to my interpretation of this phrase. But τὸ δυνατόν cannot very well be a third case to which the notion of possibility is applied, for there is no third case comparable with the two already listed. Rather, we must understand τὸ ἀναγκαῖον καὶ τὸ μὴ ἀναγκαῖον as referring to the notion of possibility proper, and understand τὸ δυνατόν as referring to the other notion of possibility, viz.

contingency. This, in fact, seems to be the way Ross understands the passage. Its meaning may hence be expressed somewhat as follows: '. . . seeing that possibility has many applications (for we call possible both that which is necessary or is not necessary either way and that which is capable of being) . . .'

This interpretation is supported by the fact that the context shows that Aristotle is here treating both the variants of possibility at the same time. If they are here mentioned in the same order in which they are subsequently treated (in the connection of the conversion of negative problematic premisses) we can scarcely separate Aristotle's references to the two variants in any way different from the one just suggested.

Our interpretation also agrees with the way δυνατόν is used elsewhere in the *Prior Analytics*. The most important passage in which this term occurs is *An. Pr.* I 15. 34ᵃ6 ff. In the next chapter I shall argue that what Aristotle there (34ᵃ13) calls 'possibility with respect to generation' is very likely just our contingency. Indeed, it is seen without further argument that anything that is generated will sometimes be (viz. after having been generated) and sometimes not be (viz. before it is generated). It is, therefore, possible in the very sense (in that of contingency) that we wanted to give δυνατόν in *An. Pr.* I 3. 25ᵃ39.

8. *Remarks on* An. Pr. I *13. 32ᵇ25–32*

What we have found in Chapter I and in this chapter can be used to interpret what Aristotle says in *An. Pr.* I 13. 32ᵇ25–32—in a passage so thoroughly misunderstood by Albrecht Becker that he wants to excise large parts of it (op. cit., pp. 32–7).

This passage is Aristotle's explanation of how his problematic (possible) premisses are to be understood. In it he seems to be saying that

(P) it is possible for *A* to apply to all *B*

is ambiguous in that it may mean either

(P1) it is possible for *A* to apply to everything to which *B* in fact applies

or

(P2) it is possible for *A* to apply to everything to which *B* possibly applies.

This cannot be his meaning, however. For one thing, he never seems to use (P1) but only (P2) in his subsequent discussion of syllogisms from possible premisses. He seems even to say that (P2) is what (P) was *defined* to mean (*An. Pr.* I 14. 33ª24–5). For another, the term Aristotle uses is διχῶς, which strongly suggests that he is not at all distinguishing two different meanings of (P). Rather, he is saying that (P) covers two kinds of cases, i.e. that (P) is tantamount to the conjunction of (P1) and (P2).

This suffices to explain everything that Aristotle says and does. It may be expected that the variant of possibility Aristotle is using in (P2) is the one he usually employs, viz. contingency. Expressed as explicitly as possible, Aristotle's point therefore is that (P) is equivalent to the conjunction of (P1) and (P21), where the latter is

> (P21) it is possible for *A* to apply to everything to which *B* applies contingently.

Now this conjunction is clearly equivalent to what we get by assuming that the variant of possibility used in (P2) is my 'possibility proper':

> (P22) it is possible for *A* to apply to everything to which *B* possibly applies (in the sense of 'possibility proper'), i.e. to everything to which *B* applies necessarily or contingently.

This explains why Aristotle seems to deal exclusively with (P2) in his syllogistic theory; for what he is really dealing with is (P22) which is equivalent to the conjunction of (P1) and (P21) and therefore also to (P).

Further evidence is found in *An. Pr.* I 29. 45ᵇ31–4. Having just explained how the different kinds of assertoric syllogisms are established, Aristotle goes on to say that apodeictic (necessary) and problematic (possible) syllogisms are established in the same way. But he adds a warning:

> In the case of problematic propositions, however, we must include those terms which, although they do not apply, might possibly do so; for it has been shown that the problematic syllogism is effected by means of these. . . . (H. Tredennick's translation in the Loeb Library edition.)

Prima facie this is completely tautologous. For problematic syllogisms contain by definition terms that do not apply but may apply. What can Aristotle mean here? It is clear that the *predicate term A* of a premiss like (P) may apply possibly but not actually. But it is not equally obvious whether the *subject term B* is to be taken to apply possibly or actually; whether, in other words, (P) is to be understood as being equivalent to (P1) or to (P22). Unless we assume that Aristotle's statement is pointless, we can scarcely interpret it except as a repetition of the point which we found him making in *An. Pr.* I 13. 32^{b}25–32, viz. as identifying (P) and (P22). Notice in particular that there is no semblance here of a distinction between two meanings.

9. *Concluding remarks*

We have discussed the most important passages of *An. Pr.* I which turn on the distinction between the various notions of possibility used by Aristotle. In so far as we have been successful in applying the results of my earlier analysis of the ambiguities of ambiguity in Aristotle, our success conversely serves as a further confirmation of the earlier analysis. In particular, it supports what was said in section 12 of Chapter I above. Aristotle's own definition of contingency (see section 4 of the present chapter) establishes a connection between contingency and possibility proper: contingent is that which is (properly) possible but not necessary. If homonymy were tantamount to the absence of any common element in definition, contingency and possibility proper would not be homonyms. The fact that Aristotle calls them homonyms shows that there is more to his notion of homonymy than that.

III

ON THE INTERPRETATION OF
DE INTERPRETATIONE 12–13

1. *Aristotle's argument*

THE Chapters 12 and 13 of *De Interpretatione* are not among the easiest in the Aristotelian corpus to interpret. The task Aristotle sets to himself there is to investigate the relations of modal expressions, such as 'possible', 'necessary', 'impossible', etc., and he is well aware of the difficulty of his enterprise (see 21ᵃ37). The interpreter's difficulties are of a somewhat unusual kind, however. It is not very hard to see what Aristotle is trying to do as far as the outlines of his argument go. In *De Int.* 12 he examines the different modal expressions with a view to establishing relations of contradictoriness among them. At the end of the chapter (22ᵃ11–ᵃ13) he summarizes the results of his discussion in the form of the following list of pairs of contradictory expressions: possible (δυνατόν)—not possible (οὐ δυνατόν); possible[1] (ἐνδεχό-μενον)—not possible (οὐκ ἐνδεχόμενον); impossible (ἀδύνατον)—not impossible (οὐκ ἀδύνατον); necessary (ἀναγκαῖον)—not necessary (οὐκ ἀναγκαῖον). In *De Int.* 13 Aristotle at first establishes a number of different relations among the modal expressions. These relations he refers to by means of the verb ἀκολουθεῖν; they are listed in 22ᵃ14–ᵃ31. Aristotle runs into difficulties, however, in trying to combine the different lists he has established on the basis of different kinds of logical intuitions of his. These difficulties are discussed at length in 22ᵇ10 ff. in a way that suggests that Aristotle perhaps was not himself completely clear about the causes of his difficulties. He ends up with an attempt to solve the difficulties by a favourite device of his, viz. by distinguishing two senses of an expression, in this case two senses of the expression 'possibly' (and of related expressions). (See 23ᵃ7 ff.)

---

[1] I shall not try to assign different translations to δυνατόν and ἐνδεχόμενον. The difference in meaning between the two, if any, is not pertinent to our enterprise in this chapter.

Although the outlines of Aristotle's argument are thus rather easy to perceive, the details of his discussion are often obscure in the extreme. It is not easy to see what the lists he offers in *De Int.* 13 are really lists of, nor to see whether they are correct or not. The nature of his difficulties is not obvious nor is the exact nature of the distinction by means of which he proposes to resolve them. Many individual passages are badly in need of elucidation.

In this chapter I shall try to throw some light on the details of Aristotle's argument. Although it is not possible to prove once and for all that a certain particular interpretation is *the* right one, I believe that a careful reading of the text enables us to make good sense of almost everything Aristotle says in *De Int.* 12–13.

2. Συμβαίνειν *as expressing logical consequence*

I shall approach my task by trying to establish the exact meaning that certain crucial verbs have in Aristotle's discussion. These verbs are ἀκολουθεῖν, συμβαίνειν, and ἕπεσθαι. Usually translators and commentators do not make any clear-cut distinction between them. Frequently translators render all three of them in terms of 'following' or 'consequence', tacitly assuming that they all serve to refer to relations of logical implication (entailment). Unless I am mistaken, however, the functions of the three verbs in the discussion of *De Int.* 12–13 differ markedly.

The meaning of the verb συμβαίνειν is relatively easy to establish. Although it has other uses (see Bonitz, *Index Aristotelicus*, pp. 713–14, and Günther Patzig, *Aristotle's Theory of the Syllogism* (D. Reidel Publishing Company, Dordrecht, 1968), pp. 21 and 41), in Aristotle's logical writings it often serves to express logical consequence. It occurs in the Stagirite's definition of logical inference or syllogism in *An. Pr.* I 1. 24^{b}18–22, and most of its other occurrences in *An. Pr.* I obviously carry this meaning (e.g. *An. Pr.* I 13. 32^{a}29; 17. 37^{a}36). The same is the case with most of its occurrences elsewhere in *De Int.* (see, e.g., 18^{b}26 and 19^{a}35). In the chapters under discussion the verb occurs in *De Int.* 13. 22^{b}16, 22^{b}19, and 22^{b}28. Although we are not yet in a position to understand the context of these occurrences, we can already see that any other meaning than that of logical consequence would be very awkward.

3. Ἀκολουθεῖν *as expressing compatibility*

The most important of the three verbs for our purposes is ἀκολουθεῖν. It occurs frequently in our two chapters (see 21ᵇ35; 22ᵃ14, 33; 22ᵇ3, 12, 15, 18, 22, 25, 26, 30; 23ᵃ20). Its basic meaning is 'to follow', and Aristotle uses it to express many different kinds of 'following' or 'going together with'. Later the Stoics used it to express relations of logical consequence (according to Bocheński, *Ancient Formal Logic* (North-Holland Publishing Company, Amsterdam, 1951), p. 89, and Benson Mates, *Stoic Logic* (University of California Press, Berkeley and Los Angeles, 1961), p. 132), and Aristotle sometimes uses it for the same purpose. (Cases in point are found in *An. Pr.* I 46 and in *Topics* II 8). He is not at all consistent, however. In many passages of *An. Pr.* the word serves to express predication, i.e. a term's applying to another. Elsewhere (e.g. *Met. Δ* 10. 1018ᵃ36, *Met. H* 1. 1042ᵇ3) it has still other functions. For our purposes it suffices to observe that there is no *a priori* method of predicting what meaning it bears in any particular passage of the Aristotelian corpus; the sense it has must in each case be gathered from the context. It is also useful to stress that for Aristotle the word was not a technical term for logical consequence; it does not occur in his definition of syllogism.

I shall begin by arguing that in the *De Interpretatione* the verb often serves to express (logical) compatibility rather than logical consequence. This may be seen, I think, from the fact that this reading gives a straight-forward sense to many passages which are otherwise very difficult to make any sense of.

For instance, *De Int.* 12. 21ᵇ35–22ᵃ1 can now be given a very natural sense:

διὸ καὶ ἀκολουθεῖν ἂν δόξαιεν ἀλλήλαις αἱ δυνατὸν εἶναι — δυνατὸν μὴ εἶναι· τὸ γὰρ αὐτὸ δυνατὸν εἶναι καὶ μὴ εἶναι· οὐ γὰρ ἀντιφάσεις ἀλλήλων αἱ τοιαῦται. ἀλλὰ τὸ δυνατὸν εἶναι καὶ μὴ δυνατὸν εἶναι οὐδέποτε ἅμα· ἀντίκεινται γάρ.

This is why 'possible to be' and 'possible not to be' may be thought to be mutually compatible. For it is possible for the same thing to be and not to be; such statements are not contradictories of one another. But 'possible to be' and 'not possible to be' are never [true?] at the same time, for they are opposites.[2]

---

[2] Here, and in most of the other quotations in this chapter, I am using the translation of J. L. Ackrill, *Aristotle's 'Categories' and 'De Interpretatione'* (Clarendon

That the verb ἀκολουθεῖν which occurs in the first sentence of our quotation really serves to express compatibility is shown by the reason Aristotle gives for his view in the second sentence of the quotation. The current interpretation of the verb as expressing implication rather than compatibility would here lead virtually *ad absurdum*. For from the fact that two expressions are not contradictories no one is tempted to infer that one of them (which one?) implies the other. Yet this is exactly the inference the current interpretation imputes to Aristotle. Moreover, the contrast Aristotle draws in the quoted passage argues strongly for the synonymy of ἀκολουθεῖν ἀλλήλαις with 'being sometimes [true] at the same time', i.e. 'being compatible'.

Further support for my reading may be found by comparing the preceding discussion with what Aristotle says later in 22ᵇ36 ff. The first sentence of our quotation is obviously based on considerations like the one Aristotle mentions in 21ᵇ12 ff.: 'However, it certainly seems that the same thing may be and not be. Thus, for instance, whatever may walk or be cut may not walk or be cut.' These considerations can support a conclusion to the effect that 'it may be' always implies 'it may not be' only if there are no cases to the contrary. Yet such cases are explicitly mentioned in 22ᵇ36 ff. The material Aristotle has can therefore support a claim of compatibility but not a claim of implication.

The same interpretation works in *De Int*. 13. 22ᵇ11–14:

τὸ μὲν γὰρ ἀναγκαῖον εἶναι δυνατὸν εἶναι· εἰ γὰρ μή, ἡ ἀπόφασις ἀκολουθήσει· ἀνάγκη γὰρ ἢ φάναι ἢ ἀποφάναι· ὥστ' εἰ μὴ δυνατὸν εἶναι, ἀδύνατον εἶναι· ἀδύνατον ἄρα εἶναι τὸ ἀναγκαῖον εἶναι, ὅπερ ἄτοπον.

For the necessary to be is possible to be. (Otherwise the negation will be compatible with it, since it is necessary either to affirm or to deny; and then, if it is not possible to be, it is impossible to be; so that the necessary to be is impossible to be—which is absurd.)

If the current reading were correct, Aristotle would be assuming here that each given proposition implies one or the other of any given pair of contradictories. This is a far cruder mistake than Aristotle was likely to commit. What is true is that each given proposition must be compatible with one or the other of any pair of contradictories; and on our interpretation this is exactly what Aristotle assumes in the quoted passage.

Aristotle Series, Clarendon Press, Oxford, 1963). The departures from Ackrill's translation to which my interpretation leads me will not be explicitly indicated.

In case further evidence is needed, such can be found, e.g. in *De Int.* 13. 22ᵇ17-22:

ἀλλὰ μὴν οὐδὲ τὸ ἀναγκαῖον εἶναι ἀκολουθεῖ τῷ δυνατὸν εἶναι, οὐδὲ τὸ ἀναγκαῖον μὴ εἶναι· τῷ μὲν γὰρ ἄμφω ἐνδέχεται συμβαίνειν, τούτων δ' ὁπότερον ἂν ἀληθὲς ᾖ, οὐκέτι ἔσται ἐκεῖνα ἀληθῆ· ἅμα γὰρ δυνατὸν εἶναι καὶ μὴ εἶναι· εἰ δ' ἀνάγκη εἶναι ἢ μὴ εἶναι, οὐκ ἔσται δυνατὸν ἄμφω.

However, neither 'necessary to be' nor yet 'necessary not to be' is compatible with 'possible to be'. For with this either may happen, but, whichever of the other two is true, this will no longer be true; for it is at the same time possible to be and not to be, but if it is necessary to be or not to be, it will not be possible for both.

If ἀκολουθεῖν served to express following in the sense of logical consequence, Aristotle would be saying that neither 'necessary to be' nor 'necessary not to be' follow from 'possible to be'. These consequences, however putative, are so patently invalid that there is little point in Aristotle's taking the pains to deny them. In contrast, the compatibility of 'possible to be' with 'necessary to be' will on any interpretation be one of the main problems of *De Int.* 13. The plausibility of our interpretation (and translation) is enhanced by the rest of the quotation.

It may be added that in *Prior Analytics* I 4. 26ᵇ6, the verb ἀκολουθεῖν clearly expresses compatibility rather than implication.[3]

4. Ἀκολουθεῖν *as expressing equivalence*

What we have seen suffices to show that the critical verb ἀκολουθεῖν sometimes expresses compatibility rather than implication in *De Int.* 12–13. It seems to me, however, that this is not the only meaning it has in these chapters. There are occurrences of the verb in which it can scarcely express logical compatibility. In particular, it seems to express something else in the lists that Aristotle gives in the beginning of *De Int.* 13 (see 22ᵃ14 and 33).

[3] Bocheński finds ἀκολουθεῖν also in *An. Pr.* I 4. 26ᵃ2, where it would carry a different sense (*Formale Logik* (Verlag Karl Alber, Fribourg and Munich, 1956), p. 74, text 13.04). The word does not occur in the manuscripts, however, only in Alexander. (See Sir David Ross, *Aristotle's Prior and Posterior Analytics* (Clarendon Press, Oxford, 1949), ad loc. We may, therefore, disregard it here. Very likely Alexander is only substituting his own term for Aristotle's.

It may be worth while reproducing the lists here to facilitate reference to them:

I	II
it may be (δυνατὸν εἶναι)	it cannot be (οὐ δυνατὸν εἶναι)
it may be (ἐνδεχόμενον εἶναι)	it cannot be (οὐκ ἐνδεχόμενον εἶναι)
it is not impossible	it is impossible
it is not necessary	it is necessarily not

III	IV
it may not be	it cannot not be
it is not impossible not	it is impossible not
it is not necessarily not	it is necessary

It does not seem possible to understand Aristotle as saying merely that the different listed expressions are logically compatible. (Are they supposed to be compatible pairwise or all together?) It is here that the alleged meaning of ἀκολουθεῖν as expressing logical consequence seems to sit most happily. Yet I think that even here the verb expresses something different from logical consequence, viz. logical equivalence. The different lists Aristotle gives in the beginning of *De Int.* 13 are not sequences of implications but groups of equivalent expressions.

This view may seem quite perverse, for some of the equivalences in question appear to be obviously false. To take a typical example: how can 'it may be' (δυνατὸν εἶναι) be equivalent to 'it is not necessary' (οὐκ ἀναγκαῖον εἶναι), as Aristotle would be claiming (*inter alia*) in 22ª24–7 (list I), according to the suggested interpretation? However, in Chapter II above it was seen that for Aristotle 'not necessary' sometimes implies 'not impossible'. When this is the case, 'it is not necessary' and 'it is not impossible' will be equivalent with each other and with 'it is possible' (or 'it may be'), in the most frequent sense of the last-mentioned expression in Aristotle. And this is exactly what Aristotle says in list I. Far from yielding unnatural results, our interpretation merely gives this list a meaning that could have been expected on the basis of Aristotle's usage elsewhere. That the other lists (especially list III) can similarly be interpreted as lists of equivalent expressions follows almost *a fortiori*.

There are several other indications that Aristotle often uses the verb ἀκολουθεῖν to express logical equivalence in the *De Inter-*

pretatione and that the lists he gives in *De Int.* 13 are really intended to be lists of equivalent expressions. Even if these lists were lists of implications, we would have to say that 'it is not impossible' implies 'it is not necessary' (see list I; this is also attested to by 22^{b}15–16). On the assumptions concerning the interrelations of modal notions that Aristotle seems to use, this may be expected to be enough to show that 'it is not impossible' at least is equivalent to 'it may be'.

A further piece of evidence to illustrate Aristotle's use of the verb ἀκολουθεῖν is found in *De Int.* 10. 20^{a}20 ff. (This piece of evidence has the advantage of being independent of all the problems that beset modal notions.) There Aristotle says that

(1) not every man is not-just

'accompanies' (ἀκολουθοῦσι)

(2) some men are just.

He cannot mean that (2) implies (1), for the reason he goes on to give for his claim can only serve as a reason for the *converse* implication: 'for there must be some' (viz. if not every man is not-just).

5. *Some assumptions of Aristotle*

Why did Aristotle hold that the expressions he gives in the three lists are equivalent? The lists II and IV offer no special problems; the difficulty lies in trying to understand why the members of the lists I and III seemed to him equivalent. I venture to suggest the following explanation. If somebody says that a certain event is not impossible *when he knows that it is necessary*, or says that it is not necessary when he knows it is impossible, he is very much liable to mislead his hearers, and can often be blamed for dishonesty. A similar situation was in fact described by Aristotle in *Topics* II 6. 112^{b}5 ff.: 'For if a necessary event has been asserted to occur usually, clearly the speaker has . . . made a mistake.' In a sense all the three expressions 'possibly', 'not impossibly', and 'not necessarily' therefore apply most naturally to one and the same kind of cases, viz. to cases that could be this way but could also be that way; and this fact may have lead Aristotle to the view that the three expressions are therefore logically equivalent.

We can at any rate easily see what logical relations between the different modal expressions are presupposed by Aristotle's equivalences. They can be conveniently summed up in the following diagram, which may be compared with lists I–IV:

Diagram 1

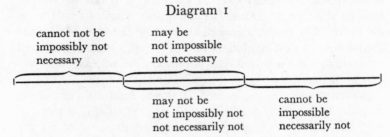

cannot not be	may be
impossibly not	not impossible
necessary	not necessary

may not be	cannot be
not impossibly not	impossible
not necessarily not	necessarily not

From this diagram we can readily see certain important implications of Aristotle's equivalences.

(*i*) We can see that not only the members of the lists I and those of III are equivalent among themselves; the members of I are equivalent with those of III, and vice versa. In the sequel we shall find more evidence to show that Aristotle sometimes followed this line of thought.

(*ii*) If the view that our diagram represents is adopted, Aristotle's list (in *De Int.* 12; cf. section 1 above) of pairs of contradictories is not correct. This earlier list presupposes an entirely different diagram:

Diagram 2

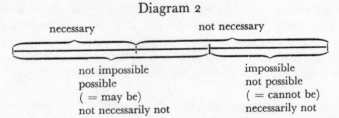

| necessary | not necessary |

not impossible	impossible
possible	not possible
(= may be)	(= cannot be)
not necessarily not	necessarily not

There need not be anything inherently wrong in either list of Aristotle's.[4] However, they are incompatible. It is, therefore, not at all surprising that Aristotle should run into difficulties as soon as he tries to combine the two lists, i.e. tries to relate the lists of equivalences in *De Int.* 13 to the list of contradictories in *De Int.* 12. (See *De Int.* 13. 22^{b}11 ff.)

(*iii*) It is seen from the two diagrams that the notion of possi-

---

[4] It must be said, nevertheless, that the use of the negative particle 'not' (οὐκ) presupposed by Diagram 1 is somewhat awkward.

bility presupposed in them is different in the two cases: in Diagram 1 whatever is necessary is also possible, whereas in Diagram 2 necessity and possibility appear as mutually exclusive notions. It is thus very natural that Aristotle should have tried to solve his difficulties by distinguishing two different meanings of the word 'possible' (δυνατόν or ἐνδεχόμενον).

Later, I shall argue that the difference between them is exactly the one suggested by a comparison of the two diagrams: one of them includes whatever is necessary whereas the other excludes it. In Chapter II above I called the former notion 'possibility proper' and the latter 'contingency'. I shall use the same terminology in this chapter whenever I have to distinguish the two meanings explicitly.

Once we have realized that the verb ἀκολουθεῖν often refers to equivalence rather than to implication or compatibility we can understand certain puzzling passages of *De Int.* 13. The following passage (22ᵇ22–4) is a case in point:

λείπεται τοίνυν τὸ οὐκ ἀναγκαῖον μὴ εἶναι ἀκολουθεῖν τῷ δυνατὸν εἶναι· τοῦτο γὰρ ἀληθὲς καὶ κατὰ τοῦ ἀναγκαίου εἶναι.

It remains, therefore, for 'not necessary not to be' to go together with 'possible to be', for this is true of 'necessary to be' also.

Aristotle's point cannot very well be that 'not necessarily not' is implied by 'possibly', which is trivial. Nor can it very well be that the two are compatible, which is still more trivial. A non-trivial sense can be obtained by taking Aristotle's words to mean that 'not necessarily not' is equivalent to 'possibly' on that interpretation of the former expression that includes whatever is necessary. As we have seen, the question whether or not 'it may be' is to be understood in this wide sense is vital to Aristotle's discussion. If our interpretation of the passage just quoted is right, this passage is especially interesting in that the notion of 'possibility proper' is there for the first time explicitly introduced to the discussion of *De Int.* 13.

The passage is also interesting in that it suggests that Aristotle spontaneously understood 'not necessarily not' in the wide sense of possibility proper even when he was still uncertain of the interpretation of the expression 'possibly'.

The same point may perhaps be expressed by saying that among Aristotle's most firmly entrenched intuitions concerning modal notions there were those we can represent by omitting from Diagram 2 all but those expressions that are in terms of necessity.

This observation helps us to understand one of Aristotle's concluding remarks in *De Int.* 13:

καὶ ἔστι δὴ ἀρχὴ ἴσως τὸ ἀναγκαῖον καὶ μὴ ἀναγκαῖον πάντων ἢ εἶναι ἢ μὴ εἶναι, καὶ τὰ ἄλλα ὡς τούτοις ἀκολουθοῦντα ἐπισκοπεῖν δεῖ.

Perhaps, indeed, the necessary and not necessary are first principles of everything's either being or not being, and one should look at the others as going together with them. (*De Int.* 13. 23ᵃ18–21)

The connection of this statement with the rest of Aristotle's discussion is not obvious. It seems to me that it can only be understood by interpreting it somewhat as follows: Of all the modal expressions, both affirmative and negative, those that are in terms of necessity are perhaps to be considered primary, and each of the others (i.e. each of the expressions that are in terms of possibility or impossibility) is to be taken to be equivalent to some expression that is in terms of necessity.

The words ἢ εἶναι ἢ μὴ εἶναι which I have rendered (for want of anything better) 'being and not being' do not mean 'existence and non-existence'. In Aristotle this phrase sometimes refers to predication (something's being something else) rather than to existence (something's being ἁπλῶς, as Aristotle puts it). Cases in point are found in *De Int.* 12. 21ᵇ14 (witness Aristotle's example which does not deal with existence at all) and 21ᵇ31. I suspect that the same is frequently the case when Aristotle uses the phrase εἶναι ἢ μὴ εἶναι in the *Posterior Analytics*. Aristotle's explanations show that in his definition of a hypothesis in *An. Post.* I 2. 72ᵃ20 the words τὸ εἶναί τι ἢ τὸ μὴ εἶναί τι do not refer to existence and non-existence but rather to affirmation and negation in general.[5] This strongly suggests that in a parallel explanation in *An. Post.* I 10. 76ᵇ35 the words εἶναι ἢ μὴ εἶναι do not refer exclusively to existential statements, either. In our present case (*De Int.* 13. 23ᵃ19) 'everything's being and non-being' may be short for something like 'the being-possible and not-being-possible of that which is or is not possible, the being-impossible and not-being-impossible of that which is or is not impossible, etc.'.

[5] Cf. Richard Robinson, *Plato's Early Dialectic* (Clarendon Press, Oxford, 1953), pp. 101–3.

Our interpretation is supported by the observation we made above to the effect that intuitions concerning necessity were in fact among Aristotle's most important starting-points. He is in the quoted passage advocating a procedure not entirely different from what he was inclined to follow himself. In terms of our diagram, it may be said that he first placed the various statements that are in terms of necessity into Diagram 2 and then placed each of the other statements into the diagram according as it is equivalent to one of them.

As you may easily see, the natural outcome of this procedure is to use the notion of possibility proper rather than that of contingency. (In Diagram 2 there is no expression that would be equivalent to 'contingently'.) This observation may perhaps help us to find some further support for our interpretation in Aristotle's text. In the *Prior Analytics* Aristotle frequently has occasion to distinguish possibility proper from contingency. One of the ways he does this is to call the former as distinguished from the latter 'possible . . . understood with reference to the necessary' (*An. Pr.* I 14. 33^{b}22). This practice now becomes intelligible. It is very difficult to understand otherwise, for Aristotle's own definition of contingency (see *An. Pr.* I 13. 32^{a}18 ff.) also refers explicitly to the notion of necessity.

6. *The common source of the two meanings of* ἀκολουθεῖν

The reader is undoubtedly still puzzled by an important question. I have argued that the verb ἀκολουθεῖν sometimes expresses compatibility and sometimes equivalence in *De Int.* 13. How can the two claims be combined? How could Aristotle use one and the same word in two entirely different meanings within a single short chapter?

It seems to me that the answer is really very simple. The basic meaning of the verb is 'to follow' or 'to go together with'. Mr. Unto Remes has reminded me that this very meaning is registered by Plato in the *Cratylus* 405 c. Now two expressions are logically equivalent if and only if they 'go together' in *all* (possible) cases (in the sense that one can be used whenever the other can); they are logically compatible if and only if they 'go together' in *at least one* (possible) case. For this reason, Aristotle's ambiguous usage is not unnatural. All that the reader has to do is to supply one of the words 'always' and 'sometimes'. The context usually helps one to make a choice between them. We could even say that Aristotle's usage is not so much ambiguous as elliptical.

It is perhaps objected that a merely logical compatibility of two expressions does not suffice to guarantee that they really 'go together' in any actual case, or that the 'going together' of two expressions in every (actual) case does not suffice to make sure that they are logically equivalent. However, for Aristotle this was no problem. Later I shall argue that he assumed that every genuine possibility will be realized sooner or later.[6] Hence if it is possible for two expressions to apply to one and the same case, there must (according to Aristotle) sooner or later be an actual case in which the expressions 'go together'.

The naturalness of our interpretation of the verb ἀκολουθεῖν as it is used in *De Int.* 12–13 is shown by the fact that there is another word that seems to have been used by Aristotle in the way we have argued he used the verb ἀκολουθεῖν. This word is the rare verb συναληθεύειν. It occurs in an important context in *De Int.* 10. 19ᵇ36. Aristotle is there comparing two groups of four propositions, viz. the following:

man is just	man is not just
man is not-just	man is not not-just

and

every man is just	not every man is just
every man is not-just	not every man is not-just.

Of the second group Aristotle says that 'here it is not possible, as in the former case, that the diagonally opposing statements should be true together (συναληθεύειν). Nevertheless it is sometimes possible.' The most straightforward meaning that I can give to these words is the following: whereas the diagonally opposing statements of the first group, viz. 'man is just' and 'man is not not-just' as well as 'man is not-just' and 'man is not just' are *always* true together, i.e. are logically equivalent, such equivalences are not possible in the second case. 'Every man is just' and 'not every man is not-just' are not equivalent (the latter is rather equivalent to 'some men are just') nor are 'every man is not-just' and 'not every man is just'. Nevertheless they may *sometimes* be true together, i.e. they are logically compatible.

A reader who nevertheless finds the ambiguity of the verb ἀκολουθεῖν confusing may find some consolation in the fact that this ambiguity was apparently a source of confusion for Aristotle, too. There was clearly a tendency in his thinking to assimilate the two meanings of the verb to each other somewhat too closely for comfort. Thus the fact that 'possibly' and 'possibly not' were found (in *De Int.* 12. 21ᵇ35 ff., cf. section 3 above) to 'go together' in the sense of being compatible may have encouraged him to think that they 'go together' also in the sense of being logically equivalent, as we have found him asserting in the lists of equivalences of *De Int.* 13. Aristotle does not warn the reader of an ambiguity as he so often does elsewhere. The ambiguity of the verb was one of the obstacles he was trying to surmount in the course of the discussion of *De Int.* 13. He never succeeded completely, and for this reason no single consistent reading of ἀκολουθεῖν can be carried out throughout *De Int.* 12–13, not to mention Aristotle's other writings.

7. *The verb* ἕπεσθαι

The last of the three verbs we proposed to examine does not occur very frequently in *De Int.* 12–13. Those occurrences there are (see 22ᵃ39, 22ᵇ30, 23ᵃ17) nevertheless enable us to make an informed guess at its meaning here. In 23ᵃ17 it is said that 'as the universal goes together with (ἕπεται) the particular, so the possible goes together with (ἕπεται) the necessary, although not in every sense of the word'. The verb ἕπεσθαι cannot express equivalence here. Nor can it very well express implication, either, for a universal statement is not implied by the corresponding particular statement. What is especially interesting in the quoted passage is Aristotle's indifference to the order of the relation which our verb serves to express. For clearly the analogy Aristotle intends is different from the one he actually announces: the necessary is related to the possible in the same way as the general to the particular. (For Aristotle this analogy may have been more than a mere analogy; in Chapter V we shall see that he came very close to identifying the necessary with the general.) The obvious explanation is that the relation the verb serves to express is symmetrical. And this in turn virtually forces us to assume that this symmetrical relation is that of compatibility (implication is not symmetrical relation!). It thus seems that Aristotle here uses the verb ἕπεσθαι to express logical compatibility rather than implication or equivalence.

Our guess is strongly supported by the fact that this interpretation enables us to understand a passage that otherwise seems very difficult to make any sense of. In *De Int.* 13. 22ᵃ38 ff. Aristotle writes:

τὸ δ' ἀναγκαῖον πῶς, ὀπτέον. φανερὸν δὴ ὅτι οὐχ οὕτως, ἀλλ' αἱ ἐναντίαι ἕπονται, αἱ δ' ἀντιφάσεις χωρίς. οὐ γάρ ἐστιν ἀποφάσις τοῦ ἀνάγκη μὴ εἶναι τὸ οὐκ ἀνάγκη εἶναι· ἐνδέχεται γὰρ ἀληθεύεσθαι ἐπὶ τοῦ αὐτοῦ ἀμφοτέρας·

But what about the necessary? Evidently things are different here: it is contraries that go together, and the contradictories are separated. For the negation of 'necessary not to be' is not 'not necessary to be'. For both may be true of the same thing.

Certain things are clear from the context. The statement 'it is necessary' has as its contrary 'it is necessarily not' and as its contradictory 'it is not necessary', and likewise for the statement 'it is necessarily not'. It is also clear that in the quoted passage Aristotle is comparing the behaviour of statements that are in terms of necessity with the behaviour of those that are in terms of possibility or of impossibility. It seems to me that we can understand fully the comparison if we interpret ἕπονται as expressing compatibility. For what Aristotle then means by saying that contraries go together with contradictories is exactly what he says in a different way in the last two sentences of our quotation, viz. that 'not necessary' and 'necessarily not' (as well as 'not necessarily not' and 'necessary') are logically compatible. This is really a point at which the notions of necessity and possibility behave differently in Aristotle's opinion. As we have seen, 'it may be' and 'it may not be' were for Aristotle equivalent (as far as those intuitions of his go that he relied on in the beginning of *De Int.* 13).[7] Hence 'possibly not' (δυνατὸν μὴ εἶναι) and 'not possible' (οὐ δυνατὸν εἶναι) were for him denials of each other, unlike 'necessarily not' and 'not necessary'.

We may perhaps also understand what Aristotle means by saying that the contradictories 'not necessary' and 'not necessarily

---

[7] This follows from the fact that the members of lists I and III are equivalent for Aristotle; see section 4 above.

not' (they are the contradictories of 'necessary' and of 'necessarily not', respectively) are χωρίς. It seems to me that we can take him to mean no more and no less than that the two expressions are not equivalent. Provided that Aristotle is relying on the intuitions represented by Diagram 2, he is right, as a glimpse at this diagram shows.

Our interpretation also enables us to make perfectly good sense of the occurrences of the verb ἕπεσθαι in 22ᵇ30:

ἀπορήσειε δ' ἄν τις εἰ τῷ ἀναγκαῖον εἶναι τὸ δυνατὸν εἶναι ἕπεται. εἴ τε γὰρ μὴ ἕπεται, ἡ ἀντίφασις ἀκολουθήσει, τὸ μὴ δυνατὸν εἶναι·

One might raise the question whether 'possible to be' is compatible with 'necessary to be'. For if it is not compatible, the contradictory will be, that is, 'not possible to be' . . .

The principle Aristotle is appealing to here is the one we found him appealing to in 22ᵇ11 ff. (section 3 above).

In the *De Interpretatione* the verb ἕπεσθαι also occurs in 11. 21ᵃ22. Although the context of the occurrence is not very easy to understand, it appears from Aristotle's subsequent remarks that its logical powers are those of a word expressing compatibility rather than those of one that expresses implication. The same interpretation works in *An. Post.* I 4. 73ᵇ22.

Lest I should seem to be claiming more than I want to do, let it be added that elsewhere in the Aristotelian corpus the verb often has other meanings including that of logical implication and logical equivalence.

The different senses of the word ἕπεσθαι hang together in the same way as the several uses (or meanings) of ἀκολουθεῖν: sometimes it is used to express 'going together' in some cases, at other times 'going together' in all cases (equivalence). Aristotle's awareness of this is shown by *An. Pr.* I 27. 43ᵇ11–13: 'But he must select not those attributes which follow some particular but those which follow the thing as a whole, e.g. what follows a particular man but what follows every man . . .'.

8. *Aristotle's different possibilities again*

As has already been pointed out, in *De Int.* 13. Aristotle tries to solve his difficulties by distinguishing different senses of the word 'possible' (δυνατόν). (See *De Int.* 13. 23ᵃ7 ff.) Now we have to have a closer look at this distinction (or these distinctions) and see how it is related to the other relevant features of Aristotle's theory of modality, including the distinction between contingency and possibility proper.

The observations made above in Chapter I are once again serviceable here. They show at once what the over-all structure of Aristotle's distinctions here is. The point is easily missed, for the Stagirite is using both the notion of homonymy and the notion of multiplicity of applications at the same time (see 23ᵃ6–7):

ἔνιαι δὲ δυνάμεις ὁμώνυμοί εἰσιν· τὸ γὰρ δυνατὸν οὐχ ἁπλῶς λέγεται . . .

Again, some capabilities are homonymous. For the capable is spoken of in more than one way. . . .

It is seen that Aristotle is here distinguishing two different senses of τὸ δυνατόν. They can be run together only on pain of homonymy. And the reason for this difference of meanings (cf. the word γάρ) is a multiplicity of different kinds of uses of δυνατόν, signalled in the text by the words οὐχ ἁπλῶς λέγεται. Aristotle explains the two different uses as follows, continuing our last quotation:

ἀλλὰ τὸ μὲν ὅτι ἀληθὲς ὡς ἐνεργείᾳ ὄν, οἷον δυνατὸν βαδίζειν ὅτι βαδίζει, καὶ ὅλως δυνατὸν εἶναι ὅτι ἤδη ἔστι κατ' ἐνέργειαν ὃ λέγεται δυνατόν, τὸ δὲ ὅτι ἐνεργήσειεν ἄν, οἷον δυνατὸν βαδίζειν ὅτι βαδίσειεν ἄν.

. . . either because it is true as being actualized (e.g. it is capable of walking because it walks, and in general capable of being because what is called capable already exists in actuality), or because it might be actualized (e.g. it is capable of walking because it might walk).

Of these two kinds of cases, both are covered by the sense of 'possible' in which it is equivalent to 'not impossible': 'Of both it is true to say that it is not impossible for them to walk, or to be— both what is already walking or actualized and what can walk.' One of the two homonymous senses of δυνατόν is thus my 'possibility proper'. By an obvious contrast, the other must be my 'contingency'. It is described by Aristotle as covering 'changeable things'—that is, precisely the things that can be other than they in fact are and thus possess the two-pronged capability characteristic of contingency.

9. *Other Aristotelian distinctions*

Although we can thus see what the upshot of Aristotle's distinctions is, the whole discussion in 23ª7 ff. is clearly somewhat tentative. It appears that it was in fact tightened up by Aristotle himself elsewhere.

One of the loose ends of Aristotle's discussion is the relation, or lack of one, of the distinction contingency–possibility proper to the sense of δυνατόν Aristotle had been relying on before he moved on to draw the distinction explained in *De Int.* 13. 23ª6 ff. In this sense, Aristotle says, the possible λέγεται κατὰ τὸ αὐτὸ εἶδος. Translators have not made much sense of these words, which literally mean something like 'by reference to one and the same εἶδος [kind?]'. Their point is nevertheless quickly betrayed by Aristotle's use of the closely similar expression πρὸς τὸ αὐτὸ εἶδος in *Met.* Θ 1. 1046ª9 in discussing the different senses of possibility (potentiality). Potencies of this sort are so called 'in reference to one primary kind of potency, which is the originative source of change in another thing or in the thing itself *qua* other'.

It would take us too far afield to try to discuss the different kinds of potency Aristotle distinguishes in *Met.* Δ 12. By and large, it seems to me that the situation is nevertheless rather simple. Aristotle contrasts potencies that are so called because they are sources of change or movement and potencies that involve no relation to movement. (See, e.g., the beginning of *Met.* Θ 6.) This distinction goes together with the famous contrast *kinesis–energeia*. These observations cannot be documented here as fully as they deserve. What concerns us here is mainly the relation of the distinctions Aristotle makes in the *Metaphysics* to the contrast contingency–possibility proper.

This question is answered by Aristotle in *Met.* Δ 12. There the senses of possible (δυνατόν) that involve a δύναμις are said to refer back to the idea of 'a source of change in the same thing *qua* other' (cf. *Met.* Θ 1. 1046ª11–12). They are contrasted to a sense in which the possible is equated with what is not necessarily false. The latter is obviously what has been called 'possibility proper', the former my 'contingency'. The parallelism between *Met.* Δ 12 and *De Int.* 13 is further strengthened when we discover as subclasses (as it seems to me) of possibility proper 'that which is true' (τὸ ἀληθές) and 'that which may be true' (τὸ ἐνδεχόμενον ἀληθὲς εἶναι). (Compare section 8 above with *Met. Δ* 12. 1019ᵇ32–33.)

This happy conformity of the different Aristotelian distinctions with each other seems to break down, however, when we return to *De Int.* 13. According to the parallelism I have suggested, capabilities *kata to auto eidos* should be classified as cases of contingency, that is, should exhibit the opposite capacity, too. But the very point Aristotle makes in *De Int.* 13. 23ᵃ5–6 is that some capabilities of this sort are not capable of opposites. Hence we apparently cannot identify capabilities *kata to auto eidos* with cases of contingency, and no clear parallelism seems to obtain between the contrast contingency–possibility proper and Aristotle's distinction between capabilities *kata to auto eidos* and those capabilities that go together with *energeiai*.

This apparent discrepancy is little more than an indication of the tentative character of Aristotle's discussion in *De Int.* 13, however. For in *Met. Θ* 8. 1050ᵇ31–4, precisely the opposite view is emphatically put forward by Aristotle by reference 'to our previous discussion' : 'But the other potencies ... are all potencies for opposites, for that which can move another in this way can also move it not in this way. ...' Hence everything can be understood in terms of my interpretation precisely in the way already indicated:

Capabilities *kata to auto eidos* go together with possibilities in the sense of contingency, whereas possibilities proper give rise to *energeiai*.

The insight we have gained into the interrelations of contingency and possibility proper in Aristotle and into the terminology (and phraseology) he used to express them may be further confirmed if we apply them to other passages in the Aristotelian corpus. An interesting test case is offered by *Prior Analytics* I 15. 34ᵃ12 ff. There, after giving a certain argument, Aristotle adds something which one translator has expressed as follows:

We must understand the terms 'possible' and 'impossible' with respect not only to generation but also to true statement and to attribution, and in all the other senses in which the term 'possible' is used ; for the same principle will obtain in all of them. (H. Tredennick in the Loeb Classical Library edition of the *Organon*)

The text reads as follows:

δεῖ δὲ λαμβάνειν μὴ μόνον ἐν τῇ γενέσει τὸ ἀδύνατον καὶ δυνατόν, ἀλλὰ καὶ ἐν τῷ ἀληθεύεσθαι καὶ ἐν τῷ ὑπάρχειν, καὶ ὁσαχῶς ἄλλως λέγεται τὸ δυνατόν· ἐν ἅπασι γὰρ ὁμοίως ἕξει.

Recent commentators have not made very clear sense of this passage. Sir David Ross (op. cit., ad. loc., p. 337) thinks that it expresses 'a mere generality' and that 'Aristotle had no particular other sense in mind'. This view is refuted, however, by Aristotle's words. Aristotle does not say that the argument he had given *may* (somehow) be generalized (or broadened in some other way), but that it *must*. Why?

The passage can be given a satisfactory sense, it seems to me, if we compare it with *De Int.* 13. 23ᵃ7 ff. discussed above. Possibility 'with respect to generation' is clearly that variant of the notion of possibility in which being possible presupposes coming-to-be in the sense of changing from potential to actual. Possibility with respect to true statement or to attribution is that sense of the word 'possible' in which a statement's being true at some moment of time suffices to show that it is possible (or a term's being attributable to another at some moment of time suffices to show that the attribution is possible). Since Aristotle says that in his argument the notion of possibility has to be taken not only in the former sense but also in the latter, he is in effect saying that in his argument the notion has to be understood in the wider sense which also includes what is necessary. In short, he is saying that in the preceding argument the notion of possibility must be understood in the sense of 'possibility proper' rather than in the sense of contingency.

It is especially instructive to note how the reference to truth in the quoted passage matches a similar reference in Aristotle's description of a subclass of possibility proper in *Met. Δ* 12. 1019ᵇ32 as 'that which is true'.

This reading makes excellent sense of the passage. For one thing, it shows that Aristotle was right about the necessity of modifying the argument he had just given. In the *Prior Analytics* he usually employs the notion of contingency rather than that of possibility proper, and is careful to point out the exceptions from this usage. However, the argument he has given immediately before the quoted passage is invalid if the notion of possibility is there taken in the sense of contingency. The argument was designed to show that necessarily (if *A*, then *B*)

entails

if (possibly *A*), then (possibly *B*),

or, on another (likelier) interpretation, entails

necessarily (if (possibly *A*), then (possibly *B*)).[8]

If 'possibly *A*' here means '*A* is contingent', i.e. '*A* is neither necessary nor impossible', the entailment Aristotle claims there obtains clearly does not obtain. (In order to see this, let *B* be any necessary fact while *A* is contingent.) However, if 'possibly *A*' means 'properly possibly', i.e. 'not impossibly', the entailment is impeccable. Aristotle obviously realized the necessity of rightly interpreting the notion of possibility in his argument. He pointed out this need of widening the scope of the notion of possibility in terms that are concise but not unintelligible.

If our interpretation is correct, we have to do with a case of the multiplicity of applications of an unambiguous word rather than with a word with several senses. Aristotle is not saying, it seems to me, that the argument he has carried out remains valid even if the word 'possible' is there given different meanings. He is saying that it remains valid only if the scope of this word is broadened so as to admit within it also cases of 'true statement and attribution'. That this view is correct is suggested by Aristotle's words. He says that the term 'possible' must be understood *not only* with respect to generation but also with respect *both* to true statement *and* to attribution.

Our interpretation thus presupposes understanding the words ἐν ἅπασι which occur in the last sentence of our quotation in a collective rather than a distributive sense. As far as I can see, such a reading is not impossible. (Liddell and Scott say that in the plural ἅπας means 'all together'.)

In this respect, our interpretation is perhaps also supported by Aristotle's use of the word ὁσαχῶς in the penultimate sentence of

[8] Łukasiewicz's interpretation of this passage, which differs essentially from mine, has been convincingly criticized by G. H. von Wright in his *Logical Studies* (Routledge and Kegan Paul, London, 1957), pp. 125–6. My interpretation differs from von Wright's in that I have utilized the results of Patzig's concerning Aristotle's usage of the phrase ἐξ ἀνάγκης (op. cit., pp. 25–8). The difference between the two alternative interpretations mentioned in the text is irrelevant for my purpose, however. (For Łukasiewicz, see his book, *Aristotle's Syllogistic from the Standpoint of Modern Logic* (Clarendon Press, Oxford, 1951, pp. 138–9.)

our quotation. For this word belongs to a family of terms (which includes πολλαχῶς, ποσαχῶς, etc.) which Aristotle typically uses to express a word's applying to a multiplicity of cases rather than to express ambiguity, i.e. a word's having several logically different meanings, as was seen in Chapter I above.

This success of my interpretation in making sense of the *Prior Analytics* passage lends further support to my reading of *De Interpretatione* 13.

IV

TIME, TRUTH, AND KNOWLEDGE
IN ARISTOTLE AND OTHER
GREEK PHILOSOPHERS

1. *Conceptual presuppositions*

IN this chapter I shall discuss a tacit presupposition, or a group of presuppositions, which seems to lurk behind certain doctrines of Aristotle's and to have been rather widespread in ancient Greece.

A generalization concerning such widespread tacit presuppositions has of necessity something self-defeating about it. If such a generalization is correct, the presuppositions it postulates were shared by the great majority of philosophers and of ordinary people within a culture. If so, there was little occasion for anyone to challenge these presuppositions, to discuss them, or even to bring them out into the open. In such circumstances, not very much direct evidence is likely to be available to show the existence of these presuppositions.

This does not go to show that broad generalizations concerning more or less unconscious ways of thinking within this or that culture are without philosophical interest. In fact, they seem to be worth a great deal more attention than professional philosophers have devoted to them of late. The difficulty I mentioned perhaps explains part of this lack of interest, however. In most cases, it is not very difficult to put forward intriguing suggestions concerning the general features of people's ways of thinking in different cultures or at different periods of intellectual history. The speculative philosophy of history from Hegel onward bristles with such proposals. However, it is usually much more difficult to substantiate them. Often it is rather difficult to connect the more or less implicit *Weltanschauung* that some philosophers of history have thought that they can perceive in the background of the Greek mind with what we actually know about Greek thinkers or of other facets of the Greek civilization.[1] Hence the largely justified qualms of professional philosophers about imputations of implicit general presuppositions to the Greeks.

It seems to me, nevertheless, that a closer study of the most articulate and systematic Greek philosophers may serve a purpose here. Such a philosopher is much more likely to make explicit some of the presuppositions he shares with his countrymen than the majority of these. He may even have to rely on these presuppositions in his philosophical arguments. A careful study of the general presuppositions of an individual Greek philosopher may therefore throw some light on the implicit conceptual presuppositions of the ancient Greeks in general.

We are primarily concerned here with certain general features of Aristotle's philosophical thinking. Some of the assumptions he makes appear to have parallels in other Greek philosophers, and hence occasion the question whether there is something in the common background of all these philosophers to which these assumptions might be related and which might partly explain them. I shall make some suggestions along these lines toward the end of this chapter.

2. *The predominance of temporally indefinite statements*

The group of presuppositions we deal with here is connected with the notion of time.[2] Many presuppositions in this group seem to stem from a characteristic tendency which permeates many different parts of Aristotelian thought. It is safer to speak of a tendency here than of an assumption, for apparently Aristotle

[1] These difficulties are illustrated by the scantiness of genuine evidence for those fashionable contrasts between the ancient Greek and the ancient Hebrew *Weltanschauungen* which have been effectively criticized by James Barr in *The Semantics of Biblical Language* (Clarendon Press, Oxford, 1961). The theoretical problems involved in inferences from linguistic to cultural data are also discussed by Joseph Greenberg in 'Concerning Inferences from Linguistic to Nonlinguistic Data', *Language in Culture*, ed. by H. Hoijer (University of Chicago Press, Chicago, 1956); reprinted in *Psycholinguistics*, ed. by S. Saporta (Holt, Rinehart, and Winston, New York ,1961), and by Max Black in 'Linguistic Relativity', *Philosophical Review*, 68 (1959), 228–38; reprinted in Max Black, *Models and Metaphors*, (Cornell University Press, Ithaca, 1962), pp. 244–57.

[2] The importance of people's attitudes to the category of time as an indication of their value orientation is brought out clearly by F. R. Kluckhohn and F. L. Strodtbeck in *Varieties in Value Orientation*, (Row and Peterson, Evanston, Illinois, 1961).

does not consciously choose this way of thought in preference to explicitly formulated alternatives. Rather, he takes this mode of thought as the only natural one, without ever becoming quite clear of the alternatives it might have and certainly without ever articulating the alternatives. If we nevertheless want to formulate this tendency as an explicit assumption we may say that for Aristotle the typical sentences used in expressing human knowledge or opinion are not among those Quine calls *eternal sentences* (or, even among *standing sentences*) but among those Quine calls *occasion sentences*.[3] That is to say, they are not sentences to which we assent or from which we dissent once and for all. They are sentences to which we can subscribe or with which we must disagree on the basis of some feature or features of the occasion on which they are uttered (or written). In particular, the sentences Aristotle is apt to have in mind are *temporally indefinite*; they depend on the time of their utterance. They may be said to be relative to the moment at which they are propounded. This relation may be implicit, but it may also be made explicit by the occurrence of such 'token-reflexive' expressions as 'now' or 'at the present moment' in the sentence in question. (Among these we have to count also such expressions as 'yesterday' or 'to-morrow' where another moment or period of time is specified by reference to the present moment.) In a sense they can be fully understood only if we know what moment this 'now' is, i.e. when the sentence in question was uttered or is thought of as being uttered. If Aristotle had been asked to give an example of an arbitrary sentence, he might have chosen something like 'Socrates is awake' or 'Socrates is walking'—and these we may express equally well by 'Socrates is now awake' and 'Socrates is walking at the present moment'.

If Aristotle's tacit assumption is expressed in this way, however, we are already siding with the moderns against him to some extent. What we have said already expresses the spontaneous reaction of almost all modern logicians and philosophers to the sentences of the kind we are discussing. A modern logician is likely to avoid the use (and the mention) of such sentences as much as possible.[4] They are usually thought of by him as in-

---

[3] W. V. Quine, *Word and Object* (M.I.T. Press, Cambridge, Mass., 1960), § 9 and § 40.

[4] Instances are far too numerous for me to give more than a sprinkling of

complete or indefinite sentences whose 'meaning' or 'content' depends on the circumstances in which they are uttered or otherwise propounded. Modern philosophers generally prefer not to deal with such temporally indefinite sentences as 'Socrates is awake' or 'Socrates is walking'; they prefer to discuss and to use instead sentences obtained from these by somehow specifying the time to which they refer independently of the moment of their utterance. The laws of logic are formulated with only or mainly sentences of the latter sort in view, and other procedures are sometimes thought of as being somehow fallacious.

3. *Statements and their objects*

It is not my purpose here to take sides for or against the Aristotelian assumptions as contrasted with the modern ones. It is important, however, to compare them to see how they differ. How would a modern thinker argue for his view that the 'content' or 'meaning' of a temporally indefinite sentence (say, 'It is now raining') varies? One way of doing so might be as follows. Suppose this sentence is uttered on two different occasions, say yesterday and today. Then the facts that make this sentence true or false are different in the two cases. Yesterday it referred to

examples here: Bertrand Russell, *An Inquiry into Meaning and Truth* (London, Allen and Unwin, 1940), p. 113; A. J. Ayer, *Philosophical Essays* (Macmillan, London, 1954), pp. 186–7; Nelson Goodman, *The Structure of Appearance* (Harvard University Press, Cambridge, Mass., 1951), p. 297; Donald C. Williams, 'The Sea Fight Tomorrow', in *Structure, Method and Meaning*, ed. by P. Henle (Liberal Arts Press, New York, 1951), pp. 282–306, especially p. 287. Further examples will be given in the course of the discussion.

My list might give the idea that only fairly recent philosophers of an analytic bend of mind favour eternal sentences over occasion sentences. This impression would be incorrect, as Appendix A to A. N. Prior's *Time and Modality* (Clarendon Press, Oxford, 1957) convincingly shows. In fact, in this respect most of our logical tastes go back to the seventeenth century at least. An early version of the doctrine that eternal sentences are superior to occasion sentences is especially interesting in that it was developed in conscious opposition to Aristotle. For Aristotle, the time relation in a sentence is carried by the verb. This doctrine is closely related to the fact that a typical Aristotelian sentence refers to the moment at which it is uttered or written, for it was the verb that carried the assertoric element in a sentence and was thought of as creating the judgement expressed by the sentence. In contradistinction to this view, it was already held by the authors of the *Port-Royal Logic* that time reference is not, logically speaking, a part of the verb. For them, the temporal aspect is, as it were, part of the subject matter and not created by creating the judgement.

Only very recently have logicians again begun to question the predominance of temporally definite statements.

yesterday's weather; today it refers to today's weather. On one day the sentence is verified or falsified independently of its verification or falsification on the other. It may be true on one day and false on the other. All these things are taken to show that the two utterances of the sentence in question cannot carry the same meaning. Although the sentence in the grammatical sense of the word is one and the same, its content or, as it is often said, the *proposition* it expresses on the two occasions is not the same.[5] Hence if we want to have a satisfactory correspondence between our thought and our language, between the logical and the grammatical form, we really must use a different form of words on the two occasions.

Whether the points I have just made are correct or not, Aristotle would not have accepted them. Aristotle would apparently have accepted the doctrine that the sentence 'It is raining' is made true or false by different sets of facts accordingly as it is uttered today or yesterday. However, he would not have been worried about the consequence that one and the same sentence may be true at one time and false at another. He would have rejected the notion of a proposition and would have stuck instead to the actual thoughts of the people who uttered the sentence on the two occasions. When doing so, he would have been willing to argue that the thought expressed by the sentence today and yesterday is one and the same. And all this he not only would have been willing to say; he as much as said so quite explicitly:

For the same statement (*logos*) seems to be both true and false. Suppose, for example, that the statement that somebody is sitting is true; after he has got up this statement will be false. Similarly with beliefs. Suppose you believe truly that somebody is sitting; after he has got up you will believe falsely if you hold the same belief about him. (*Cat.* 5, 4ª23–8)[6]

Statements and beliefs, on the other hand, themselves remain completely unchangeable in every way; it is because the *actual thing* changes that the contrary comes to belong to them. For the statement that somebody is sitting remains the same; it is because of a change in

---

[5] See, e.g., G. E. Moore, 'A Defence of Common Sense', *Philosophical Papers* (Allen and Unwin, London, 1959), p. 35.

[6] The translation is taken from J. L. Ackrill, *Aristotle's 'Categories' and 'De Interpretatione'* (Clarendon Press, Oxford, 1963).

the actual thing that it comes to be true at one time and false at another. Similarly with beliefs. (Ibid. 4^a34-4^b2)

These quotations show that Aristotle saw no difficulty in combining the two assumptions which to a typical modern thinker are likely to seem incompatible, viz. the assumption that the truth value of a temporally indefinite sentence changes with time, and the assumption that the sentence in question may nevertheless express one and the same content or proposition or, as Aristotle puts it, one and the same belief or opinion (*doxa*) on the different occasions on which it is uttered or otherwise propounded. Apparently, Aristotle did not find anything strange or awkward about his reconciliation of the two assumptions. Later, we shall examine some reasons why he felt this way.

Some comments are in order here. First of all, the authenticity of the *Categories* has sometimes been challenged. Hence the relevance of the passages we just cited is perhaps not beyond doubt. However, even if this work is not by Aristotle himself, it reproduces views current in the Lyceum at a very early date. Hence its testimony can be trusted provided that there are parallel statements in undisputably genuine works of Aristotle's. This is in fact the case. Exactly the same point that was made in the *Categories* recurs in a slightly briefer form in *Met. Θ* 10. 1051^b13 ff. Hence it is surely Aristotle's own view. Many of the passages that will be quoted in the sequel constitute evidence to the same effect.

It is also interesting to observe that the view put forward in the *Categories* is not due to Aristotle's desire to rule out recalcitrant facts or to enhance the architectonic neatness of his system. On the contrary, it would have suited the argument of the *Categories* much better if the author could have taken the modern view that the truth value of opinions and full-fledged sentences never changes. For the point made there is that substances are the only entities that can take contrary attributes at different moments of time and nevertheless remain numerically one and the same (*Cat.* 5. 4^a10 ff.). To this doctrine the changing truth values of opinions and of sentences constituted an unpleasant counter-example. The counter-example was eventually ruled out by means of a rather unsatisfactory manœuvre. (Substances are the only entities that assume contrary attributes because they themselves change; opinions and sentences do this only because the facts they refer to change.) The fact that the modern view was not even considered by the author of the *Categories*, although it would have served his purpose perfectly, illustrates the hold of the contrary view of him.

We may also register the fact that the statements we quoted from the *Categories* are completely categorical. A sentence or a belief remains 'completely unchangeable in every way' although the facts it refers to change. Furthermore, nothing is said of beliefs (opinions) and sentences which perhaps never change their truth values. Hence the author is clearly thinking in terms of temporally indefinite sentences. Because of the parallelisms between the *Categories* and other parts of the Aristotelian corpus, we may infer that the same was the case with the Stagirite.

I conclude, then, that Aristotle saw no obvious difficulties in the assumption that a temporally indefinite sentence expresses one and the same thought or opinion on the different occasions of its utterance. My main suggestion is that he tended to take temporally indefinite sentences as paradigms of all informative sentences. This led him, among other things, to define some of his key notions so as to be applicable only or primarily to temporally indefinite sentences or to 'opinions' corresponding to such sentences.

4. *Further Aristotelian evidence*

The fact that Aristotle preferred temporally indefinite sentences is not belied by the fact that in his syllogistic theory, and in his theory of scientific method which was built on his syllogistic theory, he frequently says in so many words that a general premiss has to take in all the different individuals of a certain sort, no matter whether they exist now or at some other moment of time. For instance, 'All men are mortal' is about all men, present, past, or future.[7] That Aristotle had to stress this feature of the syllogistic premisses may equally well indicate that there was a tendency among his audience and perhaps even in himself to understand these premisses in a different way. That such a tendency really existed is betrayed by the fact that Aristotle frequently uses temporally indefinite sentences as putative examples of syllogistic premisses, contrary to his own explanations.

[7] *An. Pr.* I 15, 34^{b}7–18; *An. Post.* I 4. 73^{a}28–9, and 8. 75^{b}21–36.

In at least one passage he indicates explicitly that his example is of this sort.[8]

A study of Aristotle's usage also tends to support our view of his notion of truth. He often speaks of what was or will be or would be true to say at some particular time. The following are cases in point (the italics are, of course, mine):

For when nothing was separated out, evidently *nothing could be truly asserted* of the substance that then existed. (*Met. A* 8. 989b6–7)

But there are two senses of the expression 'the primary when in which something has changed'. On the one hand it may mean the primary 'when' containing the completion of the process of change (the moment when *it is true to say* 'it has changed') ... (*Phys.* VI 5. 236a7–9)[9]

Notice also the care with which Aristotle habitually qualifies his statements of the law of contradiction: one and the same sentence cannot be true and false *at the same time*, he says.[10]

Locutions of this sort are by no means infallible evidence. Such locutions could conceivably be used by a philosopher who is not subscribing to the assumptions I have imputed to Aristotle. In connection with his explicit pronouncements on the relation of truth to time, however, they constitute useful circumstantial evidence. Their frequency shows how deeply engrained the ways of thinking were that we have found in Aristotle.

There are certain passages in Aristotle's works that may seem to call for a different interpretation. Some passages seem to suggest that in addition to temporally indefinite sentences, Aristotle sometimes considered sentences containing some kind of more definite time reference. The evidence is not conclusive, however, but points predominantly in our direction. When Aristotle says that a sentence includes a time reference, he normally means simply that its verb is in the present, past, or

---

[8] At *An. Pr.* I 10. 30b37–8 Aristotle considers a syllogistic conclusion that is not necessarily true, but is true 'so long as' (ἕως) the premisses are true. These premisses thus cannot refer to individuals existing at all the different times, for if they did, their truth value could not change. An equally revealing example occurs at 31b8–10, where Aristotle uses the terms 'sleeping' and 'waking' in a counter-example to a syllogism. These are as clear-cut examples as one might wish of terms that apply to an individual *at a time* only. Hence they contradict Aristotle's own admonitions as to how syllogistic premisses ought to be construed.

[9] Similar statements are found, e.g. in *Met. Γ* 7. 1012a27–8, *Met. Δ* 30. 1025a14–15, *Physics* VI 8. 239a28–9.

[10] e.g. *Met. Γ* 3. 1005b19–20, 23–32; 6. 1011b15–18; *Top.* II 7. 113a22–3; *De Int.* 10. 20a16–18.

future tense.[11] Such a sentence normally implies a reference to the moment at which it is uttered. There are also passages in which Aristotle has in mind some kind of closer specification of the time to which a sentence refers. But a second look at these passages shows that he is thinking of a specification (of the time of the occurrence of an event) in terms of 'the measurable stretch of time from now onwards to that, or . . . from that on to now' (*Phys.* IV 13. 222ª24–8). For instance, in *Parva Naturalia* (*De Memoria*) 2. 452ᵇ7 ff. Aristotle discusses the difference between 'exact' and 'inexact' estimate of time in connection with memory.[12] One of his examples is 'the day before yesterday', which is a specification of time in relation to the present day. In fact, the context makes it quite clear that what Aristotle is thinking of in this whole passage are exact and inexact specifications of the length of time that separates the remembered event from the present moment (cf., e.g., 452ᵇ8 ff.). Hence we again have an instance of a temporally indefinite time reference.

5. *Propositions, time, and truth in other Greek thinkers*

The same predilection for temporally indefinite sentences is found in other ancient philosophers, although not always in as explicit a form as in Aristotle. Virtually all the examples of singular sentences that were used by the Stoics as examples and are preserved to us seem to be temporally indefinite.[13] What is more important, such temporally indefinite sentences are put forward by the Stoics as examples of sentences that are taken to express a complete λεκτόν (*lekton*). These complete assertoric *lekta* or in short ἀξιώματα (*axiomata*) of the Stoics are in many respects reminiscent of the 'propositions' that many modern philosophers postulate as meanings of eternal assertoric sentences.[14]

---

[11] See *De Int.* 3. 16ᵇ6–18; *De An.* III 6. 430ª30 ff.

[12] I am indebted to Professor John W. Lenz for calling my attention to this passage.

[13] Cf., e.g., Benson Mates, *Stoic Logic* (University of California Press, Berkeley and Los Angeles, 1961, originally published as vol. 26 the University of California Publications in Philosophy) which contains a full discussion of the Stoic logic and translations of a number of sources. The closest approximations to genuine exceptions from this type of example that I am aware of are found in Cicero (*De Fato*, IX 19, and XIII 30).

[14] For examples of this sort, see, e.g., Mates, op. cit., pp. 96, 113, 118, 121, 123, etc.

However, *axiomata* differ from propositions in that they are temporally indefinite in the same way as occasion sentences. By saying 'writes', one does not yet express a complete *lekton*, we are told by the Stoics, because 'we want to know *who* [writes]'. Nevertheless, a sentence like 'Dion is walking' is said to express a complete *lekton*, in spite of the fact that it leaves room for the analogous question: '*When* is it that Dion is walking?'[15]

From this it followed that the Stoics spoke freely of changes in the truth value of a sentence and also (more properly) in the truth value of *lekta*. As is brought out very clearly by William and Martha Kneale, a *lekton* could change its truth value and even cease to exist.[16] In his list of the different senses of ἀληθής in the Stoics, Benson Mates distinguishes the use of this notion in connection with propositions (Sense I) from its use in connection with sentences that can change their truth value or, as Mates calls them, propositional functions with a time variable (Sense II).[17] The distinction does not seem to be motivated, however. In fact, some of Mates's own examples of Sense I are easily seen to involve sentences (or *lekta*) with changing truth values. Cases in point are found in Diogenes Laertius, *Vitae* VII 66, where the temporally indefinite sentence 'It is day' occurs as an example, as well as in Sextus Empiricus, *Adversus Mathematicos* VIII 10–13.[18] The latter passage is not unambiguous by itself; however, its import is brought out when Sextus later returns to the same topic (op. cit. 85, 88–9), using as an example the same temporally indefinite sentence as Diogenes.

One is also reminded here of the famous Megarian and Stoic controversies concerning the conditions of the validity of implications.[19] This whole controversy is couched in terms of sentences (or *lekta*) with changing truth values. For instance, Diodorus Cronus held that 'if *p*, then *q*' is true if and only if *q* is true whenever *p* is true.[20] If *p* and *q* were temporally definite sentences, this would reduce to our own truth-table definition of material

---

[15] See Diogenes Laertius, *Vitae* VII 63; Mates, op. cit., p. 16.

[16] William and Martha Kneale, *The Development of Logic* (Clarendon Press, Oxford, 1962), pp. 144–6, 153–5. Cf. also A. A. Long, 'Language and Thought in Stoicism' in *Problems in Stoicism*, ed. by A. A. Long (Athlone Press, London, 1971), esp. pp. 97 and 101.

[17] Mates, op. cit., p. 132.

[18] See the Loeb Classical Library edition of Sextus, vol. 2, pp. 244–7.

[19] See Mates, op. cit., pp. 42–51; Kneale and Kneale, op. cit., pp. 128–38.

[20] See, e.g., Sextus Empiricus, *Adv. Math.* VIII 112 ff.

implication. However, the Diodorean doctrine is known to have been contrasted with Philo's definition which is subsequent just our own truth-table definition. Hence Diodorus is clearly presupposing that p and q are temporally indefinite sentences.

Mates explains the Diodorean definition in terms of quantication over a time variable.[21] This is justified and illuminating, provided that we realize that there is no trace whatever of such a treatment in the Stoics themselves.[22]

6. *Knowledge, time, and immutability*

One of the most interesting things about the assumption we are dealing with is that it helps us to understand some of the most characteristic features of the Greek epistemology. Since these features are found not only in Aristotle but also in many other Greek philosophers, the existence of this connection suggests that we are really dealing with a common tendency of many Greek thinkers.

The most important feature I have in mind is the widespread Greek doctrine that we can have genuine knowledge only of what is eternal or at the very least forever changeless.[23] This doctrine becomes very natural if we consider it as the outcome of two tendencies: (1) A tendency to think of temporally indefinite sentences as typical vehicles of communication; (2) A tendency to think of knowledge in terms of some sort of direct acquaintance with the objects of knowledge, e.g. in terms of seeing or of witnessing them.

I cannot here document the second tendency as fully as it deserves. That there is something here worth being documented is already shown by the facts of the Greek language. One of the common Greek ways to claim that I know was to use the verb οἶδα which, literally taken, amounts to saying that I *have seen* the thing in question. If we are to believe Bruno Snell, this was not a mere piece of etymology but a fact the speakers of the language were aware of. According to him, 'in the Greek language we can

---

[21] Mates, op. cit., p. 45.

[22] Cf. P. T. Geach's review of Mates in the *Philosophical Review*, 64 (1955), 143–5.

[23] This tendency is one of the most striking characteristics of both Plato and Aristotle, and is found in other ancient philosophers as well. Its role and background in ancient Greek thought does not seem to have been systematically studied, however.

frequently discern that the verb εἰδέναι means, to know on the basis of one's own observation'.[24] The same applies also to the important word γιγνώσκω, especially in Homer, and to other verbs, too, as pointed out by Snell.[25]

Similar observations have often been made. W. G. Runciman sums up his patient examination of the relevant aspects of Plato's *Theaetetus* as follows: 'The general impression left by the *Theaetetus* is that Plato continued to think of knowledge as a sort of mental seeing or touching.'[26] This impression is not changed by Runciman's scrutiny of the *Sophist*: 'Although Plato says that all statements are either true or false and that all judgments are merely unspoken statements, he does not thereby . . . commit himself to any modification of what we have seen to be his earlier position on the nature and objects of knowledge.'[27]

For our purposes it is especially relevant that there was a marked tendency to conceive of the highest forms of knowledge as being somehow analogous to immediate observation as distinguished from mere hearsay. In short, the highest form of knowledge was thought of as being comparable to that of an eyewitness. In the introduction to his edition of Plato's *Meno*, R. S. Bluck says that 'the inferiority of ὀρθὴ δόξα to ἐπιστήμη as a state of awareness of the *a priori* is analogous to the inferiority of second-hand information about empirical matters to the certainty of one who has learnt from personal experience'.[28] It is also instructive to note that the kind of universal knowledge that Plato ascribes to the soul in his famous doctrine of recollection is explained by Plato (whether metaphorically or not is not at issue here) as being due to earlier personal experience: 'The soul, then, as being immortal, and having been born again many times, and having seen all things that exist, whether in this world or in the world below, has knowledge of them all' (*Meno* 81 c).

As pointed out by Snell, there is a striking example of this way of thinking in Homer.[29] When he appeals to his omniscient

[24] Bruno Snell, *Die Ausdrücke für den Begriff des Wissens in der vorplatonischen Philosophie*, (Philologische Untersuchungen, vol. ixxx, Berlin, 1924), p. 25.

[25] Bruno Snell, *The Discovery of the Mind* (Harvard University Press, Cambridge, Mass., 1953), p. 13.

[26] W. G. Runciman, *Plato's Later Epistemology* (Cambridge University Press, Cambridge, 1962), p. 52.   [27] Ibid., p. 121; cf. p. 125.

[28] R. S. Bluck, ed., *Plato's 'Meno'* (Cambridge University Press, Cambridge, 1961), p. 33.

[29] Snell, *The Discovery of the Mind* (op. cit.), ch. 7, especially p. 136.

Muses to help him, he does not represent their omniscience as a consequence of superhuman intelligence or of more insight into the laws that govern the events than mortal men possess. In Homer's own words,

> Tell me now, Muses that dwell in the palace of Olympus—
> For you are goddesses, you are at hand and know all things,
> But we hear only a rumour and know nothing—
> Who were the captains and lords of the Danaans.[30]

As Snell puts it, 'the goddesses are superior to man for the simple reason that they are always at hand, and have seen everything, and know it now . . .'. In fact, their having seen it was for the Greeks almost a prerequisite for their knowing it. Perhaps more significant than this old testimony is the fact that almost exactly the same view is echoed by Plato and Aristotle: 'You both admit, to begin with, that the gods perceive, see, and hear everything, that nothing within the compass of sense or knowledge [therefore?] falls outside their cognizance ' (*Laws* X 901 d; tr. A. E. Taylor; cf. Aristotle, *Poetics* 15. 1454^{b}2–6, and Empedocles fr. 129 (Diels–Kranz)).

What happens now if this idea of genuine knowledge as an eyewitness's knowledge is applied to the kind of knowledge that can be expressed by means of temporally indefinite sentences? One case seems to be clear: We know the things that are at the present moment within our sphere of perception. But what about things that are not under our present observation? Take, for instance, the piece of putative knowledge expressed by the sentence 'There is snow on Mount Olympus' as uttered by somebody who is not within the sight of the famous mountain. On what conditions is a man right who claims to know what this sentence asserts? The Greeks had, if I am right, a tendency to take this question as being equivalent to the question: When does his claim, 'I have seen it', amount to a conclusive evidence that the things are now as he says they are? The obvious answer is: Only if the thing in question never changes. Only on this condition does it follow from his earlier observation that things are still as they were at the time of the observation. If the purported object of his knowledge changes, it may have changed in the interval between his seeing it and his making the statement. If

---

[30] Homer, *Iliad*, beginning of the 'Catalogue of Ships' II. 484–7.

the snow sometimes melts from Mount Olympus, then the fact that I have seen the snow there does not go to show that there is snow there now. Only if the snow never melts does the 'I have seen it' assertion amount to knowledge concerning the present state of affairs. Hence, the two tendencies I mentioned made it very natural for the Greeks to adopt the view that there can be genuine knowledge only of what is unchangeable (and perhaps also of what is being perceived at the present moment).

This is in fact the way in which Aristotle argues for his doctrine that we have knowledge in the full sense of the word only of what is eternal or forever unchangeable:

Now what scientific knowledge ($\epsilon\pi\iota\sigma\tau\eta\mu\eta$) is, if we are to speak exactly and not follow mere similarities, is plain from what follows. We all suppose that what we know is not even capable of being otherwise; of things capable of being otherwise we do not know, when they have passed outside our observation, whether they exist or not. Therefore the object of scientific knowledge is of necessity. Therefore it is eternal . . . (*Eth. Nic.* VI 3. 1139^{b}18–23)

It is worth while noticing Aristotle's locution 'We all suppose'. It shows that Aristotle thought that what he was saying was not a peculiarity of his but rather a commonplace among the Greeks.

A concurrent reason why it was easy for Aristotle (and for the other Greeks) to accept the doctrine that there can be knowledge only of what is eternally the same is implicit on his view that sentences like 'Socrates sits' express one and the same opinion every time they are asserted. It is natural to say that an opinion of this sort cannot amount to real knowledge if it is sometimes false. For 'false knowledge'—even merely *sometimes* false knowledge—struck the Greeks, as it is likely to strike us today, as a misnomer.[31] Hence opinions that correspond to temporally indefinite sentences can constitute knowledge only if they are always true, i.e. only if they pertain to facts that never change. And if opinions of this kind are thought of as typical, then one may be inclined to say generally that we can have knowledge only of what is indestructible and unchangeable.[32]

---

[31] That it seemed a misnomer to Plato may be gathered from *Gorgias* 454 d, from *Republic* 476 e, and from *Theaetetus* 152 c and 186 e. Cf. also Parmenides, fr. 2 (Diels–Kranz), lines 7–8.

[32] This is to all intents and purposes the point of Aristotle's remarks in the *Cat.* 7. 7^{b}27–30: 'Destruction of the knowable carries knowledge to destruction. . . . For if

If we keep in mind that for Aristotle what is always necessary and that for him what is contingent sometimes will fail to be,[33] we can see that essentially this point is made by Aristotle in *An. Post.* I 33. 88ᵇ31–4: '. . . that which is necessary cannot be otherwise; but there are propositions which, though true and real, are also capable of being otherwise. Obviously it is not knowledge that is concerned with these . . .'

In many pronouncements of Aristotle's, both these reasons appear intertwined. The following seems to be especially worth quoting:

> For this reason, also, there is neither definition nor demonstration about individual sensible substances, because they have matter whose nature is such that they are capable both of being and of not being; for which reason all the individual instances of them are destructible. If then demonstration is of necessary truths and definition is a scientific process, and if, just as *knowledge cannot be sometimes knowledge and sometimes ignorance*, but the state which varies thus is opinion, so too demonstration and definition cannot vary thus, but it is opinion that deals with that which can be otherwise than it is, clearly there can neither be definition nor demonstration about sensible individuals. For *perishing things are obscure . . . when they have passed from our perception*; and though the formulae remain in the soul unchanged, there will no longer be either definition or demonstration (*Met. Z* 15. 1039ᵇ27–40ᵃ5; my italics).

This may be compared with *An. Post.* I 6. 74ᵇ33 ff., where a similar point is made. Here we obviously have one of the reasons why, for Aristotle, there could not be any genuine knowledge of sensible particulars, but only of universals. In *De Anima* III 3. 428ᵇ8–9 we similarly read: 'But true opinion only becomes false when the fact changes unnoticed.'

7. *Plato and the thesis 'knowledge is perception'*

Similar considerations seem to have been operative in Plato, too. In fact, Aristotle attributes exactly the same mode of argument to Plato:

Plato accepted his [Socrates'] teaching, but held that the problem [of

there is not a knowable there is not knowledge—there will no longer be anything for knowledge to be of . . .'

[33] See Chapter V below.

a universal definition] applied not to sensible things but to entities of another kind—for this reason, that the common definition could not be a definition of any sensible thing, as they were always changing. (*Met. A* 6. 987ᵇ4–7)

A few lines earlier, Aristotle alleges that Plato accepted the Heraclitean doctrine 'that all sensible things are ever in a state of flux and that there is no knowledge about them'. Whether these attributions are correct or not, similar juxtapositions of doctrines are found in Plato's writing. From our modern point of view, we may be puzzled and surprised by the facility with which Plato connects in the *Theaetetus* the view that 'Knowledge is perception' and the doctrine of Cratylus that all things are constantly changing.³⁴ This connection is introduced at 152 d, and it is frequently made use of in the argument; witness such passages as the following: 'If all things are forever in motion, every answer to any question whatsoever is equally correct' (*Theaetetus* 183 a).

Why should—how could—the constant and universal change postulated by Cratylus make true statements impossible? Clearly only if the statements in question primarily pertain to the moment of their utterance, and to other moments of time only in so far as things remain constant.³⁵

The notion of a sentence with a changing truth value may perhaps serve to explain Plato's strange doctrine of degrees of truth which Runciman finds so puzzling.³⁶ A sentence cannot at any given moment be truer than another true sentence, but it may be truer than another in the sense of being true *more often* than the latter is. Thus the different degrees of truth are in effect different degrees of unchangeability in the objects these truths are about. This connection is explicitly made by Plato in the *Philebus* (58 a–59 c).

If my interpretation of *De Interpretatione* 9 is correct, Aristotle there in fact uses the expression μᾶλλον ἀληθής meaning 'true *more often*'.³⁷

---

³⁴ For reasons other than the one we are interested in that Plato may have had for connecting the two doctrines, see Norman Gulley, *Plato's Theory of Knowledge* (Methuen, London, 1962), pp. 78–80.

³⁵ Aristotle, too, assumes that if all things were at rest, 'the same things will always be true and false', and that, conversely, if all things were in motion, 'nothing will be true and everything will be false' (*Met. Γ* 8.1012ᵇ24–8).

³⁶ Runciman, op. cit., pp. 124–5.

³⁷ See Chapter VIII below.

Another form of the same idea is that an opinion (*doxa*) is the better the more permanent it is. Thus in the *Meno* (89 c) Socrates says of a certain opinion: 'Yes, but not only a moment ago must it seem correct, but now also and hereafter, if it is to be at all sound.'

In the *Republic* (see 430 a) belief or opinion is in the same spirit compared to 'a dye, a dye designed to be as "fast" as possible'. The importance of the immutability of the Forms for Plato also becomes intelligible from this point of view. One of the most important roles of the Forms was just to provide absolutely immutable objects of knowledge and thereby secure the possibility of genuine knowledge.[38]

From this point of view we can also appreciate the firm connection there was in Plato's mind between, on one hand, the distinction between knowledge and true belief and, on the other hand, the distinction between Forms and sensible particulars:

My own verdict, then, is this. If intelligence and true belief are two different kinds, then these things—Forms that we cannot perceive but only think of—certainly exist in themselves; but if, as some hold, true belief in no way differs from intelligence, then all things we perceive through the bodily senses must be taken as the most certain reality. (*Timaeus* 51 d)

In general, we can see that there is a close connection between two apparently different and even contradictory preoccupations of Plato and Aristotle. On one hand, they paid a great deal of attention to the idea that 'Knowledge is perception', whether they in the last analysis accepted it or not. On the other hand, they were attracted by the idea that we can have knowledge only of what never changes. We can now see that these two types of knowledge were both assigned a privileged position by the Greek tendencies to conceive of knowledge as a kind of immediate awareness and to think in terms of temporally indefinite sentences. The two preoccupations are really two sides of one and the same coin.

A reference to our quotation from Homer perhaps helps us to appreciate the appeal of the idea that 'Knowledge is perception' to the Greeks. If even the superiority of the divine knowledge was essentially based on the greater share of perceptual evidence that

---

[38] Cf. *Parmenides* 135 b–c and *Cratylus* 439 d–440 c.

the gods possess, what more could there possibly be to knowledge than perception?

Our observations may also put into an appropriate perspective an argument that Plato's commentators have found puzzling and even mistaken. In *Theaetetus* 201 a–c Plato lets Socrates disprove the suggestion that knowledge can be defined as true opinion by drawing a contrast between the correct opinion of a jury which is giving the right verdict, and the knowledge of the event which is possessed by an eyewitness. This may seem puzzling because the objects of which an eyewitness to a crime has knowledge are not the kinds of things of which we can, according to Plato's (or Aristotle's) explicit doctrines, have genuine knowledge; they are not immutable Forms of which alone we can, according to Plato, have knowledge in the full sense of the word.

Now the idea that an eyewitness's knowledge is a paradigm case of genuine knowledge was seen to be one of the motives that led to the doctrine that we can have knowledge in the full sense of the word only of what is eternal. This suffices to explain Plato's apparent use of an eyewitness's knowledge as an example of real knowledge without jumping to the conclusion that we could, according to Plato, have genuine knowledge of sensible reality. The underlying reason why Plato could use the example he mentions is closely connected with the fascination that the idea that 'Knowledge is perception' had for him. Of course, Plato ended up rejecting this idea, but not before conceiving the highest form of knowledge in analogy to perception, as a kind of 'mental seeing or touching', to use Runciman's expression.

One could put the point as follows. What Plato wants to establish in *Theaetetus* 201 a–c is a distinction between knowledge and true belief. For this purpose it suffices for him to show that genuine knowledge is related to true belief in the same way as an eyewitness's 'knowledge' is related to 'knowledge' by hearsay, the last two being obviously different from one another. Cornford's view that we are here given only an 'analogous contrast' has much more to recommend itself than it has recently been given credit for.[39] It is true that Plato does speak of knowledge when he

---

[39] F. M. Cornford, *Plato's Theory of Knowledge* (Routledge and Kegan Paul, London, 1935), pp. 141–2; cf. Runciman, op. cit., pp. 37–8. It may be instructive to observe that in the passage I quoted from Aristotle's *Categories* in n. 32 above, he commits an inconsistency somewhat similar to the one Plato seems to me to commit

discusses the example, but he seems to restrict the scope of the example in so many words to 'matters which one can know only by having seen them and in no other way'.

8. *'Changing truth' and historical relativity*

The idea of 'changing truth' which we have found in Greek philosophers has to be distinguished from the modern idea of the historical relativity of truth. A historical relativist is apt to argue for an absence of any absolute criteria of truth, which results in an impossibility of obtaining truths that are not liable to be given up when the criteria are changed. What an ancient philosopher like Aristotle had in mind is almost exactly the opposite. He was not concerned with changes in our criteria of truth, but changes in the objects our truths are about. He was not concerned with changes in the opinions we have about reality, but with changes in the reality itself. Aristotle did not think that the discovery of truth is usually very difficult; the difficulty was, rather, that all the truths concerning changing things had to be discovered (as it were) all over again at each new moment.

9. *'Conjunctive' sense of present-tense statements and the idea of 'timeless present'*

Our observations concerning the notion of knowledge that naturally results from the Aristotelian presuppositions put these presuppositions themselves into a new perspective. We have so far spoken almost as if a temporally indefinite sentence in the present tense would for Aristotle normally refer merely to the moment at which it is uttered. We can see now that this is not the only way in which Aristotle was willing to understand such sentences and also why he could assume a different interpretation without any compunctions.

The alternative is to understand present-tense sentences in a 'tenseless' or perhaps better 'conjunctive' sense. In this sense, a sentence will mean that things are *always* in the way the sentence

here. Saying that the 'destruction of the knowable carries knowledge to destruction' is from an Aristotelian point of view a solecism, for of things destructible we cannot have genuine scientific knowledge (Aristotle's word is here *episteme*) in the first place.

states them to be. A number of passages in the Aristotelian corpus seem to rule out such a sense altogether. *De Int.* 3. 16ᵇ6–18 and 10. 19ᵇ11–18 as well as *De Anima* III. 6. 430ᵃ30 ff. are cases in point. However, in other passages the tenseless sense is clearly presupposed (see for instance, *Top.* V 3. 131ᵇ5–18).

The connection between the notions of time and knowledge which we have pointed out enable us to see that the difference between the two senses was much smaller for Aristotle than we might otherwise expect. For even if a present-tense statement appears to refer exclusively to the moment at which it is made, it can embody real knowledge (as we saw) only if it would have been true to make the same statement at any other moment of time. In so far as present-tense statements (without explicit temporal specifications or explicit restrictions to the present moment) are taken to represent claims to knowledge, they thus automatically assume a 'tenseless' or 'conjunctive' sense.

The conjunctive sense of present-tense statements might also be called their 'omnitemporal' sense. Recognizing its compatibility with the assumptions I have ascribed to the Greeks enables us to approach those utterances of Greek philosophers on the subject of time that prima facie might seem to go against my interpretation. There is no need for me to try to deny that Greek thinkers gradually developed doctrines of 'timeless present', as they have been called—doctrines, that is to say, according to which certain present-tense statements do not really contain any reference to time at all. Once a development in this direction got squarely under way, a sufficiently strong and independent thinker might very well have ended up with an outright denial of what I have—perhaps a shade too facilely—called tacit Greek presuppositions. It has sometimes been suggested that there was in fact in Greek philosophy a tradition essentially different in emphasis from what I have been describing—a tradition within which the idea of non-temporal existence and non-temporal predication slowly evolved.

As I have just indicated, there is nothing in the account I have given that rules out such a tradition. What my thesis implies is the direction from which this Greek tradition must be expected to have approached the idea of an atemporal sense of present-tense statements. If what gave rise to the conjunctive ('tenseless') sense was a tacit (or explicit) knowledge-claim and if this amounted to a claim of permanence, then it is to be expected that the idea of 'timeless present' was first developed by discussing 'real' knowledge as distinguished from mere belief and by postulating immutable objects of (real) knowledge. In short, we may expect to find a connection between the ideas of timelessness, knowledge, and permanence. Only secondarily, if at all, can we expect to find ideas about existence and predication that have no relation at all to time and change.

It seems to me unmistakable that, no matter precisely where we locate the different steps in this train of thought, this prediction or, rather, 'retrodiction' concerning its direction squares very well with what we find in the works of the proponents of this 'tenseless' tradition. The most important of them were undoubtedly Parmenides and Plato. In both, the marriage of the tenseless use of verbs with strong knowledge-claims and immutability is conspicuous. One piece of evidence will have to do duty for many here. G. E. L. Owen sums up his examination of 'Plato and Parmenides on the Timeless Present'[40] by saying that 'it is part of the originality of Plato to have grasped, or half-grasped, an important fact about certain kinds of statements, namely that they are tenseless whereas others are tensed. *But he tries to bring this contrast under his familiar distinction between the changeless and the changing*' (my italics).

10. *The idea of atemporal being is still underdeveloped by Plato and Aristotle*

Some sort of tenseless sense seems to be present already when Parmenides says of what is (fr. 8, line 5) : 'Nor was it ever nor will it be; for it is now, all together, single, continuous.' Hermann Fränkel has argued[41] that even here Parmenides is in effect comparing different moments of time with each other. This has provoked a sharp counter-argument from G. E. L. Owen.[42] I do not have to take sides in this controversy, however, for it concerns merely the stage reached by Parmenides in his groping toward the idea of an atemporal being.[43] The *direction* of Parmenides'

---

[40] The *Monist*, 50 (1966), 317–40; see p. 335.
[41] Hermann Fränkel, *Wege und Formen frühgriechischen Denkens* (second edition, C. H. Beck, Munich, 1960), p. 191 (note 1).   [42] Op. cit., pp. 320–1.
[43] It is nevertheless worth emphasizing that one can deny the presence of a fully

approach is what is relevant to my thesis here, and this point is clearly common ground for Fränkel and Owen. Parmenides' starting-point is clearly the idea of immutability, and equally clearly he is led to emphasize immutability because of his quest for knowledge stronger than illusory belief.

Whether and how a completely atemporal sense of present-tense statements was reached among the Greeks needs, of course, a careful separate investigation. One index of such a sense is a clear separation between *omnitemporality* and *eternity*. In Greek they would presumably be expressed by the adjectives ἀΐδιον (*aïdion*, everlasting) and αἰώνιον (*aionion*, eternal). However, the mere presence of this pair of words is not conclusive. For one thing, Plato still uses *aionion* of the 'regular motions of the astronomical clock' (as Owen puts it—see *Timaeus* 37 d). Even when he seems to have reached an explicitly atemporal concept, Plato cannot but betray the source of his idea. Thus we read (*Tim.* 37 e–38 a): 'Days, nights, months, years, . . . are all parts of time, and "was" and "will be" have come about as forms of time. We are wrong to apply them unthinkingly to what is eternal. Of this we say that it was and is and will be, but strictly only "is" belongs to it.' This sounds atemporal enough. But Plato continues: ' "Was" and "will be" should be spoken of the process that goes on in time, *for they are changes*' (my italics, of course). Plato's posture in the *Timaeus vis-à-vis* 'timeless present' has been described by Owen by saying that Plato 'is apparently ready to drop the word "now" from timeless propositions, but he imports "always" in its place (38 a)'.[44] If so, there can scarcely be said to be much of a sharp distinction between the omnitemporal and the eternal in the *Timaeus*.

In the *De Caelo* Aristotle likewise uses 'the word 'eternity' (αἰών) to describe . . . never-ending and never-changing existence', i.e. omnitemporality rather than atemporal eternity.[45]

Elsewhere, Aristotle speaks in so many words of things that are not *in time* (see *Phys.* IV 12. 220ᵇ32 ff.). It quickly turns out, however, that what he really means by this is that their existence

fledged idea of timeless being in Parmenides (including fr. 8, line 5) even if one rejects the particular arguments Fränkel uses. Cf., e.g., Leonardo Tarán, *Parmenides: a Text with Translation, Commentary, and Critical Essays* (Princeton University Press, Princeton, 1965), pp. 176–83.   [44] Op. cit., p. 333.

[45] See Friedrich Solmsen, *Aristotle's System of the Physical World* (Cornell University Press, Ithaca, N.Y., 1960), p. 157.

has no bounds in time. 'Things which are always are not, as such, in time, for they are not contained in time' (*Phys.* IV 12. 221ᵇ3–5). 'Not being in time' is thus not sharply distinguished— in fact, not distinguished at all—from omnitemporality by Aristotle.

From such indications one may thus plausibly infer that the explicitly atemporal sense of being that Owen almost ascribes to Aristotle in his essay 'Aristotle on the Snares of Ontology'[46] (Owen's *is***) is a radical anachronism. Even when employed merely as an analytical tool, this concept seems to be so foreign to Aristotle as to be of little value.

It might perhaps seem that I am watering down my thesis to a near-tautology by admitting a gradual development of the idea of atemporal existence among the Greeks. Surely such a sophisti- cated idea must in any case have developed by stages from some- thing more concrete, such as the idea of omnitemporal existence, a reader might object. In order to counteract this impression of vacuity, it is in order to indicate what sorts of ideas would tell against my thesis. Conceptually, the most telling counter- examples would not be among the entities that spring to our minds when we think of 'things eternal'. Such metaphysical entities as eternal Forms and everlasting gods often still bear marked traces of their conceptual dependence of the plain notion of omnitemporality. Conceptually, a philosopher is much further removed from the boundaries of *our* succession of actual nows when he considers *à la* Leibniz altogether different possible histories of the world than when he contemplates exotic actors— even backstage *artistes*—on the stage of *our* world history. Of this idea of possible worlds in the sense of successions of times alto- gether separate from ours it is very hard to find traces in Greek thinkers, however. On the contrary, there are indications that it was not taken into account by Aristotle at least. (Cf. Chapter IX, section 16, below.)

11. *The semantic background of the idea of changing truth*

The features of Aristotle's thinking that we have noted are related

46 See *New Essays on Plato and Aristotle*, ed. by R. Bambrough (Routledge and Kegan Paul, London, 1965). (Cf. my review article on this volume, 'New Essays on Old Philosophers', *Inquiry*, 10 (1967), 101–13.)

in more than one way to his other logical, semantic, and psychological doctrines. The idea that a temporally indefinite sentence may express one and the same opinion or belief when uttered at different moments of time is encouraged by Aristotle's idea that 'spoken sounds are symbols of affections in the soul' (*De Int.* 1. 16ᵃ3–4). It is obvious that the sentence, 'It is raining', as uttered by me today, is made true or false by a set of facts different from those that verified or falsified my utterance yesterday, 'It is raining'. But it is very natural to say that in some sense the state of mind or attitude toward my environment that is expressed by the two utterances is the same. The facts to which yesterday's utterance refers are referred to today by the sentence, 'It was raining yesterday.' But the 'state of mind' that this utterance appears to express seems to be entirely different from that expressed by yesterday's present-tense utterance, 'It is raining'. For instance, the former involves a thought about a temporal difference between the time the sentence refers to and the time of the utterance of the sentence, whereas the latter presupposes no awareness of such a difference.[47] Hence the idea that spoken words are symbols for unspoken thoughts encourages the idea that one and the same temporally indefinite form of words expresses one and the same belief or opinion at the different times when it is uttered.

It is tempting to express this point by saying that Aristotle presupposed a principle of individuation for propositions different from ours. This way of putting my point turns out to need qualifications, but it is nevertheless useful for many purposes. For instance, we can now see that one of my earlier explanations has to be qualified. The typical sentences considered by Aristotle were said to contain, explicitly or implicitly, a token-reflexive expression like 'now' or 'at the present moment'. This makes the sentences in question in a sense token-reflexive from our modern point of view. The proposition such a sentence expresses is different on different occasions. However, the very same sentences were *not* token-reflexive for Aristotle in this sense, for the belief or opinion they express at different times was for him one and the same.

[47] This is borne out by Aristotle's comments in *De Memoria*; see, e.g., 449ᵇ24–30. One is here reminded of Russell's paradoxical statement that ' "present" and "past" are *primarily* psychological terms . . .' (op. cit., p. 113).

Notice also that a defender of our modern view cannot argue that Aristotle handles temporally indefinite sentences incorrectly because they express a different meaning or thought (Frege's *Gedanke*) in different contexts. Aristotle's procedure implies that we have to individuate thoughts or opinions expressed by temporally indefinite sentences in the same way as these sentences themselves.

In the Aristotelian *Physics* we find a neat metaphysical projection of the semantic idea we have discussed. According to the latter, the belief expressed by a sentence containing the word 'now' remains ordinarily one and the same. In the *Physics*, Aristotle argues that the 'now' is in the actual sense of the word *always the same*. It is what 'holds the time together' and makes it continuous (see *Physics* IV 13. 222ᵃ10 ff. and 11. 219ᵇ10–20ᵃ4). There seems to be an interesting analogy between the way different moments of time are actualized by becoming in turn identified with the eternally identical 'now', and the way in which the content of a known 'now' statement becomes relevant to the world at the different moments of time by becoming utterable at the moment in question.

It is thus literally the case that the word 'now' was not token-reflexive for Aristotle, for each actually uttered 'now' referred to the same forever-identical actual 'now' that is postulated in the *Physics*.

12. *Cultural background*

It may be suspected that the peculiarities we have discussed are connected with the general attitudes the Greeks had toward time. It has been suggested that the Greeks 'lived in the present moment' to a larger extent than the members of other cultures.[48] It might seem tempting to see in the Aristotelian way of handling the relations of the concepts of time and truth a reflection of the same attitude. It is as if philosophers were so absorbed in the present moment that they tended to think in terms of sentences that contained a reference to the present moment and therefore dealt primarily with the present state of affairs. It is not easy, however, to find direct evidence for (or against) this suggestion.

[48] Cf., e.g., the hyperbolic statements of Oswald Spengler's in *The Decline of the West*, vol. i (New York, 1926), p. 131. 'Classical man's existence—Euclidean, relationless, point-like—was wholly contained in the instant.'

There are in any case other general features of the Greek intellectual scene relevant to our subject. Whether or not there was a direct connection between the general Greek attitude toward time and their philosophers' ways of handling this notion, there is the fact that the Greeks were not very successful with their timekeeping—much less successful than some earlier civilizations, not to speak of the Romans. Different cities could have different calendars to such an extent that the year might begin at different times and that the thirteenth month that periodically had to be added to the year was added at different times.[49] Combined with a general neglect of public timekeeping, it is no wonder that the failure of chronology sometimes amounted to a public scandal, as shown by Aristophanes in the *Clouds*. Because of these failures of chronology, there simply was no handy way for the Greeks to take the course modern philosophers generally assume to be the only satisfactory one, viz. to replace all references to the indefinite 'now' in a sentence by references to some chronology independent of the moment at which the sentence is uttered. What point would there have been in replacing the sentence 'It is raining in Athens today' by a sentence in which the day in question is specified by a reference to a calendar of the form 'On such-and-such a day of such-and-such a year it is raining in Athens' if the day and perhaps even the year were different in another city? A reference to the moment of utterance must have been as useful in general as a reference to a badly kept calendar.[50]

It is difficult not to see in this neglect of a systematic calendar a symptom of a general lack of interest in timekeeping and in

[49] See *A History of Technology*, vol. iii, ed. by C. Singer, E. J. Holmyard, A. R. Hall, and T. I. Williams (Clarendon Press, Oxford, 1954–8), p. 569.

[50] The connection between the problems of time-measurement and the logic of tenses cuts deeper than modern philosophers sometimes realize. As Y. Bar-Hillel points out in his useful paper, 'Indexical Expressions', *Mind*, 63 (1954), 359–79, the problem of converting temporally indefinite sentences into definite ones is not without its presuppositions. To express 'The sun is now shining' in temporally definite terms, I must know what time it is (at the place I am talking about). What comes up in the ancient Greek world is primarily the practical difficulty of setting up a useful frame of temporal references. But when we consider statements made at spatially distant parts, even difficulties in principle start cropping up. These are of the well-known relativistic variety. If we want to build up a tense-logic that applies to more than one world-line (as is necessary if we, for example, want to study quantified tense-logic) and is compatible with physical reality, we cannot accept the usual simple tense-logic with a linear structure but must instead have one that has the structure of Lewis's S4. On this point, see my paper 'The Modes of Modality', *Acta Philosophica Fennica*, 16 (1963), 65–81, especially p. 76.

chronology. It is perhaps not impossible to find some independent evidence of the same attitude. For instance, Hermann Fränkel's study of the early Greek ideas of time has led him to state bluntly that in the *Iliad* 'There is virtually no interest in chronology, neither in absolute chronology nor in relative one.'[51] He does not find much more interest in later writers, either. This squares rather well with the early Greek ways of expressing temporal relations that Eric Havelock has emphasized. He points out that events were located in time not with reference to any absolute chronology but rather by reference to each other: 'The basic grammatical expression which would symbolise the link of event to event would be simply the phrase "and next".'[52]

13. *Reliance on the spoken word*

It seems to me, however, that there is another closely related feature in Aristotle's background which was more important or at least easier to document. This is the fact that in some obvious though elusive sense the Greek culture was largely based on the *spoken* and not on the *written* word. In philosophical literature this oral character of the Greek thought is shown, for example, by the importance of dialogue as a method of presenting philosophical ideas. One is also reminded of the origins of logic in the technique of oral argumentation. Every reader of Aristotle's *Topics* knows to what extraordinary extent he was concerned with the tricks and pitfalls of verbal exchange.

From this emphasis on the spoken word it follows that the reasons for replacing temporally indefinite sentences by temporally definite ones which modern philosophers have were to some extent absent. If the spoken word is primary in relation to the written word, one is apt to think of and discuss logical and semantical matters from the vantage point of some situation in which the words in question are actually uttered. Now this situation supplies what is missing from a temporally indefinite sentence itself; it enables us to know what the moment of time actually is to which the spoken word 'now' refers. A logician

---

[51] Hermann Fränkel, *Wege und Formen frühgriechischen Denkens*, 2nd ed. (C. H. Beck, Munich, 1960), p. 2. Cf. Eric Havelock, *Preface to Plato* (Harvard University Press, Cambridge, Mass., 1963), pp. 192–3, notes 22 and 27.

[52] Havelock, op. cit., p. 180.

eliminates the indefiniteness of temporally indefinite sentences by projecting himself, as it were, to the audience of someone actually uttering the sentence in question. In a written text such words as 'now' and 'at the present moment' are indeterminate in a sense in which they are not indeterminate as a part of actual speech. In a written culture the replacement of temporally indefinite sentences by definite ones is more important than in an oral culture—to the extent that it might appear to its philosophers as the only 'correct' course.

The primacy of the spoken word in relation to the written word is not merely an explanatory hypothesis of a historian; it occurs as an explicit doctrine both in Plato and in Aristotle. Plato's rejection of the written word as a mere aid to one's memory and as being dead and helpless as compared with the spoken word is well known and need not be elaborated here.[53] Aristotle expresses himself in different terms but equally clearly; according to him 'written marks are symbols of spoken sounds' in the same way as the latter were in turn symbols of 'affections in the soul'.[54]

Eric Havelock has emphasized the same feature in the background of Plato that I am now stressing in the common background of the philosophers of the Socratic school.[55] The use he makes of this idea is different from mine, however. Havelock considers Plato's philosophy as an expression of a transition from a poetic oral tradition to a conceptual culture based on written records. This approach is appealing, but even if the uses Havelock makes of it are fully justified it does not exclude the possibility that many traces of a reliance on the spoken word persisted in Plato's and Aristotle's thinking. If I am right, the heavy reliance on temporally indefinite sentences as a medium of knowledge and of opinion is such a trace.[56]

It is also remarkable that in some unacknowledged sense the spoken word was for Plato and Aristotle even logically prior to the

[53] Cf., e.g., *Phaedrus* 275 d–276 a. A full documentation is given in Paul Friedländer, *Platon*, vol. i (3rd ed., Walter de Gruyter & Co., Berlin, 1964), Ch. 5, especially pp. 116–21.

[54] *De Int.* 1. 16ᵃ3–6.   [55] Havelock, op. cit., *passim*.

[56] In fact, I would go further and say that in the particular matter at hand, *pace* Havelock, Plato is an arch-conservative who in his logical semantical doctrines relies entirely on the spoken word, whatever other differences there may be between him and the 'poetic tradition'. The references given in note 53 above show how deeply Plato felt about this matter.

thoughts it expresses. Plato explained the nature of thinking by calling it 'the inward dialogue carried on by the mind with itself without spoken sound'.[57] This was not merely a metaphor, for Plato felt free to carry out arguments and considerations in terms of spoken sentences and then to transfer the results so as to apply to the corresponding thoughts as well. This is in fact the strategy of Plato's interesting and important discussion at the end of the *Sophist*.

Aristotle does not formulate the logical primacy of the spoken word as compared with thinking as an explicit doctrine. However, he sometimes does exactly the same as Plato, that is to say, he too sometimes bases his view of what we can say of people's *thoughts* on what can be said of their words. The passages quoted above from *Categories* 5 are instructive cases in point.[58] It may be observed that the word that Aristotle uses in these passages, which was translated by Ackrill as 'statement', viz. *logos*, often refers to *spoken* words and sentences.

It is perhaps not irrelevant to mention that both Aeschylus (*Agamemnon* l. 276) and Homer occasionally referred to people's thoughts as 'wingless' or unspoken words.

This primacy of concepts applying to spoken words and sentences in relation to concepts referring to thinking must have encouraged the idea that one and the same temporally indefinite sentence expresses one and the same thought (opinion, belief) even when it is uttered on different occasions. If a thought is, logically speaking, nothing but a statement addressed by the 'speaker' to himself without spoken sounds, the question whether a statement specifies a complete thought becomes tantamount to the question whether the speaker has to add something to this statement when he tacitly addresses it to himself in order to make it fully understood by the 'hearer'. The obvious answer is that no expansion is needed as compared with occasions when the same form of words is addressed to someone else, for surely a man understands his own words if they are explicit enough for others to understand them. Hence the grammatical identity of a spoken sentence (form of words) easily becomes a criterion of the identity of the corresponding thoughts, too. Thus a transition from the spoken word to thoughts it expresses does not seem

---

[57] See *Theaetetus* 190 a and *Sophistes* 263 e.
[58] *Categories* 5. 4^{a}23–8, 4^{a}34–^{b}2.

to necessitate any changes in the principle of individuation involved.

The conceptual primacy of the spoken word over thinking is related to the absence of a full-fledged notion of a proposition in Plato and Aristotle. By and large, they tended to discuss logical and semantical matters in terms of actual utterances rather than in terms of the thoughts or beliefs expressed. It is true that in the opening paragraph of the *De Interpretatione* which we discussed the order of relative importance seems to be the opposite. Aristotle says there that spoken sounds are symbols of affections of the soul. However, Aristotle seems to have rather limited purposes in mind in this passage. As Ackrill points out, what the reference to the 'affections in the soul' is primarily intended to elucidate is the fact that although spoken and written sounds are different in different languages, what the words express may be 'the same for all men', as Aristotle himself says.[59] As Ackrill also points out, 'the notion that utterances are symbols of affections in the soul does not have a decisive influence on the rest of *De Interpretatione*'. Like other Greek philosophers, Aristotle thought of logical and semantical matters primarily in terms of the spoken language.

The same point is applied to Plato by F. M. Cornford.[60]

Logicians . . . might maintain that there is a false 'proposition' . . . which has a meaning, though I cannot believe it. With that we are not concerned, but only with judgments and statements that can be actually made and believed by some rational being. Plato never discusses 'propositions' that no one propounds.

Similar remarks can be made of the Stoic concepts of a *lekton* and of an *axioma*, closely though they approximate our notion of a proposition in many other respects. Thus Mrs. Kneale writes as follows:[61]

As a previously quoted passage has shown, the Stoics wished to insist that an *axioma* which is to be described as true or false must somehow be present when it is so described; . . . in one place Sextus clearly assumes that *lekta* exist only when they are expressed or meant.

As far as Aristotle is concerned, it would not be strictly true to say he never considers propositions that no one propounds. He comes very close to envisaging one in *De. Int.* 9. 18ᵇ36. It is no

---

[59] Ackrill, op. cit., pp. 113–14.   [60] Op. cit., p. 113.
[61] W. Kneale and M. Kneale, op. cit., p. 156.

accident, however, that this passage is, if I am right, exactly the passage in which Aristotle came closest to considering statements that refer to a unique singular event and therefore need an objective chronology.[62] The other similar cases that there are in Aristotle of unasserted propositions are much less clear, and probably explainable as mere *façons de parler*.

14. *'The sense of the temporal'*

If there is anything to the contention that the Greeks 'lived in the present' to a larger extent than the members of some other tradition, the justification (and perhaps also the import) of this suggestion has to be spelled out in terms of such concrete facts as those that are known about the ways of Greek philosophers with the concepts of time and truth. Whether or not the facts we have pointed out go very far toward establishing any broad generalizations, in any case they show us how the different facets of the Greek way of thinking are related to each other. The suggestion that the Greeks were immersed in the present moment more deeply than we are easily provokes a reply that points to the preoccupation of the Greek philosophers with the eternal and the immutable. We have seen, however, that this preoccupation is closely connected with the reliance of these philosophers on temporally indefinite sentences. Far from being a counter-example to the temporality of Greek thought, this pursuit of the eternal is more of a manifestation of this very temporality—or perhaps rather an attempt to compensate for it. Plato's and Aristotle's ideal of knowledge was knowledge of eternal truths just because the vehicles by means of which truths were thought of by them as being expressed tended to make all other kinds of truths ephemeral. In a sense I am thus led to agreement with the view of R. G. Collingwood that 'the Greek pursuit of the eternal was as eager as it was, precisely because the Greeks themselves had an unusually vivid sense of the temporal'.[63]

---

[62] See Chapter VIII below.
[63] R. G. Collingwood, *The Idea of History* (Clarendon Press, Oxford, 1946), p. 22.

V

ARISTOTLE ON THE REALIZATION
OF POSSIBILITIES IN TIME

1. *The relation of modality to time in Aristotle is problematic*

AN attentive reader of the Aristotelian corpus can scarcely fail
to notice that in certain respects the Stagirite used the *modal
notions* of possibility and necessity in a manner different from our
modern ways with them. A case in point is the relation of
modality to time. That there is something not quite familiar
about the way Aristotle was wont to operate with the concepts of
necessity and possibility is already betrayed by his repeated
statements to the effect that the past is necessary.[1] Natural
though such statements sound, the sense of necessity involved
here is not a familiar part of the conceptual repertoire of today's
philosophers.

Another indication of a difference between Aristotle's modal
notions and ours is the close connection that there is for him
between necessary (apodeictic) truths and plain (assertoric)
general truths, in short between necessity and universality. This
is brought out strikingly by the role he ascribed to the assertoric
syllogism as a vehicle of scientific demonstration. Since he also
held that 'the truth obtained by demonstrative knowledge will be
necessary' (*An. Post.* I 4. 73ᵃ21–4) and that 'demonstrative
knowledge must be knowledge of a necessary nexus, and therefore must clearly be obtained through a necessary middle term'
(*An. Post.* I 6. 75ᵃ12–14), an assertoric syllogism must clearly be
capable of establishing necessity. On the other hand, Aristotle
distinguished between assertoric (simple) and apodeictic (necessary) premisses and conclusions. Since even the assertoric syllogisms were seen to be capable of establishing necessary scientific

---

[1] See, e.g., *Rhet.* III 17. 1418ᵃ3–5; *Eth. Nic.* VI 2. 1139ᵇ7–9; *De Caelo* I 12.
283ᵇ13 ff., and cf. Chapter IX below.

truths, one may expect that they are somehow related to the apodeictic syllogisms in a closer manner than we are accustomed to.

2. *The realization of possibilities in time*

There is an assumption concerning the interrelations of time and modality which has undoubtedly played a much more important role in the history of Western thought—in the history of metaphysics, theology, logic, philosophy of nature, and even speculative poetry—than any other assumption concerning their relationships. This is the assumption that *all genuine possibilities*, or at least all possibilities of some central and important kind, *are actualized in time*. Any such possibility thus has been, is, or will be realized; it cannot remain unrealized through an infinite stretch of time; in a sense, everything possible will happen in the long run.

Obviously, this assumption admits of many variants, some of which will be distinguished from each other later in this chapter. For one thing, it is not clear what kind of possibility is intended in it. Possible events? Possible courses of events? Possible kinds of individuals? Possible individuals (particulars)? Some of these distinctions turn out to be crucial for the study of the later stages of the history of this principle.[2]

If the principle is applied to possible kinds of individuals, it says that *all* possible kinds of individuals are realized in the course of time—in that particular 'possible world' that is in fact actualized, as Leibniz would have said. In a sense, the assumption under consideration thus amounts to saying that the actual world is as full as it can be, that it is the fullest or most plentiful world possible. This has led Arthur O. Lovejoy to call the assumption 'the principle of plenitude'. In the absence of any other convenient designation, I shall adopt this term, although it is important to realize that this locution can be highly misleading when used in contexts different from the rather limited one Lovejoy has primarily in mind. For us it will be a mere *terminus technicus*.

[2] See, e.g., my paper 'Leibniz on Plenitude, Relations, and the "Reign of Law"', in *Modern Studies in Philosophy: Leibniz*, ed. by Harry Frankfurt (Doubleday, Garden City, N.Y., 1972).

3. *A. O. Lovejoy on the principle of plenitude*

Lovejoy has studied the history of the principle of plenitude in his book *The Great Chain of Being*.[3] This work is impressive as a documentation of the importance of the principle of plenitude in Western thought. It has been widely influential, especially among literary historians. As a contribution to the history of philosophy, however, it leaves a great deal to be desired. Important aspects of the role of the principle of plenitude, conceived of as a precise ontological assumption, remain almost completely unexamined by Lovejoy. They include its role in Stoic thought, in the philosophy of nature of the late Middle Ages, in the methodology of early modern science, and in certain parts of the thought of Leibniz and Descartes, to mention only some of these 'gaps in *The Great Chain of Being*'. They are not the business of the present chapter, however. It is more important here to note that Lovejoy seems to be almost consistently wrong about the early stages of the principle, provided again that we understand it in a fairly literal sense, as Lovejoy in fact does himself. Lovejoy claims that Plato adopted and used the principle while Aristotle did not. The truth, it seems to me, is precisely the opposite: Plato rejected for most relevant purposes the principle of plenitude, whereas Aristotle was not only inclined to think that it is true, but made conscious use of it in philosophical arguments and gave some reasons for believing it. As far as Plato is concerned, his relationship to the principle has been discussed by Erkka Maula.[4] Here we shall concentrate our attention on Aristotle.

4. *A plenitude of formulations of the principle*

In order to bring out some aspects of the role of the principle of plenitude, it may be useful already at this stage to state some of its alternative formulations. The principle itself may (tentatively and approximately) be formulated as follows:

each possibility is realized at some moment of time.

Later, we shall see that in order to catch Aristotle's intentions it must probably be expressed in a slightly qualified form:

[3] Arthur O. Lovejoy, *The Great Chain of Being: a Study of the History of an Idea* (Harvard University Press, Cambridge, Mass., 1936).
[4] Erkka Maula, 'Plato on Plenitude', *Ajatus*, 29 (1967), 12–50.

(T) no unqualified possibility remains unactualized through an infinity of time.

Hence, if something can possibly exist, it sometimes will exist in fact. Hence the only things that *never* are, are the impossibilities. Thus we obtain the following variant of (T):

(T)$_1$ that which never is, is impossible.

By the same token, what never fails to be, cannot fail to be, that is, is necessarily:

(T)$_2$ what always is, is by necessity.

For some purposes, we might reformulate (T)$_2$ as follows:

what is eternal, is by necessity.

However, we are not entitled to mean by 'eternal' here anything more than omnitemporality. Hence if someone wants to make a distinction between what is omnitemporally and what is timelessly (eternally in *one* sense of the word), he cannot use this formulation.

In so far as we can disregard this point, however, it can be said that whoever adopts the principle of plenitude makes such attributions as 'eternal' and 'necessary' at least materially equivalent, and the same goes without qualifications for such attributes as 'necessary', 'imperishable', 'indestructible', 'omnitemporal', and 'always existing'.

As far as Aristotle is concerned, it is in fact the case that he did not distinguish 'eternal' and 'omnitemporal'. When he spoke of certain things being 'not in time', he made clear that he merely meant that they are not 'in the middle of time', so to speak, i.e. that their existence is not limited by the earlier and later moments of time. In other words, 'not being in time' was simply tantamount to 'omnitemporal'. (For evidence, see *Phys.* IV 12.)

For Aristotle what is contingently is not by necessity, and hence possibly is not. If this possibility is sometimes realized, the contingent cannot be eternal. Thus contraposition yields the following form of the principle:

(T)$_3$ nothing eternal is contingent.

By 'contingent' we mean here 'neither necessary nor impossible'.

It is clear that, with the exception of (T)$_3$, the implications we have formulated can be (on suitable assumptions accepted by

Aristotle) strengthened into equivalences. The converse implications are in fact unproblematic, and also independent of the principle of plenitude. Hence they will not be discussed here.

It must be emphasized that the equivalence of the four forms of the principle listed above is not a projection of our latter-day logic back to Aristotle. On the contrary, all the assumptions that are needed to move from one to another are explicitly formulated by Aristotle in *De Int.* 12–13 (cf. Chapter III above). Moreover, Aristotle in fact used himself the resulting possibilities of reformulating the principle (T). He frequently operates with the other forms as well in a way which indicates that he identifies them with each other and with (T). Furthermore, he occasionally sketches arguments that relate some of the variants of the principle to each other. A case in point is found in *Met.* Θ 8. 1050^{b}6–24. Thus whatever evidence (or counter-evidence) there is for (or against) one version of the principle of plenitude in Aristotle, is thus also evidence for (or against) all the others.

5. Contra *Lovejoy*

Lovejoy tries to present some evidence against thinking that Aristotle subscribed to the principle of plenitude. He refers to two passages, and to two only, in support of his view. These are *Met.* B 6. 1003^{a}2 and Λ 6. 1071^{b}13–14. Lovejoy apparently does not realize, however, that both these passages are ambiguous. They are quoted by him as follows: '. . . it is not necessary that everything that is possible should exist in actuality'; '. . . it is possible for that which has a potency not to realize it'.

These may be construed in several ways. They are statements about the failure of a potentiality to be actualized. We have to ask: Do these equivocal statements pertain to *each* potency, or only to *some* potencies? Furthermore, we have to ask: Do they refer to a mere *temporary* failure of a potentiality to be actualized, or can the failure in question *last infinitely long*? According to the answers that are given to these questions we obtain four possible interpretations of Aristotle's thesis:

(a) Some potentialities may *sometimes* fail to be actualized.
(b) Some potentialities may fail to be actualized *ever*.
(a)′ Each potentiality may *sometimes* fail to be actualized.
(b)′ Each potentiality may fail to be actualized *ever*.

The text does not seem to allow a clear-cut decision between these readings. Hence the context will have to decide.

Of the interpretations listed, (a) and (a)' are compatible with the principle of plenitude in the form in which we are here considering it, and therefore fail to support Lovejoy's claim that Aristotle rejected the principle, whereas the readings (b) and (b)' contradict the principle. Hence we have to decide which of the two kinds Aristotle is presupposing.

There is no obvious way of excogitating Aristotle's meaning in *Met. B* 6. 1003ª2; and even if there were, it would not settle the question one way or the other, for Aristotle is in this passage formulating a problem rather than giving his own considered opinion.

Although the second passage quoted by Lovejoy is also quite terse, the context there makes his sense clear. A few lines later Aristotle writes: 'Further, even if it [sc. a Platonic Form] acts, it will not be enough, if its essence is potency; for there will not be eternal movement, since that which is potentially may possibly not be' (*Met. Λ* 6. 1071ᵇ18–20; translation by Sir David Ross). The principle Aristotle is appealing to in the last clause is evidently the same he announced a few lines earlier in the passage Lovejoy quotes. The way he is using it here shows, first of all, that Aristotle is presupposing a sense of potentiality in which that which potentially is is also potentially is not. In other words, Aristotle is using potentiality in the sense of two-way possibility (contingency); for him, the possibility (in the sense of contingency) of being entails the possibility of not being.

Aristotle is using the principle to argue that a Form that exists merely potentially cannot guarantee eternal movement because (being merely potential) it may fail to be actualized at some moment of time and hence incapable of supporting the movement at that time. Obviously, the formulations (b) and (b)' are beside this avowed purpose of Aristotle's. (He is not claiming here that a potential form could *never* be a principle of motion.) Hence he does not deny the principle of plenitude in his argument, but rather assumes one of the weaker formulations (a)–(a)'.

Of the two remaining alternatives, (a) is clearly too weak to support Aristotle's argument. Aristotle wants to argue that if a Form is a mere potentiality, it may fail to exist. For this purpose, it does not suffice to assume that *some* potentialities may fail to exist, for those potentialities might then not include the forms. Hence Aristotle must assume (a)′ and not (a).

But even this is not enough for Aristotle's purposes. Even if it is true of each merely potential being that it *may* fail to exist at some moment of time, it may still *happen to* exist all through an eternity. Or, rather, it may so exist unless it is assumed that its possibility of not existing is at some time actualized. Now it is clear that Aristotle must make this assumption; for otherwise it might be alleged that the forms enjoy an accidental eternity, and hence can support eternal movement after all. (Such accidental eternity was perhaps ascribed to Plato's Forms in *Met. A* 9. 990^{b}29–991^{a}7.) In other words, Aristotle is tacitly giving the principle he mentions the following strong sense:

> (a)″ Each mere possibility (contingency) will in fact fail to be actualized at some moment of time.

This principle is an instance of the principle of plenitude; it says that the possibility that each merely possible (potential) being has of not being cannot remain unactualized for an infinity of time. Hence we may turn the tables against Lovejoy. Instead of demonstrating that Aristotle rejected the principle of plenitude (in the form in which we have been discussing it), the passage we have considered shows that Aristotle was in fact relying on it.

6. *Plenitude is not a 'unit idea'*

Lovejoy's mistakes on Plato and Aristotle can be traced to a deeper source. For some reason he considers the principle of plenitude in one context only. It is, he says, 'an attempted answer to *a* philosophical question' (op. cit., p. 14, my italic), and according to Lovejoy it could scarcely be anything else, for then it would not be a 'unit idea' in his sense any more than the concept of God is one.[5] This single question Lovejoy clearly takes to pertain to the relation of the creator to his creatures and more generally to the idea of creation.

This seems to me to be a seriously oversimplified view, however. The assumption which Lovejoy calls the principle of plenitude occurs in the history of philosophy in many different

[5] Lovejoy, op. cit., p. 4.

contexts, as an answer (as it were) to many different kinds of questions. Notwithstanding his own injunction, Lovejoy himself notes in the course of his discussion certain connections between the principle and the idea of determinism and of evolution, neither of which is necessarily connected with the idea of creation. In Diodorus Cronus the principle of plenitude occurs as an alleged consequence of a logical argument, the lost 'Master Argument' which was famous in antiquity.[6]

7. *Other apparent counter-evidence*

Apart from the evidence Lovejoy offers, there might seem to be passages and whole theories in Aristotle that contradict the principle of plenitude. A case in point is Aristotle's conception of infinity which is often formulated by saying that according to the Stagirite infinity exists merely potentially—that it is conceivable but never realized. In Chapter VI below I shall discuss the Aristotelian theory of infinity in some detail and show that it is not only compatible with the principle of plenitude but relies on it, and hence cannot be fully understood without appreciating the role of the principle in Aristotle. I also suspect that the ever-unrealized possibilities mentioned in the *De Interpretatione* are various kinds of infinity, which in fact are mentioned in *Metaphysics* in a rather similar context.

Another piece of apparent counter-evidence is Aristotle's example in *De Interpretatione* 9 : 'For example, it is possible for this cloak to be cut up, and yet it will not be cut up but will wear out first.' Here we in fact have a clear instance of possibility that according to Aristotle will not be realized. It does not go to show that the principal forms of the principle of plenitude cannot be attributed to Aristotle, however. The possibility of a particular cloak's being cut up is a possibility concerning an individual object, and not a possibility concerning kinds of individuals or kinds of events. Nor does the unfulfilled possibility Aristotle mentions remain unfulfilled through an infinity of time, for when the cloak wears out, it goes out of existence, and no possibility can any longer be attributed to it. Thus Aristotle's example does show that the 'genuine' possibilities which the principle says are actualized do not for him include possibilities concerning indi-

[6] See Chapter IX below.

vidual objects which only exist for a certain period of time. However, it does not show that Aristotle did not believe in some other forms of the principle which prima facie are much more plausible anyway.

A few further examples of apparently disconfirmatory evidence have to be disposed of. For instance, in a passage of *An. Post.* (see I 6. 75ª31–5), Aristotle says that accidental attributes (τὰ συμβεβηκότα) are not necessary, and if we draw a conclusion by their means, we therefore do not necessarily know why the conclusion is true; not even if the attributes belong always, but not *per se*, as in syllogisms through signs. Here Aristotle might seem to be denying $(T)_2$. However, this impression is rather misleading. First of all, it is not clear that Aristotle's statement is not counterfactual, for the optative εἴη scarcely commits Aristotle to holding that there *in fact* are cases of the kind he is describing. The only thing we can definitely extract from the passage is that even an attribute that always belongs to a subject is not necessarily *known* to do so, which of course does rule out that the attribute could belong (unknownst but) necessarily to the subject. In fact, the passage continues as follows (Oxford translation): '. . . for though the conclusion be actually essential, one will not know it as essential or know its reason'. Hence, no exception to the principle of plenitude is being contemplated by Aristotle here.

Some editors and commentators have tried to find room in *Phys.* III 1. 200ᵇ26 (and in *Met. K* 9. 1065ᵇ5) for potentialities that are not actualized. As pointed out by Ross in his edition of the *Physics* (Clarendon Press, 1936, ad loc.), this does not have any support in the manuscripts of the *Physics*, in the best manuscripts of the *Metaphysics*, or in Alexander, Themistius, Porphyry, Philoponus, and Simplicius.

A counter-example to the principle of plenitude might seem to be offered by *Top.* IV 5. 126ª34 ff. Although too complicated to be analysed here, this passage does not contradict the principle.

A few other apparent counter-examples can be explained away in terms of Aristotle's distinction between absolute and relative necessity and possibility. A more difficult problem is presented by the mare's nest of perplexing arguments we find in *Met. Θ* 3–4. At times, Aristotle there seems to declare his adherence to the principle and yet he also very definitely wants to criticize the Megarians who do likewise. Since the interpretation of Aristotle's polemic against the Megarians admittedly turns on collateral evidence offered by the rest of the Aristotelian corpus, I shall postpone my examination of this difficult problem to a later stage of our discussion, merely registering here my belief that *Met.* Θ 3–4 strongly supports my attribution of the principle of plenitude to Aristotle.

8. *The role of the principle of plenitude as a bridge between time and modality*

A word of warning seems to be in order here. However firmly Aristotle may have believed in the principle of plenitude, it is very dubious whether he ever considered it as giving us a definition of his concept of possibility. In other words, however strongly he assumed that something is possible if and only if it is sometimes the case, he did not on most occasions think of this as exhausting the meaning of assertions of possibility. Occasionally, he seems to have been pushed to this by the intrinsic difficulties in his own conception of possibility. (Cf. the discussion of his criticism of the Megarians below.) Furthermore, some of his occasional pronouncements point to this direction.

It is true that occasionally Aristotle seems to go as far as to be ready to *define* certain particular modal expressions in temporal terms. A case in point is found in *Top.* VI 6. 145ᵇ27 ff.: 'Whenever, then, we say that a living thing is now indestructible (ἄφθαρτον), we mean (τοῦτο λέγομεν) that it is at present a living thing of such a kind as never to be destroyed.' A closely similar explanation of the meaning of ἄφθαρτον and ἀγένητον is given by Aristotle in *De Caelo* I 12. 282ᵃ27–30: 'I use the words "ungenerated" and "indestructible" in their proper sense (τὰ κυρίως λεγόμενα), "ungenerated" for that which now is and could not at any previous moment of time have been truly said not to be; "indestructible" for that which now is and cannot at any future time be truly said not to be.'

Yet the general modal notions like possibility and necessity are apparently never defined by Aristotle (unlike Diodorus Cronus) in purely temporal terms.

Defining necessity and possibility in temporal terms, using the formulations (T) and (T)₂ of the principle of plenitude (strengthened into equivalences) as a bridge between time and modality, would have meant for Aristotle to base his modal notions entirely on what might be called a *statistical* model of modality: Something's being possible must be shown by its *sometimes* happening, and what is always must be by necessity. Applications of modal notions reduce in effect to comparisons of what happens at different moments of time. Such a classificatory approach to modal concepts was not foreign to Aristotle. A good illustration is offered by his distinction between different subcases of contingency in *An. Pr.* I 13. 32ᵇ4–18. They include what happens 'in most cases' (ὡς ἐπὶ τὸ πολύ), and what 'inclines by nature in the one way no more than in the opposite' (οὐδὲν μᾶλλον οὕτως πέφυκεν ἢ ἐναντίως). Elsewhere Aristotle adds rare events to the list. It is extremely natural to include necessary events into this statistical classification as events that *always* happen, and impossible ones as those that *never* do. In fact, Aristotle seems to do this in the very passage mentioned, for in this context 'falling short of being necessary' can scarcely mean anything but 'falling short of always happening'. If so the passage will parallel *Met. E* 2. 1026ᵇ27–37. In any case, this is what the scholastics subsequently did in so many words. The sun rises necessarily, they said, 'ut semper'.[7] The same way of thinking was not far from Aristotle's mind, either, as shown by his acceptance of the principle of plenitude. We shall in fact find further indications in the sequel that the whole statistical model can be said to have been one of the conceptual paradigms of Aristotle's theory of modality. It was not the only one, however, and hence did not quite yield to him *definitions* of the different modal notions.

9. *Confirming evidence*

After all the apparent counter-examples have been refuted, it is in order to marshal the positive evidence for the attribution of the principle of plenitude to Aristotle, over and above the references already given.[8]

---

[7] See Anneliese Maier, 'Notwendigkeit, Kontingenz und Zufall' in *Die Vorläufer Galileis in 14. Jahrhundert: Studien zur Naturphilosophie der Spätscholastik*, Edizioni di Storia e Letteratura (Rome, 1949), pp. 219–50.

[8] The attribution of the principle of plenitude to Aristotle has been discussed (with reference to my earlier work) by C. J. F. Williams in 'Aristotle and Corruptibility', *Religious Studies*, 1 (1965) 95–107, 203–15, especially 210–14. I am in several respects indebted to Williams's comments.

Here are some passages supporting the attribution: '. . . that which is capable of not existing is not eternal, as we had occasion to show in another context' (*Met. N* 2. 1088ᵇ23–5). It is not clear what the address of Aristotle's reference is, although it illustrates the attention Aristotle paid to the principle. In any case, Aristotle offers a kind of proof for the principle in *De Caelo* I 12. 281ᵃ28–282ᵃ25. Here Aristotle is mainly concerned with the thesis (T), although occasional other versions come into play as well: 'Anything then which always exists is absolutely imperishable' (*De Caelo* I 12. 281ᵇ25). Here we have an instance of $(T)_2$. The same version is found in *De Gen. et Corr.* II 11. 338ᵃ1–3: 'Hence a thing is eternal if it is by necessity; and if it is eternal, it is by necessity. And if therefore the coming-to-be of a thing is necessary, its coming-to-be is eternal; and if eternal, necessary.'

As to the version $(T)_3$, it is announced in so many words in *Met.* Θ 8. 1050ᵇ7–8 and 20: 'No eternal thing exists potentially' (ἔστι δ' οὐθὲν δυνάμει ἀΐδιον); 'Nor does eternal movement, if there be such, exist potentially' (οὐδὲ δὴ κίνησις, εἴ τίς ἐστιν ἀΐδιος).[9]

The form $(T)_1$ seems to make its appearance in *Met.* Θ 3. 1047ᵃ12–14: τὸ δ' ἀδύνατον γενέσθαι ὁ λέγων ἢ εἶναι ἢ ἔσεσθαι ψεύσεται (τὸ γὰρ ἀδύνατον τοῦτο ἐσήμαινεν) . . . Sir David Ross translates this: 'He who says of that which is incapable of happening either that it is or that it will be will say what is untrue; for this is what incapacity means.' Here Aristotle seems to go as far as to say that the principle of plenitude yields the very meaning of modal terms like 'impossible'. In this respect, however, the passage is perhaps somewhat inconclusive, for ἐσήμαινεν might possibly be a weak term here, to be translated in terms of 'indicating' rather than 'meaning'. In any case, the principle of plenitude *is* asserted here by Aristotle in no uncertain terms, barring of course the possibility that the quotation does not represent Aristotle's considered opinion. This lingering doubt will be dispelled later when we return to the interpretation of *Met.* Θ 3–4.

---

[9] I fail to understand why C. J. F. Williams thinks that Aristotle is here saying that 'the eternal must lack the potentiality of *being*' (op. cit. p. 211). Aristotle says in so many words that in the sense he is presupposing 'every potency is at the same time a potency of the opposite'. Hence a lack of potency of being in this sense is *ipso facto* lack of potency of not being. Be this as it may, Williams agrees that Aristotle is here presupposing some form or other of the principle of plenitude.

In *De Int.* 9. 18^{b}11–15 we find another passage which in its most literal sense agrees very well with the principle of plenitude, but whose interpretation is such a notorious mess that only an extended subsequent argument (to be given below in Chapter VIII) can ascertain that it, like J. L. Austin, means what it says. Aristotle there infers 'it *could* not not be so' from 'it was *always* true to say that it is so or would be so' (my italics in both cases). Further evidence is found in a number of passages, for instance in *Top.* II 11. 115^{b}17–18 (what is destructible *haplōs* will be destroyed), *Phys.* III 4. 203^{b}30 (in the case of eternal things what may be is not different from what is), and *Phys.* IV 12. 221^{b}25–222^{a}9.

In some passages 'necessary' and 'always' are not in so many words asserted to be equivalent, but rather lumped together by Aristotle without explicit comment. Cases in point are the following: *Top.* II 6. 112^{b}1 ff.; *De Gen. et Corr.* II 9. 335^{a}32–^{b}7; *De Part. An.* I 5. 644^{b}21–3; *Met. E* 2. 1026^{b}27–37; *Met. K* 8. 1064^{b}32 ff. They support my ascription especially when combined with Aristotle's remarks in *An. Pr.* I 13. 32^{b}4 ff. on the classification of events into necessary, general, indeterminate, and rare, and with *De Caelo* I 12.

Additional evidence will be found in later chapters, especially in Chapter VI, and in sections 11 and 13 of the present one. In the absence of any counter-examples that would withstand critical scrutiny, we can safely ascribe the principle of plenitude to Aristotle. His formulations suggest, moreover, that the version of the principle involved is just our (T), that is, the version that rules out an infinitely long frustration of a possibility. Even possibilities concerning individual objects fall within the scope of this principle, provided of course that the individual in question does not pass away, for there are in Aristotle's view no possibilities concerning non-existent particulars.

10. *Why the principle of plenitude?*

As Aristotle himself could have said, it is one thing to establish *that* someone adheres to the principle of plenitude and another thing to show *why* he does. It is not easy to appreciate Aristotle's reasons for holding the principle of plenitude, it seems to me. The most explicit argument, or approximation to an argument, is

found in *De Caelo* I 12. 281ᵃ28–282ᵃ5. It has been analysed by
C. J. F. Williams,[10] and will also be commented on in Chapter
IX below. There certain connections between the principle
of plenitude and other Aristotelian doctrines will likewise be
pointed out.

The reasons for adopting the principle which are aired in *De
Caelo* I 12 seem to me to be connected with the type of reason that
we shall find later in this chapter (see section 12 below).

Aristotle's other reasons for holding the principle are more
difficult to pinpoint, and may not have been completely articulated by him. One of them is connected with his analysis of
change or movement (*kinesis*). It would require a fuller discussion than can be given here. Suffice it therefore to indicate the
most salient points. As Aristotle's very definition of *kinesis* shows,
the only way in which a potentiality can exist for him without
already being realized is as a movement towards the realization.
(*Kinesis* is the full reality of potentiality, in so far it is a [mere]
potentiality, according to *Phys.* III 1. 201ᵃ10–11.) What exists
potentially in such a change is its outcome, for instance 'house'
in the case of 'building', to use Aristotle's own example.

The most striking feature of Aristotle's theory of *kinesis* is that
the change always has as its beginning an actual instantiation of
the same 'form' as the outcome existing potentially during the
change. This actual individual may be a member of the same
species as the outcome ('man begets man') but it may also be the
'form' realized in the mind of a conscious producer of the outcome according to a plan. In all cases, however, there will have
to be such an antecedently existing form which initiates the
kinesis. 'The mover or agent will always be the vehicle of a form
. . . which, when it acts, will be the source and the cause of the
change . . .' (*Phys.* III 2. 202ᵃ9–11). The same doctrine is explained, e.g., in *Met. Z* 7 and in *Met. Θ* 8.

From this it follows that whenever it is true to say that a
certain universal ('form') exists potentially, there must have been
an earlier exemplification of the same universal actually existing.
But this is but one version of the principle of plenitude.

This version is weaker than the ones we have been discussing so
far, for it concerns only the realization of the possible kinds of
individuals and events. It looks weaker also in that the kind of

[10] Op. cit. (note 8, p. 103 above).

possibility it pertains to is apparently some sort of *natural* possibility rather than a *logical* one. (The weaker the kind of possibility is that a version of the principle of plenitude claims to be instantiated, the more sweeping the version.) In Chapter VI, section 6, below, it will be seen that there was no sharp distinction in Aristotle between logical and natural possibility. Hence the form of the principle of plenitude which was just found to be a corollary to Aristotle's theory of *kinesis* is no weaker in this respect than others. Needless to say, it belongs to an entirely different order of ideas than the pseudo-logical argument for the principle of plenitude in *De Caelo* I 12. Perhaps for this very reason, the convergence of those entirely different lines of thought served to reinforce Aristotle's belief in the principle.

I suspect that the Stagirite had further reasons for adopting the principle of plenitude. However, as I have emphasized, they are rather elusive. What has been said already suffices to indicate the deep connections between the principle and such central Aristotelian ideas as the priority of actuality with respect to potentiality and the permanence of species.

11. *The interpretation of* Metaphysics Θ 4

Very strong support for our ascription of the theses $(T)-(T)_3$ to Aristotle also seems to be forthcoming from *Met.* Θ 4. 1047ᵇ3-6:

If what we have described is identical with the potential or convertible with it, evidently it cannot be true to say 'this is possible but will not be', which would imply that things incapable of being would on this showing vanish.

The text reads:

εἰ δέ ἐστι τὸ εἰρημένον τὸ δυνατὸν ἢ ἀκολουθεῖ, φανερὸν ὅτι οὐκ ἐνδέχεται ἀληθὲς εἶναι τὸ εἰπεῖν ὅτι δυνατὸν μὲν τοδί, οὐκ ἔσται δέ, ὥστε τὰ ἀδύνατα εἶναι ταύτῃ διαφεύγειν·

The evidential value of this passage is not undisputed, however. It has been pointed out by G. E. L. Owen and by Martha Kneale that another reading of Aristotle's words is also possible here (private communications). We can 'understand the ὥστε-clause (ὥστε with infinitive, not with indicative) in lines 5–6 as qualifying the preceding τὸ εἰπεῖν . . . οὐκ ἔσται δέ and not as stating a consequence that could be inferred from it. We then understand the sentence as follows: "It cannot be true to say that this is possible but will not happen and to say this *to such effect* that the existence of the impossible will escape us in this way" ' (Martha Kneale, private communication).

Both the original quotation and Mrs. Kneale's translation are philologically possible. In order to use the evidence of *Met. Θ 4.* 1047^{b}3–6 for my purposes, I must hence rule out the latter reading. This can be done as follows. In the passage under consideration, Aristotle is warning us against a mistake. This mistake is different on the two different interpretations. On the former, Aristotle tells us that whatever is possible will be the case, i.e. he warns us against assuming that something is possible but will never be. On Mrs. Kneale's interpretation, Aristotle is allowing for a possibility never to be realized, as long as this assumption does not let the impossible escape us altogether— whatever that means.

The sequel shows which of these warnings Aristotle has in mind:

Suppose, for instance, that a man—one who did not take account of that which is incapable of being—were to say that the diagonal of the square is capable of being measured, but will not be measured, because a thing may well be capable of being or coming to be, and yet not be or be about to be. (1047^{b}6–9, Oxford translation)

This shows quite clearly, it seems to me, that the mistake Aristotle is worried about is assuming that a possibility can remain for ever unrealized. (See especially the last clause of the quotation.) The reading he is presupposing is therefore the one originally given and not the one Mrs. Kneale is favouring.

It may be thought that this does not completely rule out Owen's and Mrs. Kneale's interpretation, if supplemented by the assumption that the mistake he is warning us against is 'to suppose that *whenever* we can say "It will never happen" we can also say "It is possible" ' (Mrs. Kneale). For several reasons this nevertheless cannot very well be what Aristotle means. For one thing, he is not envisaging a man who says that a diagonal can be measured because it never will be, but one who says that it can be measured and yet (μέντοι) will not be measured. For another, I do not see that a fallacious general inference from 'never' to 'possibly' is what Aristotle's alleged formula 'to say that something is possible but will never be—and to say this to such effect that the existence of the impossible will escape us' can naturally express. This formula deals with one case only, not with the general fallacy—which Aristotle could have described much more simply anyway. A third reason is that a view as far off the mark as the fallacious inference in question is very unlikely to have merited Aristotle's explicit rejection. (There is no indication anywhere else in Aristotle that he was worried about this fallacy.) Furthermore, a separate analysis will show that there is nothing in *Met.* Θ 3 that commits him even to the view that sometimes a possibility can remain unrealized for ever so as to encourage the fallacy in question, contrary to what the critics of my interpretation seem to assume.

Hence it seems to me clear that the current reading of 1047^{b}3–6 with which I agree is correct. This means that this passage offers us strong evidence for Aristotle's adherence to the principle that each genuine possibility is sometimes realized.

12. *Plenitude and Aristotle's definition of possibility*

If the reading favoured here is correct, further interesting conclusions will ensue. One fact that may have led interpreters astray is that Aristotle's example about the diagonal seems to involve a principle altogether different from the realization of all possibilities in time. What Aristotle argues for there is apparently not that each possibility *will be* realized, but that it *can be assumed to be realized* without implying any contradictions. What has been found strongly suggests that Aristotle is here assimilating the two principles together. (Note that Aristotle had just before appealed to the latter principle in *Met.* Θ 3. 1047^{a}24–9.) This observation is important for understanding his theory of modality in general. Aristotle's view is probably motivated by the idea that the only way in which we can think of a possibility to be realized is at some moment of time in our actual 'history of the world'. But if other things than those assumed actually take place at that moment, a contradiction does seem to result. Hence the second principle may seem to imply the first.[11]

Be this as it may, we can now see why Aristotle thought that a

[11] This suggestion will be elaborated below in Chapter IX. Note that *De Caelo* I 11. 281^{a}5–7 shows clearly that the assumption which Aristotle took to give rise to impossibilities was that a commensurate diagonal should exist *at some particular moment of time.*

denial of his thesis of the realization of all possibilities in time would have lost sight of all instances of impossibility in a very strict sense of the phrase. Aristotle's very definition (working characterization) of possibility is as follows: 'I use the terms 'possibly' and 'the possible' of that which is not necessary but, being assumed, results in nothing impossible' (*An. Pr.* I 13. 32ᵃ18–20). Because of the assimilation of the two principles to each other, an unrealized possibility would have meant for Aristotle a possibility that cannot ever be assumed to be realized without running into impossibilities, and would therefore have involved the destruction of Aristotle's principal characterization of what is possible and (by implication) what is impossible. This would indeed involve losing sight of what is impossible and what is possible according to Aristotle's definition of these notions.

In fact, the above characterization of possibility is likely to be precisely the assumption Aristotle has in mind in the continuation of our quotations from *Met.* Θ 4:

But from the premises this necessarily follows, that if we actually supposed that which is not, but is capable of being, to be or to have come to be, there will be nothing impossible in this; but the result *will* be impossible, for the measuring of the diagonal is impossible. (1047ᵇ9–13; Ross's italics)

The piece of reasoning is in precise agreement with *An. Pr.* I 13. 32ᵃ18–20.

We can thus understand very well what Aristotle meant by 'the vanishing of the things that are incapable of being'. If we accept his characterization of possibility, as well as his assimilation of the two principles mentioned above to each other, possibilities can remain unrealized only at the expense of declaring a good number of impossibilities not to be impossible at all—perhaps all of them.

We can also now see, albeit only in its general features, another reason why Aristotle was tempted to assume the principle of plenitude, besides the ones mentioned above in section 10. It was encouraged by Aristotle's way of understanding his own definition of possibility. The kind of assumption that a possibility is realized which was used in the definition meant for Aristotle assuming that it is realized at some moment of *our* time (the actual succession of 'nows'). This, for reasons that we can here only surmise, encouraged Aristotle to assume that every possibility *is in fact* realized in time.

13. *The interpretation of* Metaphysics *Θ 3–4*

What has been found does not presuppose the emendation of Zeller who wants the text to read: εἰ δ' ἐστί, τὸ εἰρημένον, δυνατὸν ⟨ᾧ ἀδύνατον⟩ μὴ ἀκολουθεῖ. . . . Needless to say, Zeller's emendation and interpolation are encouraged by observations of the same kind we have made.

Another consequence is that no reason remains not to take the evidence of *Met. Θ* 3 at its face value. It was already noted above in section 9 that *Met. Θ* 3 yields one of Aristotle's most outspoken assertions of the principle of plenitude. (See 1047ª11–14.) Now we can see that this was not retracted by Aristotle, and may even suggest his partial willingness to put the principle to use as supplying us with definitions of modal notions. Further remarks on *Met. Θ* 3 will be offered later in Chapter VIII.

14. *Consequences of the principle: Aristotle on his predecessors*

Aristotle's acceptance of the principle of plenitude was not without consequences for the rest of his philosophy. Here only one of them—a particularly important one—will be noted.

It has often been pointed out that Aristotle's attitude to his predecessors is unhistorical. He did not discuss their views as an antiquarian exercise, but as material from which he could extract his own position by means of critical and comparative analysis. As a consequence, he has been accused of reading his own problems and doctrines back to earlier philosophers.

No matter how these charges of unhistoricity against Aristotle's frequent historical surveys are to be judged, it must be emphasized that his attitude was not due to blind prejudice. The principle of plenitude gave Aristotle an important theoretical reason for his peculiar relation to his predecessors. If no possibility can remain unactualized for an infinity of time, every possible truth must presumably have been thought of some time or other. Hence a sufficiently comprehensive survey of the opinions of earlier thinkers will comprise each desired truth within its scope. The central problem thus lies in the sifting of the true opinions from the false ones rather than in the difficulty of discovering the truths in the first place; and, of course, also in collecting a large enough sample of well-established earlier opinions.

This rationale of Aristotle's method of discussion is explained in *Met. Λ* 8. 1074ᵃ38–ᵇ14. Especially instructive is the following passage:

> But if one were to separate the first [original] point from these [later] additions and take it alone . . . *and reflect that, while probably each art and each science has often been developed as far as possible and has again perished*, those opinions, with others, have been preserved until the present like relics of the ancient treasure. It is only in this way that we can explain the opinions of our ancestors and forerunners. (My italics, of course.)

In *Politics* VII 10. 1329ᵇ25–35 Aristotle expresses a closely related idea as follows:

> We must also believe that . . . most other institutions . . . have been invented in the course of years on a number of different occasions— indeed an infinite number. . . . We ought to take over and use what has already been adequately expressed before us, and confine ourselves to attempting to discover what has hitherto been omitted. (tr. Barker)

This passage is especially interesting in that it hints at the source of Aristotle's antiquarian interest which led him, *inter alia*, to compile the famous lost collection of constitutions. In this way, we begin to understand the relation of Aristotle's search for factual material to his theory of induction.

The same idea is expressed in *Politics* II 5. 1264ᵃ1–5 as follows: 'We are bound to pay some regard to the long past and the passage of years. . . . Almost everything has already been discovered, though some of the things discovered have not been coordinated, and some, though known, have not been put into practice' (tr. mostly Barker's). A similar point is made in *Meteor.* I 3. 339ᵇ27 ff.

15. *Consequences of the principle: modal and non-modal logics are inseparable*

Another consequence of the principle of plenitude is that if there *can* be exceptions to a temporally unrestricted generalization, there *will in fact* be such exceptions. In other words, the only *true* unrestricted generalizations will be the necessary ones. Since Aristotle assumed that in syllogistic premisses one is quantifying over individuals past, present, and future without any temporal restrictions (see *An. Pr.* I 15. 34ᵇ7–11), this holds for the generalizations Aristotle dealt with in his syllogistic and also in his theory of science. Thus one of the puzzles mentioned in the beginning of this chapter receives a definitive explanation.

Indeed, we have a contrary problem in our hands. The outcome of our analysis is almost paradoxical. The very difference between assertoric and apodeictic generalizations seems to disappear for Aristotle. This is paradoxical, for Aristotle was the founder of modal logic. Furthermore, modal notions played a vitally important role in his philosophy. Yet for him, as for anyone who accepts the principle of plenitude, there should not be any sharp distinction between modal logic and plain syllogistic. In the last analysis, all modal statements should admit of reformulations in temporal (but otherwise wholly extensional) terms. On the contrary, the thinkers who (like some of the characteristically modern ones) reject the principle are the ones who might be expected to occupy themselves with modal logic and modal notions in general. For them, there can be a distinction between merely contingently true generalizations ('eternal accidents') and necessary ('lawlike') generalizations, as there cannot be for Aristotle. Yet the historical situation is to a large extent a mirror image of this legitimate expectation. There is something of a correlation between the demise of the principle and the decline of modal logic.

I do not have a simple answer to this problem. Maybe it is indicative of the deep tensions that seem to have been operative in Aristotle's thinking. He believed in indeterminism and in the special role of modal notions. Yet in his very own conceptual apparatus there were factors that tended to push him towards determinism and towards an extensional (tense-logical) reduction of modal notions to non-modal ones. In the next few chapters we may perhaps catch a few glimpses of the problems and manœuvres to which Aristotle was led because of these tensions.

VI

ARISTOTELIAN INFINITY

1. *Aristotle's theory of infinity and the principle of plenitude*

In the preceding chapter, it was argued that Aristotle accepted and used, in some form or other, the principle that has been called by A. O. Lovejoy 'the principle of plenitude'.[1] That is to say, he accepted the principle that every genuine possibility is sometimes actualized or, more likely, a qualified form of the same principle according to which no genuine possibility can remain unactualized through an infinity of time.[2]

Aristotle's theory of infinity might seem to constitute a counter-example to this interpretation. In many expositions of this theory, it is said that according to Aristotle infinity had merely potential existence but was never actualized. (The very terms 'actual infinity' and 'potential infinity', which are still used, hail from Aristotle's terminology.) As one author puts it, for Aristotle infinity is 'never realized, though conceivable'. If this were all there is to the subject, we should in fact have here a clear-cut counter-instance to the principle of plenitude in Aristotle.

This interpretation is encouraged by certain remarks Aristotle himself makes. For instance, in *De Int.* 13. 23ᵃ23–6 he writes: 'Some things are actualities without capability . . . , others with capability . . . and others are never actualities but only capabilities.'[3] Aristotle's remarks in *Met. Θ* 6. 1048ᵇ9–17 are sometimes construed in the same spirit (mistakenly, I shall argue later).

In view of the wealth of evidence that there is for ascribing the principle of plenitude to Aristotle, his views on infinity need a

---

[1] See also my paper, 'Necessity, Universality, and Time in Aristotle,' *Ajatus,* 20 (1957), 65–90. In that early paper, I did not use the term 'principle of plenitude'. For the principle, see A. O. Lovejoy, *The Great Chain of Being* (Harvard University Press, Cambridge, Mass., 1936).

[2] An earlier warning is worth repeating here. The term 'principle of plenitude' is highly misleading, if taken literally. It has to be understood here as a *terminus technicus.*

[3] The context of this passage is studied above in Chapter III.

closer scrutiny.[4] I shall argue that Aristotle did not give up this principle in his theory of infinity, but rather assumed it in certain important parts of the theory. I shall also argue that by noticing this we can understand better certain issues that come up in the course of Aristotle's discussion of infinity in his *Phys.* III 4–8.

2. *The sense in which the infinite exists*

As so often in Aristotle, we cannot take his preliminary discussion of reasons for and against the existence of infinity at its face value.[5] The arguments presented in this discussion, like the corresponding preparatory arguments in other Aristotelian discussions, primarily serve to set the stage for Aristotle's own solution of the difficulty. Usually, such preliminary arguments give rise to apparently contradictory conclusions. These contradictions are normally resolved by means of a conceptual distinction. In the case at hand, it is a distinction between the different senses in which the infinite may be asserted or denied to exist (206ª12–14).

Aristotle first indicates that an infinite potentiality must be said to exist (206ª14–18). He goes on to suggest, however, that in order to understand the sense in which the infinite exists potentially we have to heed the different senses of existence (206ª21–3). In other words, it is not true (*pace* Evans)[6] that 'potentiality has here a special sense', different from the sense in which finite things may be potential. Rather, the infinite *is* (potentially *and* actually) in a sense different from the one in which a finite thing *is*. In the latter sense of being, the infinite does not exist even potentially: 'Potentially it [the infinite] exists in the same way as matter, but not independently as the finite does' (206ᵇ14–16, trans. by Sir Thomas Heath). The text reads καὶ δυνάμει οὕτως ὡς ἡ ὕλη, καὶ οὐ καθ' αὑτό, ὡς τὸ πεπερασμένον.

In what sense, then, does the infinite exist? It exists, Aristotle

---

[4] In fact, a form of the principle of plenitude is assented to by Aristotle at the beginning of his discussion of infinity: 'In the case of eternal things what may be must be' (203ᵇ30).

[5] The structure of Aristotle's discussion of the infinite may be compared, e.g., with the structure of his discussion of the problem of future contingents in *De Int.* 9. The latter discussion is analysed in Chapter VIII below, which originally appeared in the *Philosophical Review*, 73 (1964), 461–92, esp. 468–72. In reading Aristotle, it is vital to keep constantly in mind his characteristic method of approaching a problem.

[6] Cf. Melbourne G. Evans, *The Physical Philosophy of Aristotle* (University of New Mexico Press, Albuquerque, 1964), p. 47.

says, in the sense in which a day 'is' or the Olympic Games 'are'. These are not actualized in their entirety at any given moment of time in the way an individual is. Rather, their parts come to existence successively one by one. As Aristotle says, 'one thing after another is always coming into existence' (206ᵃ22–3). In other words, infinity is not a term that applies to individual things, such as men or houses, in any sense, either actually or potentially. Rather, it is an attribute of certain sequences of individual things or individual events—'definite if you like at each stage, yet always different' (206ᵃ32–3). This is the gist of the Aristotelian theory of infinity.

Saying that the infinite exists potentially might perhaps be used to express that it exists in this derivative sense. Occasionally Aristotle allows himself the luxury of this locution. It is a very misleading way of speaking, however, not merely because it does not fully express the mode of existence of the infinite according to Aristotle, but even more so because it muddles an important distinction. As Aristotle is well aware, the distinction between actuality and potentiality applies also to the kind of existence that is enjoyed, *inter alia*, by the infinite, by a day, and by the Olympic Games: 'For of these things too the distinction between potential and actual existence holds. We say that there are Olympic Games, both in the sense that they may occur and that they are actually occurring' (206ᵃ23–5). When this distinction is made clear, the principle of plenitude is seen to apply. Although there perhaps is a (rather loose and inappropriate) sense in which the infinite may be said to exist only potentially, in the exact and proper sense in which, according to Aristotle, it exists potentially, it also exists actually. 'The infinite is actual in the sense in which a day or the games are said to be actual' (206ᵇ13–14); and this, we have seen, is just the proper sense in which the Aristotelian infinite exists.[7] For instance, the infinity of time does not mean for Aristotle merely that later and later moments of time are possible; it implies that there will actually be later and later moments of time.

---

[7] Hence Aristotle in fact assumed the existence of actually infinite sets of objects (in the modern sense of actual infinity), though not the existence of infinite sets whose members all exist simultaneously. This is even more remarkable in view of Aristotle's assumption that in syllogistic premisses one is quantifying over all individuals past, present, and future. (See *An. Pr.* I 15. 34ᵇ17–18.) Hence the 'universes of discourse' of Aristotelian logic are in a sense actually infinite.

In a way, the Aristotelian theory of infinity has thus been found to entail exactly the opposite to what it is usually said to assert. Usually it is said that for Aristotle infinity exists potentially but never actually. In the *precise* sense, however, in which the infinite was found to exist potentially for Aristotle, it also exists actually. Far from discrediting my attribution of the principle of plenitude to Aristotle, an analysis of Aristotle's theory of infinity serves to confirm it.

3. *The finitude of Aristotelian universe*

The fact that Aristotle abides by the principle of plenitude in developing his theory of infinity is not without consequences for the theory. One of these is that he cannot accept any infinite spatial extension (except as the inverse of infinite divisibility), not even in the 'potential' sense of the infinite in which an infinite division or an infinity of numbers is possible. For the potential infinity of extension would mean that arbitrarily large extensions are possible. But if they were possible, they would have to be actual at some time or other. There cannot, however, be any actually existing extended magnitude greater than the universe itself (says Aristotle at 207^{b}19–21), hence there are no arbitrarily large (actual) extensions; and hence there is not even a potential infinity with respect to extension. As Aristotle puts it, 'A potential extension can be only as large as the greatest possible actual extension' (207^{b}17–18).[8] Aristotle's universe is thus finite in an especially strong sense: no extension beyond it is even possible.[9]

---

[8] This feature of Aristotle's theory of infinity is pointed out by Harold Cherniss in *Aristotle's Criticism of Presocratic Philosophy* (Johns Hopkins Press, Baltimore, 1935), p. 34: 'That is, infinity by addition, in the sense that any given magnitude may be surpassed, does not exist even potentially [according to Aristotle]. And the reason he himself gives is that it is impossible for an infinite body to exist actually.'
What is being added to Cherniss's account here is an explanation *why* Aristotle inferred the non-existence of arbitrarily large *potential* magnitudes from the non-existence of arbitrarily large *actual* extensive magnitudes. This inference was clearly mediated by the principle of plenitude.
A closely related explanation is offered (without explicitly mentioning the general principle on which Aristotle is relying) by Friedrich Solmsen in *Aristotle's System of the Physical World* (Cornell University Press, Ithaca, N.Y., 1960), p. 168, esp. n. 35.
[9] Aristotle's way of thinking is rather amusingly illustrated by the words ἔξω τοῦ ἄστεος at 208^{a}18 which were taken by Alexander, Themistius, and Philoponus

Aristotle's argument would make no sense if he were not actually making use of the principle of plenitude. By possibility he could not mean here mere conceivability, for he admits at 203^b23-5 that we can think of extensions reaching beyond the boundariès of the physical universe.

4. *Aristotle's theory* v. *mathematical practice*

What we have found about Aristotle's theory of spatial magnitude shows that the problem of reconciling his theory of infinity with mathematical practice is a much more serious one than commentators have usually realized. Aristotle thought that he could get away with saying merely this:

Our account does not rob the mathematicians of their study, by disproving the actual existence of the infinite in the direction of increase, in the sense of the untraversable. In point of fact they do not need the infinite and do not use it. They postulate only that the finite straight line may be produced as far as they wish. It is possible to have divided in the same ratio as the largest quantity another magnitude of any size you like. Hence, for the purposes of proof, it will make no difference to them to have such an infinite instead, while its existence will be in the sphere of real magnitudes. (*Phys.* III 7. 207^b27-34)[10]

(see Ross, *Aristotle's Physics, a Revised Text with Introduction and Commentary* (Clarendon Press, Oxford, 1936), p. 562) to mean 'outside the city'. They suggest that Aristotle was worried about too large a magnitude's 'sticking out' of the boundaries of the physical universe, in the same way too huge a man would have to be 'outside the city'. If this is right, there do not seem to be good reasons for omitting τοῦ ἄστεος and ἤ from 208ᵃ18.

10 Evans (op. cit., p. 49) and Sir Thomas Heath, in his *Manual of Greek Mathematics* (Clarendon Press, Oxford, 1931), p. 199, omit, when quoting this passage, the sentence 'It is possible . . . any size you like.' They are thus presupposing that the infinite extension which according to Aristotle's last sentence suffices 'for the purpose of proof' is the possibility of producing lines 'as far as one wishes'. This is not, however, what the passage says; the last sentence of the quotation clearly refers to the penultimate one, saying that what suffices for the purposes of proof is the infinite extension that exists merely as the inverse of infinite divisibility. This kind of infinity Aristotle discusses at 206ᵇ3–12, a passage which is echoed by the penultimate sentence of our quotation.

The point is correctly made by Cherniss (op. cit., p. 35 n. 129) and to some extent also by Heath in his *History of Greek Mathematics*, vol. i (Clarendon Press, Oxford, 1921), p. 344. Heath there suggests that Aristotle's statement is incompatible with the mathematical practice of his time. This is criticized by Sir David Ross in his edition of *Aristotle's Physics* (note 9 above), p. 52. Ross is right in the case of the particular assumption he is discussing (the so-called axiom of Archimedes), but there are other mathematical assumptions that are in fact vitiated by Aristotle's theory.

Aristotle is not saying here merely that a mathematician does not need an infinite magnitude all of whose parts are simultaneously actualized. If this were all that he were saying, he would have a plausible argument. The quoted passage shows him doing much more, however; he is also argueing that a geometer does not even need arbitrarily large potential extensions. He is suggesting in effect that all that the geometer needs is the kind of infinite extension that exists merely as the inverse of infinite divisibility, and that a geometer therefore does not even need arbitrarily large potential extensions. All that he needs according to Aristotle is that there be *arbitrarily small* potential magnitudes.

What Aristotle's statement therefore amounts to is to say that for each proof of a theorem, dealing with a given figure, there is a sufficiently small similar figure for which the proof can be carried out. In short, each geometrical theorem holds in a sufficiently small neighbourhood. From this it does not follow, however, that the theorem really holds. There are in fact geometrical assumptions requiring arbitrarily large extensions. The best-known case in point is of course Euclid's fifth postulate, the famous 'axiom of parallels': 'If a straight line falling on two straight lines makes the interior angles on the same side less than two right angles, the two straight lines, *if produced indefinitely*, meet on that side on which are the angles less than the two right angles' (trans. by Heath). If there is a maximum to the extent to which lines can be produced, this postulate fails. What we can justify on Aristotle's principles is merely the statement that, given the situation described by Euclid (line AB falling on the straight lines AC and BD, angle CAB + angle ABD being less than two right angles), there is a point A' on AB sufficiently near A such that a parallel to BD through A' meets AC on the side Euclid specifies. This does not, however, guarantee that the resulting geometry is Euclidean.

It might be thought that this nevertheless makes no difference to the truths that we can prove about those geometrical configurations that in fact exist, that is to say, about those configurations that are 'in the sphere of real magnitudes' (207^b33-4), in other words, that are wholly contained within the finite Aristotelian universe. This claim is not justified, however, for very often we can prove something about a given figure only by means of auxiliary constructions. (Aristotle was aware of this need and in fact keenly appreciated the role of these constructions.) These auxiliary constructions may require the existence of longer lines than any of the ones involved in the given figure. Hence we are back at the same difficulty.

Was Aristotle perhaps misled by his own terminology? In *Met.* Θ 9 he refers to a certain auxiliary construction as a 'division' (διαίρεσις), and similar locutions occur elsewhere, too.[11] This suggests that he might have thought that our auxiliary constructions are mere 'divisions' in the sense that they never transgress the limits of the given figure. This assumption is gratuitous, however.

Thus we have to conclude that Aristotle's peculiar doctrine of the existence of a maximal spatial extension made it impossible for him to justify fully the practice of the geometers of his time. In particular, the use of Euclid's fifth postulate could not be reconciled with his doctrine. If understood according to the letter of Aristotle's statements, his physical universe is non-Euclidean: the axiom of parallels is not satisfied in it.[12]

Naturally, Aristotle could not have been himself aware of this conclusion. In fact, it may be doubted whether he would have argued in the way he did if he had known that Euclid's fifth postulate is even prima facie an indispensable part of the usual system of geometrical postulates and axioms. In other words, Aristotle's theory of infinity makes us doubt whether the indispensability of this postulate was realized in Aristotle's time (or at any rate by Aristotle) as clearly as it was realized by Euclid. It may be indicative that in *Phys.* II 9. 200ª16–18, Aristotle traces one of the theorems which turns on the axiom of parallels to the straight line's being 'such as it is' without specifying its nature in any more detail and without mentioning the axiom of parallels. In the form in which it was stated by Euclid, the axiom of parallels would scarcely have been taken by Aristotle to express a part of the essence of the straight line, as the subsequent criticism of the postulate brings out. It has a form entirely different from the Aristotelian definitions that according to him expressed the essence of this or that thing.[13]

[11] The same word is used by Aristotle at 203ᵇ17 of those 'divisions' of mathematicians that sometimes induce belief in the existence of the infinite. Here, too, mathematical *constructions* are probably meant.

[12] Cf. Solmsen, op. cit., p. 173 n. 57.

[13] For one thing, typically Aristotelian definitions were equivalences, whereas the converse of the fifth postulate was demonstrable in Euclid's system.

Far from containing 'a sort of prophetic idea' of a non-Euclidean geometry, as Heath suggests,[14] this passage might on the contrary indicate that the role of the axiom of parallels was not particularly clear to Aristotle. Elsewhere Heath argues himself, with reference to Aristotle, that the fifth postulate was not known before Euclid.[15]

Aristotle's compunctions about geometrical constructions were apparently shared by at least one well-known mathematician of antiquity. Heron *mechanicus* tried to dispense with the production of particular straight lines as much as possible, motivated by the idea that there might not always be enough space available to carry out such a production.[16] (It does not matter for my purposes whether Heron was himself worried about this or whether he was trying to reassure others.) In fact, Heron gave proofs of certain propositions in Euclid alternative to Euclid's own proofs. They were designed to dispense with the applications of Euclid's second postulate which justifies the production of straight lines. This line of thought is potentially very interesting, for if it had been pushed far enough, it would have led into difficulties not only in connection with Euclid's second postulate but also in connection with the fifth.

It is not impossible, however, that mathematicians' attention was unfortunately directed away from the fifth postulate by its explicitly hypothetical form: '*if* [the two straight lines are] produced indefinitely . . .' This may have led Heron and others to think that the second postulate is the only one in Euclid that leads into trouble in connection with the finitude of the universe.

5. *Apparent counter-examples*

There are statements elsewhere in the Aristotelian corpus that seem to contradict the doctrine of the largest possible geometrical extension that we have found in *Phys.* III 7. The most important one is *De Caelo* I 5. 271^{b}28–272^{a}7, which was in fact referred to by Proclus in his attempt to prove the fifth postulate.[17] There

[14] T. L. Heath, *Mathematics in Aristotle*, pp. 100–1.
[15] Idem, *The Thirteen Books of Euclid's Elements*, vol. i, 2nd ed., (Cambridge University Press, 1925), p. 202.
[16] See Heath, *Euclid's Elements*, vol. i, pp. 22–3.
[17] Cf. ibid., p. 207.

Aristotle says that the space between two divergent straight lines is infinite. This passage is, however, inconclusive. The principle Aristotle there seems to appeal to, if it can be accepted, suffices for Proclus' purposes. Aristotle's apparent argument for it is fallacious, however. Moreover, Aristotle is in any case conducting there a *reductio ad absurdum* argument against the alleged infinity of the world, and hence may have appealed to the principle in question merely because he thought that his opponents were committed to it. In any case, his argument is carefully couched in explicitly hypothetical terms: '*If* the revolving body be infinite, the straight lines radiating from the centre must be infinite.'

Apostle suggests that, according to Aristotle, a mathematician need not worry about problems occasioned by the finitude of the universe because 'it belongs to the physicist to investigate the shape and magnitude of the universe'.[18] The remarks of Aristotle to which he refers (*Phys.* II 2. 193^{b}22–35) do not warrant this complacency, however. Aristotle's doctrine is that 'the geometer deals with physical lines, but not *qua* physical' (194^{a}9–11). In other words, a geometer deals with physical lines by abstracting from certain of their attributes. (This is also suggested by *Parva Naturalia* (*De Mem*) 1. 449^{b}30–450^{a}7.) Now the real problem here is that some of the lines that a geometer needs do not seem to be forthcoming at all, and of course *this* existential problem is not alleviated by the possibility of abstracting from certain attributes of lines. If the requisite lines do not exist, there is nothing to abstract from. In fact, Aristotle's words at 204^{a}34 ff. show that he included the mathematical senses of infinity within the scope of his discussion, at least when he was arguing λογικῶς.

To return to the problems connected with the principle of plenitude, the doctrine that the infinite is in a sense actualized is apparently denied by Aristotle at 206^{a}18–21: 'But possibility can be understood in more than one way. A statue exists possibly in that it will in fact exist. But the infinite will not exist actually.' This does not yet give us Aristotle's settled view of the matter, however, for he hastens to emphasize the peculiar sense of existence which is involved here, not the sense of potentiality that is being used. Hence the quotation does not disprove my interpretation.

[18] Hippocrates George Apostle, *Aristotle's Philosophy of Mathematics* (University of Chicago Press, Chicago, 1952), p. 79.

In the last analysis, Aristotle's references to the 'merely potential' existence of the infinite tell us less of his notion of infinity than of his idea of genuine full-fledged existence. This was the separate, independent (καθ' αὐτό) existence of an individual substance. All the other modes of existence were viewed by him with some amount of suspicion, and were sometimes liable to be assimilated to 'merely potential' existence. The mode of being that belongs to the infinite is a case in point. Here the crucial consideration was clearly that there is no moment of time at which one can truthfully say: the infinite is *now* actualized, in the way we can say of an existing individual that it is *now* actually existent. Hence the burden of such Aristotelian remarks as the one just quoted is perhaps not so much that the infinite is not actualized but that it does not exist *as an individual*—that no infinite body exists or can exist. As Aristotle formulates his point:

We must not regard the infinite as a 'this' (τόδε τι), like a man or a house, but must suppose it to exist in the sense in which a day or the games are said to exist—things whose being has not come to them like that of a particular substance (οὐσία τις), but consists in a process of coming to be and passing away. (206ᵃ29–33)

When Aristotle says that the infinite 'will not exist actually', what he has primarily in mind is therefore merely the fact that there will not be any moment of time at which it can be said to be actualized. This does not go to show, however, that the infinite is not actualized in some other sense.

It would nevertheless be too rash to disregard contrary evidence altogether. There are indications that Aristotle is himself hesitating between different views. It may be significant that some of the clearest statements to the effect that for Aristotle the infinite was in a sense actualized come from passages that appear somewhat parenthetical. This is clearly the case with the passage that was just quoted from 206ᵃ29–33; it is in fact considered by Ross as 'an alternative version which . . . was at an early date incorporated in the text' (p. 556). The same may be the case with the words ἄλλως μὲν . . . πεπερασμένον at 206ᵇ12–15 which do not contribute anything to what Aristotle is discussing there. It is also interesting to note that the passage we quoted earlier from 206ᵃ23–5 is missing from one of the manuscripts (sc. E). It almost looks as if we had caught Aristotle here in the process of changing his mind, or perhaps rather changing his emphasis. This assumption would also serve to explain Aristotle's reliance on the descriptions of the infinite as 'potential but not actual' which we have found to be unrepresentative of Aristotle's definitive statements on the subject.

The line of thought that these statements to some extent replace seems to turn on assimilating the mode of existence that the infinite enjoys to that of the material which, for example, may become a statue. This line of thought is seen from 206^{b}14–16, 207^{a}21–32, and 207^{b}34–208^{a}4. It is not obvious that it has to contradict the emphasis on the principle of plenitude which we found elsewhere; the two ideas seem to coexist happily in 206^{b}14–16. The contrast between matter and form, however, is elsewhere (for example *Met.* Θ 6. 1048^{b}1–8) assimilated by Aristotle to that between potentiality and actuality. Hence this seems to lead at least to a different emphasis in the case of infinity.

6. *Conceivability and realizability in Aristotle*

Another problem with wider implications comes up in the course of Aristotle's discussion of infinity. I quoted a statement to the effect that for Aristotle infinity is 'conceivable though never realized'. This was found to be a misleading formulation in that the infinite is in a sense realizable for Aristotle. It may now be asked whether the formulation is perhaps equally misleading in so far as the conceivability of the infinite is concerned. I shall argue that it is.

In general, there appears to have been little difference for Aristotle between actual physical realizability and realizability in thought. The difference between these two, should one make a distinction here, would be in effect a distinction between two senses of possibility, a distinction which bears some resemblance to our distinction between logical possibility and physical possibility. In most cases Aristotle completely fails to appreciate distinctions of this sort, even in cases where he would find it convenient to use it. How foreign the general trend of his thought is to such a distinction is perhaps seen by considering the equivalent distinction between two senses of necessity (the impossibility of conceiving the contradictory to something versus the impossibility of actually realizing the contradictory). The main burden of the *Posterior Analytics* is to make definitions, or truths essentially like definitions, the ultimate starting-points of each science.[19] The way of coming to know the basic principles of a science is described by Aristotle as a way of coming to have the basic concepts of that science.

This idea has a neat counterpart in Aristotle's psychology. There we learn that thinking is an actuality and that the thinking mind is formally identical with the object of which it is thinking. 'Actual knowledge is identical with its object' (*De Anima* III 6. 431^{a}1–2). In other words, in thinking of x the mind assumes the form of x and even in a sense *becomes* this form.[20] For this reason, the conceivability of a form entails that this form is in a sense actualizable. In being thought of, this form is actualized in the mind of the thinker: being conceivable is a form of being realizable.[21]

Of course, what is realizable in the mind need not for that reason be realizable outside the mind, according to Aristotle. What makes the difference in such cases is apparently the material factor; what for Aristotle was realizable in one medium was not necessarily realizable in another. This is shown, for instance, by his remarks on the Socratic paradox in the *Eudemian Ethics* I 5. 1216^{b}6 ff. A man may know what virtue is—that is, the form of virtue may be present in his mind—but he may nevertheless fail to become virtuous. This is explained by Aristotle in terms of the material factor, which therefore is to be blamed for the failure of realization in this case. A similar point is made in *Phys.* II 2. 194^{a}21 ff.

When we discuss realizability without qualifications, however, we are discussing actualization in any material whatsoever, and for this purpose actualization in one's mind seems to serve perfectly well in Aristotle's view. In being able to bring about a certain result x the main thing was to have in one's mind the form of x. This was taken for granted by Aristotle; what he argues

[19] See, e.g., *An. Post.* I 8. 75^{b}31; II 3. 90^{b}23; II 17. 99^{a}22. For a discussion of some of the many intricate issues involved here, see my paper 'On the Different Ingredients of an Aristotelian Science', *Nous*, 6 (1972), 55–69.

[20] See, e.g., *De Anima* III 4–5.

[21] Apostle (op. cit., p. 79) claims that, according to Aristotle, 'we may have thoughts of impossibilities'. In support of this view he refers to *Met. E* 3. 1027^{b}25–7. But in this passage Aristotle is not discussing possibility and impossibility at all, merely truth and falsity, which are said to be 'not in things . . . but in thought'.

for in the *Eudemian Ethics* is the further point that one must *also* have knowledge of the material 'out of which' x is to be formed.

It is not quite clear, however, exactly how Aristotle thought of the actualization of the various forms in one's mind. In what kind of material are these forms realized? Is a bodily change involved? Is Aristotle dealing with the images that he says must accompany all thinking, or with thinking proper? What exactly is the distinction between these two? We cannot discuss these difficult and involved questions here. It may be pointed out, in any case, that the realization in one's mind takes place in a material different from the ones in which forms are normally embodied outside us. Hence knowing an individual x, which involves having its form in one's mind, does not necessarily give us a capacity of realizing the same (numerically the same) individual in one's mind or in any other medium, but only the capacity of reproducing the same form in some material or other.

What is also clear is that Aristotle repeatedly insists that actualization in one's mind is in principle as good a sort of actualization as any other. Aristotle wants to apply his principle that 'everything comes out of that which actually is' (*De Anima* III 7. 431^{a}3–4) to artificial products like houses or to such results of skilful activity as the health that a doctor has brought about. In order to do so, he has to say that the process of building or of healing has as its starting-point another actual instance of the form of house or of the form of health—namely, the form that exists in the mind of the builder or of the healer. In *Met.* Λ 4. 1070^{b}33–4 he writes: 'For the medical art is in some sense health, and the building art is the form of the house, and man begets man.' The analogy presented here shows that the form of a house that exists in the builder's mind is for Aristotle as good an instantiation of the form in question as the father of a son is an instance of the form of man. Essentially the same point is made more fully in *Met.* Z 7. 1032^{b}1–14 (cf. also *Met.* Z 9. 1034^{a}21–3). The obvious connection between these passages and Aristotle's discussion of the temporal priority of the actual in *Met.* Θ 8. 1049^{b}18–29 shows that the thought (or image) that one has in one's mind when one knows x is for Aristotle as fully actual an instance of the form of x as an external object exemplifying this form.

This parity of actualization in thought with actualization in external reality is what leads me to say that for Aristotle conceivability implied actualizability. According to Aristotle, to conceive of a form in one's mind was *ipso facto* to actualize it.

7. *The conceivability of infinity*

This idea is also applied by Aristotle to mathematical entities. They exist only in thinking, but since thinking is an actuality, they are not any less real for this reason.[22]

A case in point is the existence of the auxiliary constructions or 'divisions' that are often needed in a geometrical proof. These divisions are obviously of the same kind as the divisions that are contemplated by Aristotle when he discusses infinite divisibility and are hence of immediate relevance to his theory of infinity. Of the 'divisions' or constructions needed in geometrical proofs Aristotle writes in *Met. Θ* 9. 1051ᵃ21–31 :

It is by an activity also that geometrical constructions [or theorems, διαγράμματα] are discovered, for we discover them by dividing. If the figures had been already divided, the constructions [theorems] would have been obvious; but as it is they are present only potentially. . . . Obviously, therefore, the potentially existing constructions are discovered by being brought to actuality: the reason is that a geometer's thinking is an actuality.[23]

Now this idea of conceivability as realizability in one's mind seems to fare very badly in Aristotle's discussion of infinity. Initially, Aristotle appeals to it in the way he might be expected to use it on the basis of what we have found:

Most of all, a reason which is peculiarly appropriate and presents a

[22] Cf. esp. *Met. Θ* 9. 1051ᵃ21–33, to be quoted (in part) below, and *Met. M* 3. There is something of a contrast between these two passages, however. At *Met. M* 3. 1078ᵃ30–1 it is implied that mathematical objects exist ὑλικῶς—i.e. by way of matter—whereas in the *Met. Θ* 9 passage it is stressed that 'a geometer's thinking is an actuality'. This appears to be a matter of emphasis, however. Cf. also Apostle, op. cit., pp. 11–17, and Anders Wedberg, *Plato's Philosophy of Mathematics* (Almqvist and Wiksell, Stockholm, 1956), pp. 88–9.

[23] In interpreting *diagrammata* as theorems, I am following Heath (*Mathematics in Aristotle*, pp. 216–17) who refers to *Cat.* 12. 14ᵃ39 and *Met. Δ* 3. 1014ᵃ36 for further evidence. The context itself shows rather clearly that this is what Aristotle has in mind here. Cf. also Eckhard Niebel, *Untersuchungen über die Bedeutung der geometrischen Konstruktion in der Antike*, (Kant-Studien, Ergänzungshefte, vol. lxxvi, 1959), especially pp. 92–5, where further references to the literature on this subject are given.

difficulty that is felt by everybody—not only number but also mathematical magnitudes and what is outside the heaven are supposed to be infinite because they never give out in our thought. (*Phys.* III 4. 203^{b}22–5)

Aristotle's words reflect the importance he attached to this argument. Nevertheless, it seems to be rejected in *Phys.* III 8. 208^{a}14–19:

To rely on mere thinking is absurd, for then the excess and defect is not in the thing but in thinking (ἐπὶ τῆς νοήσεως). One might think that one of us was bigger than he is and magnify him *ad infinitum*. But it does not follow that he is bigger than the size we are, just because someone thinks he is.

In fact, these words seem to indicate that Aristotle made a clear distinction between conceivability and actual realizability. If this were really the case, this passage would have important consequences for our interpretation of Aristotle's thought in general.

We can see, however, that Aristotle's purpose here is severely restricted, and that it cannot therefore support any general conclusions concerning the relation of conceivability and realizability in Aristotle. The fact that Aristotle formulates his point in terms of 'excess or defect' shows that he has in mind only quantities, and indeed only spatial magnitudes. He hastens to point out (at 208^{a}20–1) that his remarks do not apply to movement or time. There is no trace anywhere of an application of this idea to the other concepts that Aristotle had been considering and had mentioned at 203^{b}22–5—for example, to number or to divisibility. On the contrary, at 207^{b}10–13 he seems to rely on the conceivability of a higher and higher number of divisions to establish infinite divisibility:

But it is always possible to think of a larger number (ἐπὶ δὲ τὸ πλεῖον ἀεὶ ἔστι νοῆσαι); for the number of bisections of a magnitude is infinite. Hence (ὥστε) the infinite exists potentially, although never actually, in that the number [of bisections] always surpasses any assigned number.

It is also significant that in reassuring us of the infinity of time and movement at 208^{a}20 Aristotle adds thinking to the list. His point seems to be that in the case of time and movement, infinity in thought and infinity in fact go together. In fact, time and movement are at once contrasted by Aristotle to magnitude, which 'is not infinite either in the way of diminution *or of magnification in thought*' (208^{a}21–2).

What Aristotle has in mind in 208^{a}14–19 is his idea that although in thinking of *x* one's mind assumes the form of *x* (or, alternatively, makes use of an image having the form of *x*), it need not assume this form in the same size as the original. The replicas of outside forms that one has in one's mind are merely scale models of these forms, as it were. That this is what Aristotle had in mind is shown by *Parva Naturalia* (*De Mem.*) 2. 452^{b}13–17:

How, then, when the mind thinks of bigger things, will its thinking of them differ from its thinking of smaller things? For all internal things are smaller, and as it were proportional to those outside. Perhaps, just as we may suppose that there is something in man proportional to the forms, we may assume that there is something similarly proportionate to their distances.

Hence Aristotle's whole point turns out to be this. Because of limitations of size ('all internal things are smaller') a human mind can think of large things only as being large in relation to something else. Because of this, it does not follow that an imaginable size is realizable, because what is realized in one's mind is merely large in relation to something else, but not absolutely. It does follow that there is no limit to *relative* size; and this is in fact a conclusion in which Aristotle acquiesces at 206^{b}3–9.

Thus Aristotle does not give up the general principle that conceivability (or imaginability) implies realizability, but only that this principle applies to the realizability of (absolute) sizes. It is only in the case of spatial 'excess and defect' that Aristotle can say that they lie 'not in the thing but in conceiving'. The form that is being thought of ordinarily lies *both* in the thing and in the conceiving or imagining mind.

There is even more direct evidence that for Aristotle infinity was not 'conceivable though never realized'. Properly speaking, for Aristotle infinity was inconceivable. In *Met.* ∝ 2. 994^{b}20–7, Aristotle denies in so many words that we can apprehend an infinity. 'The notion of infinity is not infinite', Aristotle says, thus emphasizing that in the sense in which the infinite is not actualized in external reality it is not realized in thinking, either, for that would involve the realization of an infinite form in one's

finite mind. In the sense in which the infinite was for Aristotle
unactualizable, in that sense it was also inconceivable.[24]

8. *Absolute* v. *relative possibility*

In general it may be said that Aristotle has a distinction which
prima facie looks very much like a distinction between conceivability and actual realizability (or perhaps our modern distinction between logical and physical possibility), and which
serves some of the same purposes but which from a theoretical
point of view is entirely different. This distinction is used, *inter
alia*, in *De Motu Animalium* 4. 699^{b}17–22, and *De Anima* II 10.
422^{a}26–9. The corresponding (in effect, equivalent) distinction
between two different kinds of necessity is even more familiar.
It is often referred to as a distinction between absolute and
hypothetical necessity. It is explained, *inter alia*, in *Phys.* II 9, *De
Partibus Animalium* I 1. 639^{b}25 and 642^{a}8, as well as in *An. Pr.* I
10. 30^{b}31–4, 38–40.

The distinction between two senses of possibility can be
characterized as a distinction between what is possible absolutely
speaking (that is, in so far as we merely consider its own nature)
and what is possible on certain conditions—for example, possible
to us in our present circumstances. To use Aristotle's own example,
if there are men on the moon, they will be visible in the ordinary
unqualified sense of the word, though *we* cannot see them. It is
important to realize that Aristotle is not here postulating two
different irreducible senses of possibility but rather two senses, one
of which is in effect definable in terms of the other. This interpretation is confirmed by Aristotle's terminology; he refers to
the distinction by means of such locutions as ποσαχῶς λέγεται
(204^{a}2–3) and λέγεται πλεοναχῶς (699^{b}17). As I have shown elsewhere, Aristotle uses these expressions not of outright ambiguities,
but rather of interrelated but different uses of one and the same
word.[25]

---

[24] By the same token, in the sense in which the infinite was in Aristotle's view
conceivable, it was also actualizable. At 208^{a}20–1 *noesis* is accordingly said to be
infinite in the same sense as time and movement, viz. 'in the sense that each part
that is taken passes in succession out of existence'. It is well known that time and
movement are according to Aristotle's doctrine in a perfectly good sense *actually*
infinite, viz. in the sense that there actually has been and will be an infinite
number of moments of time and movements of bodies, although Aristotle does not
usually express himself in this way.   [25] Chapter I above.

The fact that Aristotle deals in this way with cases that we might characterize in terms of a difference between logical and physical possibility suggests that he either had no recourse to the latter distinction or else did not want to use it. In the unqualified sense of the word, conceivability implied for him realizability somewhat in the same way as it did later for Descartes.

There are in any case indications that Aristotle's distinction between intrinsic possibility and possibility under certain circumstances is different from the distinction he makes in his discussion of infinity between possibility in thought and possibility in actual physical reality. In the course of this very discussion, Aristotle also uses the former distinction, applied to a special case:

We must begin by distinguishing the various ways in which the term 'infinite' is used. (1) What is incapable of being gone through, because it is not its nature to be gone through. . . . (4) What naturally admits of being gone through, but is not actually gone through or does not actually reach an end. (*Phys.* III 4. 204ᵃ2–6)

A comparison with Aristotle's remarks elsewhere suggests that this distinction between the different senses in which it is impossible to go through something is an instance of the distinction he makes elsewhere between different uses of possibility. Nevertheless, it is in no way related by Aristotle to the distinction between realizability in thought and realizability in actual reality which he makes later in his discussion of infinity. This strongly suggests that the two distinctions were not connected by Aristotle with each other.

Our discussion of the sense in which the infinite was conceivable for Aristotle shows that his theory of infinity does not constitute a counter-example to this relation between conceivability and realizability in Aristotle.

9. *Infinity in* Metaphysics Θ

Our conclusions also help us to understand what Aristotle is really up to in his brief pronouncement on infinity in *Met.* Θ 6. 1048ᵇ14–17, and are confirmed by what we find there. If I am right, what Aristotle says in this passage may be expressed as follows:

The infinite does not exist potentially in the sense that it will ever exist actually and separately; it exists only in thinking. The potential existence of this activity ensures that the process of division never comes to an end, but not that the infinite exists separately.

This version follows Ross's translation fairly closely. Nevertheless it requires a few explanatory comments.

(1) The first and foremost thing to be noted in this passage is Aristotle's main conclusion. Understanding this conclusion is completely independent of the difficulties that we may have in understanding the passage in other respects. The conclusion is that the infinite does not exist *separately* (Aristotle's word is χωριστόν). Now what would such a separate existence mean for Aristotle? It is contrasted by him not with potential existence but to the kind of non-separate existence that, for example, qualities enjoy in relation to the substances whose qualities they are.[26] The Platonists had supposed that the forms exist separately, Aristotle tells us, and goes on to argue that they were wrong and that the forms exist only in those things whose forms they are and on whose existence their being is dependent.[27] In the same way, Aristotle is here pointing out the peculiar way in which the infinite exists. According to him, it depends for its existence on the finite beings which one after another come into being.

In short, he makes here the same point we found him making in *Phys.* III 7. He is pointing out that the infinite *exists* in an unusual sense of existence, not that it is potential in a new sense of potentiality. As he says himself in introducing the subject of infinity, 'but also the infinite and the void and all similar things are said to exist potentially *and actually* in a sense different from that which applies to many other things' (1048ᵇ9–11).

(2) The second clause of the first sentence is sometimes taken to mean that according to Aristotle the infinite exists *separately* only in thinking (or knowledge, γνώσει). This is surely wrong. As we have seen, Aristotle's doctrine is that the infinite does not exist as an individual (that is, separately) in any sense at all.

Ross translates the clause by 'it exists *potentially* only for knowledge'. This may quite well be right, although it does not quite

---

[26] It is also contrasted with the mode of existence of mathematical objects which do not exist apart from sensible particulars and which can be separated from them only in thinking; see *Met. E* 1. 1025ᵇ27; *K* 1. 1059ᵇ13; *M* 3. 1078ᵃ21–31; *M* 6. 1080ᵇ17; *M* 9. 1086ᵃ33. Cf. (2) below.

[27] Cf. e.g., *Met. Z* 14–16.

square with Aristotle's avowed purpose of showing that the infinite exists potentially *and actually* in an unusual sense. The difference does not matter, however, since for Aristotle each potentiality eventually actualizes. For then we might equally well render Aristotle's thought by saying 'it exists (potentially and therefore also actually) only in thinking'. What Aristotle is bringing out here is not any special way in which the infinite exists, but rather the way in which all mathematical objects exist according to him.

(3) The second sentence of our quotation is very difficult to understand and to translate. We shall not discuss here the philological details but refer the reader once and for all to Ross's comments in his edition of the *Metaphysics* (ii. 252–3). The main problem is whether the subject of the sentence is the phrase that may be translated 'the potential existence of this actuality' (or 'activity') or the phrase that may be translated 'the fact that the division never comes to an end'. Accordingly, we shall have a choice of two translations which run somewhat as follows: 'for the potential existence of this activity ensures that the process of division never comes to an end' and 'for the fact that the process of dividing never comes to an end ensures that this activitity always exists potentially'. Ross points out that the philological evidence favours the former interpretation, but he finds in favour of the latter on topical grounds. These grounds are inconclusive, however, for they amount to taking Aristotle's statement at 203ᵇ22–5 as being accepted by him and viewed 'as a given fact'. We have already seen that Aristotle returns to the same subject in 208ᵃ14–19 and qualifies his earlier statement in certain respects. It is true that we have also seen that these qualifications are not nearly as sweeping as commentators have often taken them to be; but perhaps they should nevertheless warn us not to rely too much on 203ᵇ22–5.

The question is really this. In *Phys.* III 4. 203ᵇ18–20 Aristotle mentions as a putative proof of the actual (better: separate) existence of the infinite the idea that an endless coming-to-be (μὴ ὑπολείπειν γένεσιν) can only take place if there (actually) exists an infinite supply from which the things that are coming to be are coming from. In *Phys.* III 8. 208ᵃ8–11 Aristotle points out that this explanation is not needed (οὔτε γὰρ ἵνα ἡ γένεσις μὴ ἐπιλείπῃ, ἀναγκαῖον ἐνεργείᾳ ἄπειρον εἶναι σῶμα αἰσθητόν). At

208ᵃ8–11, however, he does not give any alternative explanation, perhaps because such an explanation is implicit in the rest of his discussion of infinity in the *Physics*.

Now, the statement in *Met*. Θ 6. 1048ᵇ15–17 can be understood as offering just such an alternative explanation, formulated in terms of infinite division. The endless coming-to-be of further and further divisions is 'ensured' (Aristotle's verb is ἀποδίδωμι) by the potential existence of the activity of dividing. Hence it is compatible with everything Aristotle says to follow the philological evidence and to parse Aristotle's sentence in a way different from the one Ross endorses.

It is seen, however, that something is still missing here. (This insufficiency of our interpretation so far may have been instrumental in leading Ross to the other reading.) How can the merely potential existence of the activity of dividing ensure that the actual process of dividing never comes to an end? The answer is, of course, that no genuine potentiality is for Aristotle a *mere* possibility: if it continues to exist as a potentiality, it will ultimately be actualized. Hence the principle of plenitude supplies the link which our interpretation might prima facie seem to fail to provide.

Far from being incompatible with the principle of plenitude, the passage we have been discussing again turns out to presuppose it.[28]

---

[28] In writing the first version of this chapter I profited from the friendly criticism to which Richard Sorabji and Peter Geach subjected it, although I have probably failed to meet most of their criticism.

VII

ON ARISTOTLE'S MODAL SYLLOGISTIC

1. *The multiplicity of Aristotelian modal principles*

ARISTOTLE's modal syllogistic—that is to say, his theory of syllogisms from premisses some or all of which are apodeictic (necessary) or problematic (possible) as distinguished from plain non-modal (assertoric) premisses—is presented in *An. Pr.* I 9–12. The most general problem it poses is a methodological one. How can we understand what Aristotle is doing in those chapters? What kinds of concepts and conceptualizations are relevant here?

A timely reason why this methodological question is important is the existence of several recent attempts to reconstruct Aristotle's system of modal syllogisms, or some important part of it, in terms offered to an interpreter by modern symbolic logic. The best-known attempted reconstructions of this sort are those by Storrs McCall,[1] Jan Łukasiewicz,[2] Albrecht Becker,[3] and Nicholas Rescher.[4] These interpretations, especially those by McCall and Łukasiewicz, illustrate a methodological pitfall that has not attracted much notice recently. This pitfall is not, as some historians would probably expect, an anachronistic reliance on the tools of modern logic in studying an ancient logician like Aristotle. On the contrary, it seems to me that the insights we have recently gained into logic and especially into what is known as logical semantics have opened valuable new possibilities of understanding earlier logicians. The mistake I have in mind is a

---

[1] Storrs McCall, *Aristotle's Modal Syllogisms* (North-Holland Publishing Company, Amsterdam, 1963).

[2] Jan Łukasiewicz, *Aristotle's Syllogistic from the Standpoint of Modern Formal Logic* (second edition, Clarendon Press, Oxford, 1957), Chapters 6–8.

[3] Albrecht Becker, *Die Aristotelische Theorie der Möglichkeitsschlüsse* (Junker und Dünnhaupt, Berlin, 1931).

[4] Nicholas Rescher, 'Aristotle's Theory of Modal Syllogisms and Its Interpretation', in *The Critical Approach: Essays in Honour of Karl Popper*, ed. by Mario Bunge (The Free Press, Glencoe, Illinois, 1963), pp. 152–77.

more specific one. It is due to what I shall call the multiplicity of Aristotle's approaches to modal logic. In different parts of his modal syllogistic, he relies on different principles, often based on independent insights into the logic of modal notions. There is no reason to believe that these principles are all compatible, even though each of them embodies a valid insight or at least an idea that is in itself unobjectionable. I shall indeed argue later in this chapter that the different principles Aristotle uses are in fact incompatible.

From this it follows that those discussions of Aristotle's modal syllogistic that concentrate on systematizing the syllogisms (syllogistic modes) accepted by Aristotle are completely misplaced.[5] If the principles by means of which Aristotle accepts and rejects different syllogisms are not only different but incompatible, no insight whatsoever can be gained by systematizing the accepted syllogisms: with different applications of the same principles, the set of accepted syllogisms would be different. Axiomatizing a set whose membership is sometimes based on sheer accident is a pointless exercise.

2. *The apodeictic-assertoric distinction confounded*

In order to substantiate these points, a brief discussion of some of the principles Aristotle uses in his modal syllogistic is needed. No complete inventory of Aristotle's syllogistic methods will be attempted. For instance, nothing will be said of the highly interesting method of *ecthesis* (ἔκθεσις) which he uses both in his assertoric and in his modal syllogistic. We are only concerned with showing the inconsistency of Aristotle's modal principles.

One important principle has already been studied in Chapter V. There it was seen that Aristotle accepted what we referred to as the principle of plenitude, that is to say, the assumption that every possibility is realized sooner or later. As a consequence, whatever is always true is true necessarily according to Aristotle.

Now, Aristotle also insists that universal assertoric (non-modal) premisses, i.e. premisses of the form

(1) *A* applies to all *B*,

have to be understood with no limitation with respect to time, for instance so as to be restricted to the present moment. (See *An.*

---

[5] A case in point is McCall's book (note 1, p. 135, above).

Pr. I 15. 34ᵇ7–18.) What this means is that premises like (1) will have to take in all individuals, past, present, and future. From the principle of plenitude it therefore follows that if (1) is true, it is necessarily true.

Thus the dividing line between assertoric (plain) and apodeictic (necessary) universal premisses apparently disappears. This contradicts directly Aristotle's initial statement in his discussion of apodeictic syllogisms in *An. Pr.* I 8. 29ᵇ29–35 to the effect that 'since there is a difference according as something belongs, necessarily belongs, or may belong to something else . . . , it is clear that there will be different syllogisms to prove each of these relations'. Nor does this conflict affect only Aristotle's general pronouncements. We can see that several of the mixed syllogisms Aristotle accepts as valid are fallacious unless assertoric premisses are assumed to have the same force as they had if they were prefixed by 'necessarily'.

Several examples are found in *An. Pr.* I 15. For instance, Aristotle accepts there a syllogism with the premisses

(2a) *A* possibly applies to all *B*

and

(2b) *B* applies to all *C*,

and with the conclusion

(2c) *A* possibly applies to all *C*.

No matter how you try to interpret the premisses, there is no hope of turning the syllogism into a valid one unless you somehow lend modal (apodeictic) force to (2b). This is also what Aristotle in effect does. He explains the syllogisms as follows: 'Since *C* falls under *B*, and *A* possibly applies to all *B*, clearly it possibly applies to *C* also.' (See *An. Pr.* I 15. 33ᵇ34–6.) Here it is assumed that *B* would still apply to all *C* if the possibility were realized that *A* should apply to all *B*. (Otherwise it might happen that then the *B*s to which *A* possibly applies are not *C*s any more when this possibility is actualized.) This can be assumed without further explanation only if *B* *necessarily* applies to *C*.

An alternative explanation would be to surmise that Aristotle thought that (2c) follows from (2a) and (2b) because each *C* is in fact a *B* (in virtue of the latter premiss) and hence a possible *A* in virtue of the former. This interpretation presupposes that (2a) is to be understood as having the form

A possibly applies to everything to which *B* in fact applies and (2c) therefore as having the form

A possibly applies to everything to which *C* in fact applies.
It might seem to be encouraged also by an analogy with Aristotle's treatment of mixed apodeictic and assertoric syllogisms, to be discussed in the next section. However, Aristotle stipulates elsewhere (*An. Pr.* I 13. 32ᵇ25–32, for the interpretation of which see Chapter II, section 8 above) that the force of the putative conclusion (2c) must be such that it speaks of everything to which *C* *possibly* applies, whereas the interpretation under discussion implies that it only speaks of those individuals to which *C in fact* applies. Hence something else must be involved here. What this something else is is shown by the structure of Aristotle's discussion. The requirement which Aristotle puts forward later in the same chapter (see 34ᵇ7–18) and which was mentioned earlier, to the effect that assertoric premisses be understood omnitemporally, covers in Aristotle's treatment the present syllogism. Aristotle's procedure becomes understandable if we assume that the possibilities he is dealing with are thought of as being realized at some particular moment of time and that his assertoric premisses cover all moments of time. (For the former assumption, see Chapter V, section 12 above.)

Examples of the same kind as our syllogism (2) can be multiplied; see for instance *An. Pr.* I 15. 34ª34–ᵇ2 (to be discussed briefly in Chapter IX, section 7). In fact, most of the syllogisms discussed later in *An. Pr.* I 15 are cases in point.

3. *How are Aristotle's apodeictic premisses to be understood?*

Thus we have found one important problem in Aristotle's modal syllogistic. It perhaps does not amount to an outright inconsistency, however, for Aristotle seems to have invested what he called universal apodeictic premisses with a structure different from those that result from assertoric ones even when their necessary character is spelled out. This may be seen as follows: Aristotle accepts syllogisms of the form

(3a) *A* necessarily applies to all *B*

(3b) *B* applies to all *C*

(3c) *A* necessarily applies to all *C*

but rejects syllogisms of the form

(4a) *A* applies to all *B*

(4b) *B* necessarily applies to all *C*

(4c) *A* necessarily applies to all *C*.

It has often been pointed out that the only natural way to explain this seems to be to say that an universal apodeictic premiss, such as (3a), really had for Aristotle the form

(5) *A* necessarily applies to everything to which *B* in fact applies.

If we use modern notation and abbreviate 'necessarily' by N, this may be written

(5a) $(x)(B(x) \supset NA(x))$

or, perhaps more explicitly,

(5b) $(x)(y)((B(x) \,\&\, x = y) \supset NA(y))$.

That something like (5) is what Aristotle is assuming here is shown by his explanation why syllogism (3)—that is, inference from (3a) and (3b) to (3c)—is valid: 'For since *A* necessarily applies . . . to *B*, and since *C* is one of the *B*'s (τὸ δὲ Γ τι τῶν Β ἐστί), clearly *A* necessarily applies . . . to *C*.' (See *An. Pr.* I 9. 30ª21–3.) The point here expressed is that since each *C* is in fact a *B*, and since whatever in fact is *B* is necessarily an *A*, each *C* is necessarily an *A*. This presupposes (5) as the structure of the major premiss.

What makes the interpretation (5) or (5b) especially natural is that of universal apodeictic premisses it represents what is known as the *de re* interpretation of modal statements.[6] This interpretation is in several respects very straightforward, for it, so to speak, takes off from considering certain individuals as being given and then moves on to discussing what can be said of them in modal terms. This was an especially natural attitude for Aristotle to take in any case. There is nothing surprising or awkward about his adopting this kind of interpretation of apodeictic premisses.

[6] For the *de dicto–de re* distinction, see Jaakko Hintikka, *Models for Modalities: Selected Essays* (D. Reidel Publishing Company, Dordrecht, 1969), pp. 97, 120–1, 141; and William Kneale, 'Modalities *de dicto* and *de re*', in *Logic, Methodology, and Philosophy of Science*, ed. by Ernest Nagel, Patrick Suppes, and Alfred Tarski (Stanford University Press, Stanford, 1962), pp. 622–33.

What is awkward is that this interpretation which Aristotle obviously presupposed in dealing with the syllogisms (3) and (4) invalidates some of the conversion rules he relies on constantly in his syllogistic theory. From

(6) *A* necessarily applies to nothing to which *B* in fact applies

we cannot infer

(7) *B* necessarily applies to nothing to which *A* in fact applies

so as to convert apodeictic universal negative premisses.

Nor can we obtain

(8) *B* necessarily applies to something to which *A* in fact applies

from

(9) *A* necessarily applies to something to which *B* in fact applies

so as to convert an apodeictic affirmative particular premiss. Moreover, the reasons Aristotle gives for the conversion of universal negative premisses show that he is there presupposing a different structure for apodeictic universal premisses: 'If *A* necessarily applies to no *B*, *B* also necessarily applies to no *A*. For if it is possible that it apply to some, it is also possible that *A* apply to some *B*.' Here 'necessarily' has to be taken to qualify in effect the whole clause '*A* applies to no *B*', for the contradictory of '*A* necessarily applies to no *B*' is clearly assumed to be 'it is possible that *A* applies to some *B*'.

Thus there is no hope of interpreting consistently Aristotelian apodeictic premisses. Sometimes he has one interpretation in mind, sometimes another. As a consequence, which syllogisms he accepts depends on which interpretation happens to predominate on different occasions.

It may also be pointed out that the assertoric premiss (4a) must not be assumed to have apodeictic force, unlike the assertoric universal premisses used in Aristotle's mixed problematic-assertoric syllogisms which were discussed above in section 2. For otherwise the syllogism (4) would be valid after all. Here we have an additional indication of inconsistencies in Aristotle's modal syllogistic.

4. *Aristotle's principles for rejecting apodeictic syllogisms*

This does not exhaust the difficulties one has in trying to understand Aristotle's theory of syllogisms from an apodeictic (necessary) and an assertoric (simple) premiss (*An. Pr.* I 9–12). In some cases, Aristotle says, premisses of this kind yield an apodeictic conclusion, in some cases only an assertoric one. What makes the difference?

Let us try to find an answer to this question by examining another main tool Aristotle uses in his modal syllogistic. He has an explicit rule for rejecting certain putative apodeictic conclusions. He rejects those and only those apodeictic conclusions that would in turn yield, together with the apodeictic premiss, an apodeictic conclusion concerning the terms occurring in the assertoric premiss. The premiss '*A* (simply) applies to all *B*' must be compatible with 'possibly *A* applies to no *B*', no matter what relation *A* (or *B*) happens to bear to a third term *C*; and similarly for other kinds of premisses. This, obviously, is a way of insisting that there is a distinction between assertoric and apodeictic premisses: by no series of syllogisms can a premiss of the former kind imply anything necessarily true about the two terms of the assertoric premiss in question. In section 2 above, it was suggested that there are contrary motives in Aristotle's thinking tending to destroy the distinction between assertoric and apodeictic general premisses. We therefore have to return to the question: did Aristotle succeed in keeping the two apart?

Quite a few reasons have already been found for thinking that Aristotle was not always quite successful. The best reason, however, remains to be discussed. The fairest standard by which Aristotle's success or failure can be judged is his own. If he fails by *this* standard, there is no way of denying that there is an essential inconsistency in his system. And the purpose of this section is to show that this in fact is the case.

The syllogism

(10) *A* applies to all *B*

$$\frac{B \text{ necessarily applies to all } C}{A \text{ applies to all } C}$$

is accepted by Aristotle, and for a good reason: we would get the same conclusion even if the second premiss were assertoric.

But if the conclusion is correct, we can set up the following syllogism:

(11) B necessarily applies to all C

A applies to all C
___

A necessarily applies to some B.

In fact, a syllogism which differs from (11) only in having as its conclusion

(12) B necessarily applies to some A

is accepted by the Stagirite in 31^a31–3, and the conversion of affirmative particular apodeictic propositions is recognized in 25^a32–4. The syllogism is justified by Aristotle by converting the assertoric premiss 'A applies to all C' into 'C applies to some A' and thereby reducing it to the syllogism (3):

(3a) B necessarily applies to all C

(3b) C applies to some A
___

(3c) B necessarily applies to some A

which is accepted by Aristotle in 30^a33–$^b1$.

But the reason why the stronger syllogism (4)—that is, inference from (4a)–(4b) to (4c)—which is like (10) except for having an apodeictic conclusion is rejected by Aristotle, is that if (4) were correct, we could validly infer from the conclusion and the second premiss that

(13) A necessarily applies to some B

This is taken by Aristotle to be impossible, 'for B may be such that it is possible for A to apply to no B' (*An. Pr.* I 9. 30^a27–8). But the same illegitimate conclusion was seen to result from the weaker syllogism (10) which was accepted by the Stagirite. Thus there is an inconsistency in Aristotle's theory.

How can this inconsistency be remedied? Can it be remedied? It would be absurd to reject (10) on account of the inconsistency, for the modal element in (10) is actually redundant. Hence there remain two ways out; (i) one may reject (11); or (ii) one may accept (4). The rejection of (11) would mean rejecting either (13) or the conversion of (12) into (13). The second alternative is the only one open for those who accept the most popular current reconstruction of Aristotle's modal premisses, viz. the reconstruction originated by A. Becker. This is the interpretation, mentioned above, which interprets universal apodeictic premisses as amounting to (5). Under this reconstruction, '*B* necessarily applies to all *C*' is in the present context understood to mean the same as the formula $(x)(C(x) \supset NB(x))$, and (12) is read as if it were $(Ex)(A(x)\ \&\ NB(x))$, '*N*' being the necessity-operator and the rest of the notation obvious. It was already seen that this reconstruction makes (3) valid and (4) invalid, and that it fails to verify the conversion of (12) into (13). If we take Aristotle to say at 30ª27–8 that every conclusion from '*A* applies to all *B*' must be compatible with $(x)(B(x) \supset M \sim A(x))$ (where '*M*' is a shorthand for 'possibly') then this is inconsistent with the conclusion (12) but not with the converted conclusion (13).

But this harmony is only apparent. The reason why Aristotle says at 30ª27–8 that it is possible for *A* to apply to no *B* is presumably that *no* apodeictic conclusion can result from a single assertoric premiss. By the same token, '*A* applies to all *B*' must be compatible with '*B* possibly applies to no *A*', which amounts, on Becker's interpretation, to the formula $(x)(A(x) \supset M \sim B(x))$. And this formula is clearly inconsistent with the conclusion (12) of the valid syllogism (3). In other words, Becker's reconstruction gives rise to syllogisms that are unacceptable by the very standard by means of which Aristotle rejected the invalid syllogisms from an apodeictic and an assertoric premiss. This reinforces our suspicions about the whole interpretation: Becker's interpretation may well make those and only those syllogisms valid that were accepted by Aristotle in *An. Pr.* I 9, but the Stagirite's reasons for accepting and for rejecting syllogisms are so different from Becker's reasons as to be inconsistent with them. In general, I think, we should hesitate before rejecting any rule of conversion Aristotle uses. Since they are usually his most important tools, rejecting them would mean abandoning all hope of understanding how he actually goes about developing his syllogistic.

This leaves us with the choice of either rejecting (3) or accepting (4). With the first choice, a good number of syllogisms accepted by Aristotle go by the board. Moreover, it is difficult to see any reason for accepting (10) if (3) is rejected; Aristotle's reasons for accepting (10) would automatically justify (3), too.

The result would be that no apodeictic conclusion can be drawn from premisses one of which is assertoric. Something like this course was actually taken by Theophrastus for reasons that we can only guess at.

The second choice would mean giving up Aristotle's method of rejecting certain apodeictic conclusions from an apodeictic and an assertoric premiss. This would force him to accept syllogisms that he now rejects. In the end, the distinction between assertoric and apodeictic premisses would probably be obliterated for all practical purposes.

There is no way of telling which horn of the dilemma Aristotle would have preferred. There is, in general, no way of telling what people would do if they were confronted by the dilemma of rejecting one of two assumptions they have been taking equally for granted.

There are, however, a few things that we can say. If Aristotle had been anxious to make his theory of syllogisms from an apodeictic and an assertoric premiss consistent with what he says later about syllogisms from an assertoric and a problematic (possible) premiss (see *An. Pr.* I 15. 34ᵃ34–ᵇ31) he would have been likely to take the second alternative. This is best seen by considering his other, subsidiary method of rejecting some syllogisms of the former kind, viz. the method of counter-examples. Many of these counter-examples are in terms of assertoric premisses which apparently are only assumed to hold during some particular period of time; and in at least one counter-example this assumption is made explicitly (see 30ᵇ33–40). Now assertoric premisses of this kind are said to be illegitimate in 34ᵇ7–18. This overt contradiction strongly suggests that Aristotle's reasons for rejecting the syllogisms he rejects in *An. Pr.* I 9–11 are inconsistent with the view he later adopts.

What we get, then, is one more indication of a tendency in Aristotle to obliterate the distinction between apodeictic and assertoric propositions. This tendency is so strong that Aristotle's attempt in *An. Pr.* I 9–12 to maintain the distinction was not successful even by his own standards.

5. *Conclusions*

These inconsistencies of Aristotle's modal syllogistic do not reduce its interest. Each of the different principles with which

Aristotle operates can be understood so as to embody a valid insight or at least a viable assumption. However, Aristotle gave these insights and assumptions formulations which simply are not compatible with each other. In particular, he did not have a very firm grip of the internal structure of modal syllogistic premisses. It looks as if he did not think of there being something in these premisses that could be captured by the relative order of modal operators and quantifiers so as to distinguish, say,

(14) $N(x)(B(x) \supset A(x))$

from

(15) $(x)(B(x) \supset NA(x))$.

This important distinction, incidentally, is not unrelated to the famous *de dicto–de re* distinction.

It is true that in *An. Pr.* I 13. 32^b25–32 Aristotle explicitly postulates a kind of 'fine structure' for problematic premissses. (This interesting passage was analysed above in Chapter II, section 8.) However, nothing like this explicit attention to the 'fine structure' of problematic premisses is devoted by Aristotle to apodeictic premisses.

Some reasons for this rejection may be conjectured. First, as was already mentioned, Aristotle was probably working with some sort of intuitive tense-logical model of possibility and necessity. What is possible was thought of by him as being realized at some point of a one-dimensional sequence of moments of time. In fact, tense-logical reconstructions of Aristotle's problematic syllogisms offer more promising possibilities than interpreters have so far made use of.

Secondly, Aristotle undoubtedly relied as much on oral formulas with their intuitive 'semantics' as on the structure of their written codifications, which likewise would have distracted him from distinctions such as that between (14) and (15). In fact, just because both the *de re* reading and the *de dicto* one are very natural interpretations of the verbal formula '*A* necessarily applies to all *B*' they were easily run together by Aristotle.

As was already said, all this does not make Aristotle's theory uninteresting. What it means is that we should concentrate on the intuitive insights on which Aristotle was gradually and partially articulating in the different parts of his modal logic rather than on the haphazard set of syllogisms he ended up accepting.[7]

---

[7] McCall (op. cit., pp. 22–7) nevertheless claims that there is a general reason for distinguishing between valid and invalid syllogisms in the way Aristotle does and even (pp. 96–7) that Aristotle had clear 'intuitions' about this difference. He fails to provide a single reference to Aristotle's actual discussion of modal syllogisms to back this up, however. This is not surprising in view of the fact that the basic idea of his interpretation is totally un-Aristotelian. McCall thinks that in apodeictic syllogisms, the major premiss represents some sort of general rule and the minor premiss some sort of special case to be established by perception or by some similar means. This view seems to me to make nonsense of Aristotle's theory of science, as it is presented in the *Posterior Analytics*. According to this theory, scientific explanations rely on chains of syllogisms. Hence one and the same premiss must sometimes occur as the major premiss and sometimes as the minor. Of course, one and the same premiss cannot represent both 'a necessary rule' and an intuitively given 'special case'.

VIII

THE ONCE AND FUTURE SEA FIGHT: ARISTOTLE'S DISCUSSION OF FUTURE CONTINGENTS IN *DE INTERPRETATIONE* 9

'It will not happen for hundreds of years, but both of us will come back. Do you know what is going to be written on your tombstone? *Hic jacet Arthurus Rex quondam Rexque futurus.* It means, the once and future king.'

    T. H. WHITE, *The Once and Future King*, Book II, section 10

1. *Aristotle's problem is problematic*

THE most important problem raised by Aristotle's discussion of singular statements concerning the future in *De Interpretatione* 9 is the question: what is the discussion all about? Scholars disagree not only about the details of Aristotle's discussion; they have given different answers to the question: what is Aristotle's problem in *De Int.* 9?[1] What is the view he wants to refute there, and what is the view for which he wants to argue?

I do not propose to review here the whole spectrum of answers that have in fact been given to these questions. I think we can answer the questions just posed with a fair amount of confidence by considering what Aristotle says in *De Int.* 9 against the background of certain other doctrines and usages of his—a source of information rarely resorted to in recent discussion. Furthermore, I think that the main point of Aristotle's discussion has been missed by all the recent commentators. In order to throw my interpretation into sharper relief, I shall nevertheless contrast it with certain prevalent views of the nature of Aristotle's discussion.

---

[1] Some recent literature bearing on the subject of this chapter is listed in an appended Bibliography on pp. 176–8. A sense of the variety of answers to the question concerning Aristotle's problem is perhaps evoked by a comparison of Abelard's and Miss Anscombe's discussions with the others. Bibliographical details of words, cited where these are not given in footnotes, will be found in the Bibliography.

2. *The traditional interpretation*

The type of view I mainly want to criticize may be expressed by saying that in *De Int.* 9 Aristotle denied the applicability of the law of excluded middle to statements concerning individual future events.[2] According to this view, which I shall call the traditional interpretation, Aristotle argues that the sentence

(1) *p* or not-*p*

may fail to be true when *p* deals with a particular future event. In order to bring this interpretation into line with Aristotle's own formulations, which lean heavily on such modal expressions as ἀναγκαῖον,[3] the defenders of the traditional interpretation will presumably have to say that he was discussing

(2) necessarily (*p* or not-*p*)

as much as he was discussing (1). In any case, he was discussing either the truth or the necessity (or both) of the whole disjunction (1). According to the traditional view, he was not discussing the necessity or non-necessity of the two disjuncts.

How Aristotle's alleged rejection of the law of excluded middle in *De Int.* 9 is supposed to square with his defence of the law in *Met.* Γ 4 has never been spelled out in satisfactory detail.

What, then, on the traditional view, is the difficulty about (1) or (2) that worried Aristotle? It must have been what might be called the *problem of future truth*. Assume, for the sake of argument, that (1) or (2) is true universally. Then it will be the case, as Aristotle says, that if someone declares that a certain individual event will take place and someone else declares that it will not take place, one of them will clearly be making a true statement while the other will be making a false one; necessarily so, if (2) is universally true. For instance, it will either be true to say that a sea fight will take place tomorrow or else true to say that it will

---

[2] Some writers—e.g., Łukasiewicz and Mrs. Kneale—distinguish between the law of excluded middle (every sentence of the form '*p* or not-*p*' is true) and the principle of bivalence (every sentence is true or false). A few, including Mrs. Kneale and Colin Strang, think that Aristotle is striving to make this very distinction in *De Int.* 9. Whatever the merits of the distinction are in the abstract, I cannot find it in Aristotle's text. My main reason for thinking that the distinction is not Aristotle's is given below in the first few paragraphs of section 8. In the bulk of this chapter, I shall simply ignore it.

[3] See, e.g., *De Int.* 9. 19ª28, ª31, ᵇ1.

not take place tomorrow. Suppose, for the sake of argument, that the former alternative happens to obtain. Then it is true (*already* true) that there will be a sea fight tomorrow. But if this is already true today, how can the occurrence of tomorrow's sea fight be contingent? If it is already true that there will be a sea fight tomorrow, the sea fight cannot conceivably fail to come about. By the same token, if it will not take place, then it will be false today to say that it will be fought; and this seems to make it impossible for it to take place. Hence the unrestricted applicability of *tertium non datur* to statements about future events seems to commit us to holding that all future events are predetermined, and thus to lead us to determinism.

This is what I dub the problem of future truth. It has been charmingly described by Gilbert Ryle in his Tarner Lectures.[4] If this problem is what occupies Aristotle in *De Int.* 9, it is indeed plausible to hold that his solution of the problem consists in giving up the assumption that every statement about the future must be true or false. I suspect that a preoccupation with the problem of future truth has coloured recent discussion on Aristotle and has made the hold of the traditional interpretation very difficult to break. It seems to me, nevertheless, that the problem of future truth is for Aristotle a subordinate one, and that there is a great deal more to his discussion in *De Int.* 9 than this problem, if it is a problem.

3. *Aristotle's ways with time and truth*

Some of the flaws of the traditional interpretation will be discussed later (mainly in section 8). Here I shall merely contrast it with an interpretation of the objectives of Aristotle's discussion that seems to me to come much closer to the truth. In order to explain it, it is useful to recall some pertinent facts about the way Aristotle handles the notion of truth. I cannot recount all the evidence here; let it suffice to indicate the most relevant conclusions.[5] One of the most striking features of the Aristotelian

---

[4] Gilbert Ryle, *Dilemmas*, Chapter II.

[5] Some remarks on the subject are made in Chapter IV above. The main point is also made by Mrs. Kneale (see Kneale and Kneale, pp. 48–51) who points out that Aristotle's argument in *De Int.* 9 turns on the assumption that the truth value of a sentence may change. Mrs. Kneale does not point out, however, that this assumption permeates Aristotle's whole way of thinking about statements, truth,

concept of truth is that it is not applied in the first place to what we should call propositions. Nor is it usually applied by Aristotle to the kind of sentences to which some modern philosophers and logicians would like the concept of truth to apply primarily, namely, to sentences whose contents are independent of the occasions on which they are uttered.[6] When Aristotle is thinking of sentences that serve to express our knowledge or our opinions, he is typically, and indeed almost exclusively, thinking of sentences that are token-reflexive, in that they contain an explicit or implicit reference to the moment of time at which they are uttered—of sentences that, in other words, contain implicitly or explicitly the word 'now'. Aristotle's examples are likely to be of the type 'Socrates is now sleeping' rather than 'Socrates is (was, will be) sleeping at such and such a time on such and such a day'. As far as sentences that deal with individual events are concerned, there are in the whole Aristotelian corpus no instances of sentences whose contents are tied to some objective chronology and are thus independent of the moment of their utterance. From this it follows that the sentences with which Aristotle is normally dealing may change their truth value.[7] Since Aristotle's criteria for the identity of thoughts expressed by different utterances largely parallel his criteria for the sentences thereby uttered, the same will hold for thoughts (or, as Aristotle puts it, for opinions).[8] A form of words like 'Socrates is (now) sleeping' will for him express the same opinion when uttered tonight and when uttered tomorrow afternoon. And if so, then frequently one and the same

and time. Hence it would be historically unsatisfactory to dismiss this assumption as a simple mistake, as Mrs. Kneale in effect does, even if it were necessarily mistaken. The fact is, however, that Aristotle's way of thinking about the truth of sentences in their relation to time is *per se* no more fallacious than ours. It necessitates certain adjustments in the other semantical notions, and it is likely to be much clumsier than the preferred modern way of treating the same problems, but it is not bound to lead one to any absurdities. Thus it seems to me that Mrs. Kneale does not follow the interesting lead she puts forward far enough to throw as much new light on Aristotle's argument as she might have done.

[6] Such sentences are called *standing sentences* (in the case relevant here, *eternal sentences*) by W. V. Quine, in *Word and Object* (M.I.T. Press, Cambridge, Mass., 1960), pp. 35–6, as distinguished from *occasion sentences*. For the modern logicians' preference of them, see Prior, *Time and Modality*, Appendix A.

[7] See *Cat.* 5. 4ᵃ23–30, ᵃ34–61. Whatever doubts there may be concerning the authenticity of the *Categories* do not affect my point, for similar statements are found elsewhere in Aristotle's writings, e.g. in *Met.* Θ 10. 1051ᵇ13 ff.

[8] *Cat.* 5. loc. cit. See also Ch. IV, sections 3–4, above.

sentence (λόγος) and one and the same opinion (δόξα) will of course be sometimes true and sometimes false.

4. *Necessity and time in Aristotle*

If this is the way Aristotle normally thinks of our vehicles of linguistic communication, it is likely that he has the same paradigms in mind when he defines or characterizes his fundamental logical and philosophical notions. An important case in point is what he says of the notions of necessity and possibility. In passage after passage, he explicitly or tacitly equates possibility with sometime truth and necessity with omnitemporal truth.[9] Given enough Aristotelian assumptions, this is a very natural identification. But it is bound to land him into trouble as soon as he begins to consider sentences of type

(3) p at time t_0,

where t_0 is specified independently of the moment of utterance of the sentence in question, in addition to sentences of type

(4) p now

or simply p, where 'now' is tacitly included. (Notice that such sentences as 'p tomorrow' or 'p yesterday' go with (4) in that they contain a reference to the present moment.) Aristotle's troubles are increased by the fact that he neither clearly realized how closely he was committed in his conceptual system to considering (4) rather than (3) as a paradigm of an informative sentence nor fully realized what alternatives were open to him. I want to suggest that in *De Int.* 9 the difficulties broke to the surface.

The way in which the difficulties arise is obvious enough. Take any sentence about an individual event that is tied to an objective time scale (chronology)—that is, a sentence of type (3). If this sentence is true once, it is true always. If necessity equals omnitemporal truth, this means that (3) will be necessarily true if true at all; and by the same token it will be impossible if false. Hence all statements about events that are individual in the sense

---

[9] Perhaps the most explicit passage is *Met.* Θ 3. 1047[a]10–14. An instructive passage in which Aristotle explains the 'proper' sense of 'indestructible' along these lines is found in *De Caelo* I 12. 282[a]27 ff. Further evidence for this connection in Aristotle between time and possibility is found in Chapter V above which in this respect supersedes my earlier paper 'Necessity, Universality, and Time in Aristotle', *Ajatus*, 20 (1957), 65–90.

of being tied to a particular moment of time, will be either necessarily true or necessarily false. Everything that happens thus apparently happens necessarily, and we seem to end up in a complete determinism.

It will perhaps be objected that the main verb of the statement *p* must be in some tense or another. In whatever tense it is, the objection continues, it cannot be the right form of words throughout the infinity of past *and future* time. We must say 'Napoleon was defeated by the Russians in 1812', not that he is or will be defeated, whereas a contemporary may have asserted the same thing in the present or future tense. The Stoics and the schoolmen later stressed this point.[10] It would not, however, help Aristotle very much. There will in any case be a statement in the future tense that has remained true for an infinity of past time. And Aristotle believed firmly that whatever has remained unchanged for an infinity of past time cannot ever be changed.[11] Thus the statement 'Napoleon will be defeated by the Russians in 1812' would have been true to make at any previous moment of time, and hence what it expresses cannot possibly be otherwise than it is.

If we thus realize how deeply engrained Aristotle's habit of thinking in terms of temporally indefinite sentences of type (4) must have been, we also realize that he had a perfectly genuine problem about predictions concerning particular future events different from the problem of future truth. It is likely that the latter also worried him; but in the main his motives seem to have been different. Aristotle's main problem was not a metaphysician's vague worry about whether present truth about the future prejudges future events; it was the difficulty of a systematist who had defined his notions for too narrow a range of cases and was then forced to accommodate awkward new cases in his framework.

On this interpretation, Aristotle's problem was not primarily due to the apparent difficulties involved in the application of

[10] See, e.g., P. Boehner, *The 'Tractatus de praedestinatione et de praescientia Dei et de futuris contingentibus' of William Ockham*, esp. pp. 57–8. It is not obvious, however, whether this point was meant as a solution of Aristotle's difficulty.

[11] See, e.g., *De Caelo* I 12. 282ª30 ff. and 283ᵇ13 ff. Aristotle might here seem to discuss only the possible existence of individuals, not their possibly having this or that property. The arguments he gives are applicable to both cases, however, and Aristotle himself stresses their generality. Hence this is one more instance of Aristotle's use of the word 'being' as a undifferentiated expression which covers both existence and being such and such—i.e. having attributes.

tertium non datur to statements about future events. It was generated rather by the fact that statements about individual future events have *always* been true if they are true at all, and *always* false if false at all. Statements of this kind were thought of by Aristotle as being true or false *necessarily*. Aristotle's problem is thus primarily that of *omnitemporal* truth—or, more accurately, that of *infinite past* truth—rather than that of *future* truth.

5. *The structure of Aristotle's argument*

This, in any case, is what we are made to expect on general grounds by Aristotle's ways with time and truth. The first task for the rest of the chapter is to show that the problem I have ascribed to Aristotle is really found in the text of *De Int.* 9. Some piecemeal evidence against the traditional interpretation, and for my own, will be offered later (see section 8 below). In order to deduce this interpretation from the text we have to do something more, however, than discuss individual passages. We have to consider the structure of Aristotle's argument in *De Int.* 9.

What is the typical strategy of an Aristotelian argument? Often the difficulty of understanding his remarks is due not to their complexity, but to the fact that he is proceeding dialectically. He presents arguments and well-founded opinions first for one side and then for the other. The clash between the two gives rise to an *aporia* to be solved. Aristotle's own position is normally achieved by a conceptual analysis of the arguments that gave rise to the *aporia*. Very often it is achieved by pointing out distinctions between the different senses of some word or phrase figuring in the arguments. In reaching his own position, Aristotle is normally trying to preserve as much as possible of the apparently contradictory arguments he has explained, provided they 'pass the appropriate scrutiny'.[12] As pointed out by G. E. L. Owen, ἔνδοξα or well-founded opinions were for Aristotle among the 'phenomena' to be 'saved' by his own solution.

This simple scheme seems to apply very well to *De Int.* 9. Even if we do not yet understand the substance of what Aristotle says

[12] See G. E. L. Owen, 'Τιθέναι τὰ φαινόμενα', in *Aristote et les problèmes de méthode*, in the series *Aristote, traductions et études* (Publications Universitaires, Louvain, 1961), pp. 83–103, esp. pp. 84–92. I am much indebted to Owen's essay here. Cf. also Benedict Einarson, 'On Certain Mathematical Terms in Aristotle's Logic I', *American Journal of Philology*, 67 (1936), 33–54, esp. 38.

there, the main parts of his discussion stand out clearly enough. First, Aristotle presents the case for the deterministic view (18^a34–$^b16$). Then he points out the awkward consequences of the deterministic view (19^a7–22). His own solution is expounded from 19^a23 on. From the form of words Aristotle uses here, it appears that the solution turns on a distinction between the meanings of two closely related expressions.

The transition from the argument for the deterministic view to the statement of the case against it is effected by an elaboration of the consequences of the deterministic standpoint (18^b26–19^a6). In a parenthetical passage (18^b17–25) Aristotle rules out an alternative solution to his problem.[13]

So far, the structure of Aristotle's argument is clear enough.[14] However, appreciating this structure does not yet throw much light on his solution.

In order to understand Aristotle's solution we must turn to 19^a23–$^b4$. Here we find, it seems to me, the most important peculiarities of the present argument of Aristotle's. The dénouement clearly comes at 19^a23–7, a passage which will be analysed in detail below. As usual, Aristotle hastens to point out how his solution does justice both to the arguments for the deterministic position and to the arguments against it. As usual, he says in effect that in one sense one party is right and in another sense the other is also right. What distinguishes the present passage from many others in Aristotle is that here he makes the same point three times, merely addressing himself to a slightly different version of the problem each time. First, he states what is true and what is false in the deterministic arguments as far as they concern *an individual future event* (19^a23–7). Then he repeats the same points as applied to *a pair of contradictory future events* (19^a27–32). Finally he goes through the same motions all over again as applied to *a pair of contradictory statements* about an individual future event (19^a32–$^b4$). These three parts of Aristotle's exposition of his own solution will be referred to in what follows as stages I–III of his solution.

---

[13] This much is clear independently of the precise interpretation of the passage, which does not have to be discussed here.

[14] So far, my analysis of the structure of Aristotle's argument coincides mainly with Colin Strang's; see his 'Aristotle and the Sea Battle', *Mind*, 69 (1960), 447–65. I shall not discuss here his interpretation of individual passages, however.

The transitions from each of these stages to the next one are conspicuous in the text. In each case Aristotle makes it clear that he is merely going to reformulate a point he has already made. 'And the same account holds for contradictories also' (19^a27–28; transition from stage I to stage II). 'So, since statements are true according to how the actual things are, it is clear that wherever these are such as to allow of contraries as chance has it, the same necessarily holds for the contradictories also' (19^a32–5; transition from II to III). It is also conspicuous that the notions of truth and falsity ($\dot{\alpha}\lambda\eta\theta\dot{\eta}\varsigma$ and $\psi\epsilon\upsilon\delta\dot{\eta}\varsigma$) re-enter the discussion at stage III after having been absent at I and II.[15]

A comparison between the three stages of Aristotle's solution may therefore be hoped to throw light on all of them. We may also bring in the preliminary arguments *pro* and *con* as the fourth member of the comparison. At each stage, Aristotle states what is true and what is false in the deterministic viewpoint and sometimes also adds further comments on the relation between both. These remarks may be profitably compared with the initial arguments for and against determinism, which will be referred to collectively as the preparatory stage (stage O) of Aristotle's solution.

In order to facilitate a comparison between the four stages, some of the parallelisms between the key passages are brought out by the schematic outline of Aristotle's solution on pp. 156–7. The preparatory stage of Aristotle's solution is of course represented only by a few characteristic passages. The outline graphically shows the close parallelism that obtains between the different stages.

6. *The nature of Aristotle's main distinction*

Before we can pause to examine the analogies that the outline brings out we must try to perceive the nature of Aristotle's solution. As we have seen, the crucial passage is 19^a23–7, which figures in the outline as the second column. The key sentences are thus the following:

> (I.1) What is necessarily is, when it is; and what is not necessarily is not, when it is not.

[15] The difference between stages I–II on the one hand, and stage III on the other has been pointed out many times. See, e.g., J. L. Ackrill, *Aristotle's 'Categories' and 'De Interpretatione'*, pp. 137–8, and J. T. Oesterle, *Aristotle: On Interpretation. Commentary by St. Thomas and Cajetan*, p. 121 (St. Thomas Aquinas, commentary on *De Interpretatione*, pt. I, lesson 15, § 1).

OUTLINE OF ARISTOTLE'S SOLUTION

O	I
The facts of the case are presented.	The main distinction is made in terms of an individual future event.

---

0. For we see that . . . in things that are not always actual there is the possibility of being and of not being.

1. But if it was always true to say [of what now is] that it was so, or would be so, it could not not be so, or not be going to be so. But if something cannot not happen, . . . it is necessary for it to happen.

1. What is necessarily is, when it is; and what is not necessarily is not, when it is not.

2. [Nevertheless] not everything is or happens of necessity: some things happen as chance has it.

2. But not everything that is necessarily is; and not everything that is not necessarily is not.

3. For to say that everything that is is of necessity, when it is, is not the same as saying unconditionally that it is of necessity.

4. [Then] of the affirmation and the negation neither is truer than the other; with other things one is truer and happens as a rule, but still it is possible for the other to happen instead.

II	III
The same distinction is made in terms of contradictory events.	The distinction is applied to the corresponding statements.

0. And the same account holds for contradictories.	0. This happens with things that are not always so or are not always not so.
1. Everything necessarily is or is not, and will be or will not be.	1. With these it is necessary for one or the other of the contradictories to be true or false.
2. But one cannot divide and say that one or the other is necessarily.	2. Not, however, this one or that one, but as chance has it.
	4. Or for one to be truer than the other, yet not already true or false.

(I.2) But not everything that is necessarily is; and not everything that is not necessarily is not.

(I.3) For to say that everything that is is of necessity, when it is, is not the same as saying unconditionally (ἁπλῶς) that it is of necessity.

In (I.3) Aristotle introduces the distinction by means of which he proposes to solve his problem. This distinction is between saying on one hand that something is of necessity *when it is* and on the other hand that it is of necessity *haplōs*. What exactly is this distinction? What, first of all, is the force of the word *haplōs* in Aristotle? In its basic and normal sense it does not so much indicate the absence of conditions as the absence of qualifications. The translation 'without qualifications', taken in the literal sense of the phrase, thus seems to catch the Aristotelian meaning of the word quite accurately.[16] For Aristotle, something is said *haplōs* if it is said *simpliciter*—that is, said without any additional qualifying word, phrase, or clause. The contrast Aristotle is here drawing is therefore between statements of the form

(5) necessarily *p*

and certain statements that result from (5) by adding qualifications. Qualifications of what kind? Aristotle's formulations in (I.1) and in (I.3) ('*when* it is') shows that they are *temporal* qualifications. The contrast must therefore be between (5) and statements of the form

(6) necessarily (*p* at time t_0).

Statements of the form (6) are, it seems, said by Aristotle to be true whenever (3) is true, while statements of the form (5) are apparently considered false by him in many similar circumstances.

This might seem a rather strange doctrine, were it not exactly the same as the suggestion made above in section 4 concerning the causes of Aristotle's difficulty. It was pointed out there that Aristotle's assumptions concerning the notions of necessity and possibility and their relation to time seem to have tempted him to declare true statements of type (3) necessary, whereas true

[16] See *Topics* II 11. 115^{b}11 ff. and 29 ff., *Soph. El.* 5. 166^{b}38 ff., and Bonitz, *Index Aristotelicus*, on *haplōs*. Cf. also the trenchant formulation by C. S. Lewis in *Studies in Words* (Cambridge University Press, Cambridge, 1960), pp. 167–9. Ackrill, too, elsewhere translates *haplōs* by 'without qualifications'; cf. *De Int.* 13. 23^{a}16.

statements of type (4) (or of the simpler type obtained by omitting 'now') normally were not believed by him to be necessary. But saying this is exactly the same as saying that Aristotle was led to consider (6) true whenever (3) is true, but to consider (5) in most cases false. The distinction Aristotle makes in (I.3) is thus one that we are entitled to expect him to make by what we find elsewhere in his writings.

This way of reading the crucial sentence (I.3) might nevertheless seem to involve several difficulties. A couple of them will be discussed later. There is, however, further support for our reading. One piece of evidence is the fact that in contexts comparable to the one we have here, *haplōs* is often used by Aristotle to indicate the absence of *temporal* qualifications that would limit the scope of a statement to some particular moment or interval of time. Thus we read at *An. Pr.* I 15. 34ᵇ7–11:

We must understand the expression 'applies to all' not as qualified with respect to time (κατὰ χρόνον ὁρίσαντας) e.g. 'now' or 'at such-and-such a time' but without qualifications (ἁπλῶς). For it is by means of premisses taken in this latter way that syllogisms are effected.

Similar contrasts occur elsewhere. For instance, at *De Int.* 1. 16ᵃ18 we have a contrast between ἁπλῶς and κατὰ χρόνον. Further evidence is found at *De Int.* 13. 23ᵃ16; *An. Pr.* I 10. 30ᵇ31–40 and I 15. 34ᵇ17–18; *Topics* I 5. 102ᵃ24–6; *De Anima* III 10. 433ᵇ9; *De Part. An.* I 1. 639ᵇ25; and *Met.* Δ 5. 1015ᵇ11–14.

7. What does Aristotle's solution solve?

Although we have thus succeeded in deducing from the text the interpretation that Aristotle's usage elsewhere had made us expect, our reading of the text still calls for several comments. For one thing, does the distinction Aristotle makes in (I.3) help him at all? If my interpretation is right, the distinction looks much more like a restatement of Aristotle's problem than a solution to it. All true statements about genuinely individual future events still remain necessary; is this not as troublesome as any problem he may have had earlier?

The crucial passage (I.3) is the first one in which the causes of his difficulty are made clear by Aristotle. He seems to have thought that he could escape the worst merely by making the distinction between temporally unqualified sentences and sentences referring to a particular moment of time (which is specified independently of the moment of utterance of the sentence). This mere distinction does not, however, enable him to escape the deterministic conclusions he is worried about unless it is also assumed that it is the necessity or contingency of sentences of the former kind that really counts for the issue of determinism or indeterminism, not the necessity or contingency of sentences of the latter kind. In other words, Aristotle's proposed solution turns on the presupposition that it is the truth or falsity of statements like (5) that really counts here, not the truth or falsity of statements like (6).

Again, the interpretation we have found ourselves defending might prima facie seem quite implausible. For contemporary logicians, it is undoubtedly obvious that the necessity of individual events should be discussed in terms of statements of the form (6) rather than (5). A closer examination of the situation nevertheless suggests that this assumption may not have been equally obvious to Aristotle. It has already been pointed out that Aristotle habitually thought of logical matters in terms of temporally unqualified sentences of form (4) or (5) rather than in terms of temporally qualified sentences of form (3) or (6). Is it surprising, then, that he should have preferred, deliberately or unwittingly, to discuss the necessity of future events in terms of the former rather than of the latter?

Surprising or not, the fact that Aristotle does just this is betrayed by his formulations. It is well-nigh axiomatic for Aristotle that possibility equals sometime truth, or, as he puts it, whatever is not always actual is contingent. This assumption is set forward by him as the first general fact that shows the inadequacy of the deterministic position, as we can see from (O.o)—that is, from 19^a9-11. It is thus one of the 'facts of the case' to which any satisfactory solution has to conform. In (III.o), Aristotle accordingly returns to this requirement and points out that it is satisfied by his solution.

There are also further items of evidence for my interpretation. In the next chapter, I shall discuss certain similarities and dissimilarities between Aristotle and Diodorus Cronus.[17] One of the main points that emerged from the discussion was that Aristotle apparently escaped certain conclusions of the early

---

[17] See especially section 11.

Megarians only by resorting to a notion of possibility on which a statement that something is *now* possible really refers to all future times. In order for *p* to be possible *now* it suffices that it *will be* true; and in order for it to be impossible now it must *never* be true in the future. As Aristotle illustrates his point, when an animal is said to be indestructible *now*, what is really meant is that it is now an animal that *will never* be destroyed.[18]

The details of this move were never completely articulated by Aristotle, any more than the details of the move Aristotle makes in (I.3). It is obvious, however, that the two moves are parallel. In order to avoid the collapse of possibility into actuality, which the early Megarians had advocated, Aristotle had to say that what really counts as showing what is possible at a moment is not what is true of this one moment of time. In a sense, whatever happens at a moment could not fail to happen at it; 'possibly *p* at t_0' implies '*p* at t_0'. In Aristotle's view, this nevertheless does not prove determinism, for what really counts as showing that something is possible at a given moment of time is whatever happens in similar circumstances at other (future) moments of time. Such happenings Aristotle tended to discuss in terms of temporally unqualified sentences of the type '*p* now' or '*p* simpliciter'. Hence the two moves amount essentially to the same; in both cases, Aristotle tries to avoid deterministic conclusions by shifting the focus of his attention from statements of type (3) to temporally unqualified statements. In both cases, he seems to think that this shift suffices to solve his problem. He does not worry, we may say, about the implication 'if (possibly *p* at t_0) then (*p* at t_0)', because he either forgets or disparages the kinds of sentences that occur as its antecedent and consequent.

This parallelism supports the interpretation advocated here. The fact that, for us, Aristotle's move does not in either case seem to remove the deterministic conclusions in a satisfactory manner is no objection to my interpretation, although it may be an objection to Aristotle. For us, the extensionalistic account of possibility to which Aristotle resorts scarcely serves to clear up any questions as to what can or cannot happen at some particular moment of time. Given Aristotle's habits of thought, such as we have found them to be, the situation might have seemed rather different to him.

[18] Cf. *Top*. VI 6. 145^{b}27–30 and *De Caelo* I 12. 282^{a}27–30.

One way of making Aristotle's view comprehensible, if not acceptable, to contemporary philosophers is to interpret him as thinking that it does not make much sense to speak of possibilities concerning a single moment of time. Statements of possibility were taken by Aristotle to be primarily statements of frequency, wherefore they involve a range of cases. Saying that an individual event is possible is for him normally an elliptical way of saying that the relative frequency of similar events on similar occasions is different from zero.

From this point of view, Aristotle's doctrine of possibility is analogous to his treatment of certain other notions. For instance, Aristotle does not think that there really is such a thing as a velocity or even a movement *at an instant,* except perhaps in some secondary sense.[19] Aristotle's 'reply to Zeno rejects all uses of "movement" other than that which can be described in terms of periods of time'; does he depart any more radically from common sense when he discredits those uses of 'possibility' which cannot be described in terms of a variety of cases?[20] If Aristotle is 'unable to speak of a speed at an instant', we should not be surprised to find him reluctant to speak of a possibility at an instant.

Be this as it may, it seems to me obvious that Aristotle's criticism of the position of the determinist does not consist in pointing out a fallacy in the latter's argument. It consists in a reinterpretation of the conclusion of the argument. This is as it should be; Aristotle's procedure here parallels his criticism of the Megarians. This observation effectively disposes of an acute objection which has been levelled against an interpretation of Aristotle's argument along the lines we are here following. It has been objected that on such an interpretation Aristotle neither rejects the determinist's premiss nor exposes the fallacy of his argument.[21] We can now see that there is no need for him to do either. An exposé of a fallacy is not required by Aristotle's strategy, for a reinterpretation of the conclusion of an argument is an even better way of reconciling the argument with apparently contradictory doctrines than is the disclosure of a fallacy.

---

[19] See *Phys.* IV 14. 222^{b}30–223^{a}15; VI 8. 239^{a}23–^{b}4.
[20] See G. E. L. Owen, 'Zeno and the Mathematicians', *Proceedings of the Aristotelian Society,* 58 (1957–8), 199–222.
[21] Cf. Ackrill, *Aristotle's 'Categories' and 'De Interpretatione',* pp. 139–40.

8. *Some uses of the analogies*

Further light on the details of Aristotle's discussion is thrown by the analogies that our outline of his solution brings out. For one thing, if our analysis of the structure of Aristotle's argument is right, the interpretation of Aristotle's discussion that has been defended by, among others, Colin Strang and Mrs. Kneale is seen to be mistaken.[22] According to their view, the point of Aristotle's discussion is to assert the truth of the disjunction (1) even when p is a sentence dealing with an individual future event but to deny that either p or not-p should therefore be true. Even if we disregard the intrinsic absurdity of this alleged doctrine of Aristotle's, which has provoked the deserved ridicule of Cicero (*De Fato* XVI 37) and W. V. Quine (*The Ways of Paradox* (Random House, New York, 1966), p. 21), this interpretation is made implausible by the fact that initially Aristotle's key distinction has nothing to do with disjunctions. This distinction is made at stage I; and at this stage Aristotle is discussing an individual future event, not a pair of contradictory events nor yet any statements about them, whether in the form of disjunctions or not.

On our interpretation, we can see that a distinction similar to, but different from, the one just rejected ensues from Aristotle's basic distinction between (5) and (6). For many a temporally unqualified sentence p, neither p nor not-p is *always* true; hence neither of them is true necessarily, and the sentence

(7) (necessarily p) or (necessarily not-p)

is false. Nevertheless, for every p the sentence (1) is *always* true, and the sentence (2) therefore true. If Aristotle's views are formulated in terms of pairs of contradictories, he is thus on our interpretation discussing the necessity or non-necessity of the individual disjuncts of (1), not the necessity or non-necessity of the disjunction (1) itself. He has, however, to disentangle his problem from that concerning the truth of (2); and this is exactly what he does at stages II and III. The distinction he there makes is thus primarily between (2) and (7). In (II.1) he considers the necessity of the disjunction, that is, considers (2); in (II.2) he considers the necessity of the individual disjuncts separately

---

[22] See note 2, p. 148 above, and the works by Strang and by the Kneales listed in the Bibliography.

(διελόντα), that is, considers (7). This is attested by such passages as *Categories* 10. 12ᵇ38–13ᵃ3, 13ᵃ9–13. It is true that in the *Categories* Aristotle uses the expression ἀφωρισμένως and not διελόντα, but this does not seem to make them less similar to (II.2).[23]

These observations also help us to adjudicate the claims of the traditional interpretation, and of mine, to explain the details of Aristotle's text. According to these observations Aristotle is, on the traditional interpretation, denying (2) whereas, on my interpretation, he is denying (7). In order to see which of these he is actually doing, let us consider some of the relevant passages:

(*i*) In the opening sentence of *De Int.* 9 Aristotle says that

(8) With regard to what is and what has been it is necessary for the affirmation or the negation to be true or false (18ᵃ28–9).

This is soon contrasted with

(9) particulars that are going to be.

The contrast between 'what is and what has been' on the one hand and 'what is going to be' on the other is of course the contrast between present and past on the one hand and the future on the other. Aristotle is worried solely about (9). The case is different from what it is in (8); certain laws which hold for past and present events lead to difficulties when applied to (9) and will therefore eventually be rejected. These laws are formulated in (8). The formulation is not unambiguous, however, in that the law in question might either be of form (2) or of form (7). We have to resort to what Aristotle says elsewhere in order to find out what he means.

An indication is given by the fact that Aristotle more than once asserts that all true statements about the past are necessary (and that all false statements about the past are by the same token impossible).[24] In one passage he seems to say that the same holds for statements about the present.[25] Hence Aristotle undoubtedly believed that (7) holds for statements about the past. Rejecting

---

[23] Notice that the phrase ὁπότερ' ἔτυχε occurs both in the passages referred to in the *Categories* and in (O.2) as well as in (III.2).

[24] *De Caelo* I 12. 283ᵇ12–14, *Eth. Nic.* VI 2. 1139ᵇ7–9. There is no trace of a suggestion that Aristotle is in these passages employing a sense of possibility different from his usual one.   [25] *Rhet.* III 17. 1418ᵃ3–5.

it for statements about the future would amount to pointing out an interesting difference between the past and the future. This suggests, albeit not yet very strongly, that Aristotle probably had in mind (7) rather than (2).

(*ii*) Stronger evidence is forthcoming. Aristotle's discussion in *De Int.* 9 is symmetrical in the same way as a proposition in Euclid: he ends by repeating the main assertion he made in the introductory paragraph. Thus we read:

> (10) Clearly, then, it is not necessary that of every affirmation and opposite negation one should be true and the other false. For what holds for things that are does not hold for things that are not but may possibly be or not be; with these it is as we have said (19^a39-^b4).

Because of the symmetry, the first sentence of this passage must mean the same as the initial denial for the law expressed in (8). Prima facie, this sentence is ambiguous in the same way as the initial one. Here, however, the context offers a number of clues. On any interpretation, Aristotle is here summing up his own solution ('it is as we have said'). Now the body of the text does not contain any clear denial of the law of excluded middle. Our analysis of Aristotle's solution comes in handily here: a glance at (II.2) or (III.3) satisfies one that what is being denied as a part of Aristotle's solution is not (2) but (7). Furthermore, a comparison of (I.1), (II.1), and (III.1) shows that (2) is consistently affirmed by Aristotle at all stages of his solution. The last time it is asserted is in the very statement immediately preceding (10). Hence there does not seem to be any room for doubting that in (10) Aristotle wants to deny (7) but not (2). Since his closing statement (10) is obviously intended to match the initial denial that 'particulars that are going to be' are true or false of necessity, the same must hold for the latter, too.

This point is strengthened further by observing that the 'things that are not but may possibly be or not be' which are mentioned in (10) are identical with the 'things that are not always so or are not always not so' which are mentioned in (III.0) and discussed in (III.1)–(III.4). This is shown by a comparison with *De Int.* 13. 22^b36-23^a20. What 'holds for things that are' is, Aristotle informs us at 23ᵃ12–13, that some of them are changeless—that is, are always so or always not so. In contrast, 'things that are not but may possibly be or not be' are all changeable—that is, neither always so nor always not so; compare also (O.o). Thus (III.2) is concerned with the very same things as (10) and is one of the likely references of Aristotle's phrase 'as we have said' in (10). Since the former denies (7) but not (2), the same must be the case with the latter.

An objection might be based on the reference at 18ᵃ30 back to *De Int.* 7. 17ᵇ26–7, for in the latter passage Aristotle is clearly speaking of truth and falsity, not of necessity and impossibility. All the parallelism shows, however, is that the introductory statement at 18ᵃ28–33 is ambiguous, as has indeed been acknowledged above. It does not offer any firm guidance as to how (and to what extent) Aristotle dissolved the ambiguity.

(*iii*) Our difficulties, however, are not over yet. It may seem to go against our interpretation that Aristotle classifies 'universals taken universally' together with past and present events among the things for which (8) holds (see 18ᵃ29–31). The fact that he does so without apparently using any modal terms at all may seem even more alien to our interpretation. How can Aristotle state (7) without using the word 'necessary' or any of its relatives?

What Aristotle actually says can be taken to mean that with universals 'taken universally' (that is, in the normal sense) one of the contradictories is *always* true and the other *always* false. On the basis of the Aristotelian identification of necessity with omnitemporality this is just what interpretation (7) requires. In fact, the expressions ἀεί and ἀνάγκη seem to be on a par at 18ᵃ28–33. From Aristotle's statements elsewhere it also appears that he did think of unrestrictedly universal statements as being necessarily true if they are true at all.[26] Hence everything squares with my interpretation here.

(*iv*) It has sometimes been suggested that the point of Aristotle's discussion is that statements about future singulars are not yet true or false although they will later become true or false. This view is disproved by the fact that Aristotle explicitly includes

---

[26] Cf. Hintikka, 'Necessity, Universality, and Time in Aristotle', pp. 66–7, and Chapter V above. Notice also that for Aristotle a genuinely universal sentence refers to all the individuals existing at different moments of time (*An. Pr.* I 15. 34ᵇ6 ff.). Hence if it is true once, it is true always, and therefore necessarily true according to the Aristotelian assumptions.

statements concerning the future in his affirmations of (2). This is the case with (II.1)—witness the words 'everything . . . will be or will not be'—and it is also the case with an earlier passage which is as effective a counter-example to the traditional interpretation as one may wish: 'Nor, however, can we say that neither is true—that it neither will be nor will not be so' (18ᵇ17–18). The only hope of disqualifying this statement would be to allege that it does not represent Aristotle's final point of view. This allegation is shown to be invalid by my analysis of the structure of Aristotle's solution.

(*v*) Aristotle's fullest statement of his problem suggests very strongly that he is primarily worried about the fact that a true prediction must have remained true through an infinity of past time:

Again, if it is white now it was true to say earlier that it would be white; so that it was *always* (ἀεί) true to say of anything that has happened that it would be so. But if it was *always* (ἀεί) true to say that it was so, or would be so, it could not not be so, or not be going to be so. But if something cannot not happen it is impossible for it not to happen; and if it is impossible for something not to happen it is necessary for it to happen. (18ᵇ9–14; my italics)

A little later Aristotle writes: 'Hence, if *in the whole of time* (ἐν ἅπαντι τῷ χρόνῳ) the state of things was such that one or the other was true, it was necessary for this to happen. . . . For . . . of what happens it was *always* (ἀεί) true to say that it would be the case' (19ᵃ1–6; my italics). Again, we have a clear indication of what is on Aristotle's mind. With these statements of Aristotle's problem —and with our interpretation of his solution—one may compare Cicero's conclusion of his discussion of the same problem: 'Reason itself will insist *both* that certain things are true from all eternity *and* that they are not involved in a nexus of eternal causes but are free from the necessity of fate' (*De Fato* XVI 38).

The passages just quoted become especially poignant when read in conjunction with *De Caelo* I 12. There Aristotle argues at some length that what has *always* existed cannot possibly fail to exist. His arguments are so general as to allow the parallel conclusion that what has *always* been one way rather than another cannot possibly change in the future, either. Singular future events like a sea fight are by all appearances legitimate cases in point. Hence Aristotle is not in the quoted passages appealing only or mainly to a layman's unarticulated intuitions about contingent future events, but also to his own very conclusions in a (presumably earlier) work.

The way in which Aristotle reaches the passages that we have quoted, in which he formulates his main difficulty, nevertheless shows that, to some extent, he is also worried about the problem of future truth and not only the problem of infinite past truth. In fact, starting from the assumption that *tertium non datur* holds for all statements, Aristotle first derives a version of the problem of future truth (see 18ᵃ34–ᵇ9). Only then does he derive from the same assumption the formulation of the problem of omni-temporal truth which we have quoted (see 18ᵇ9–16). The fact that two different problems are initially considered together by Aristotle has added to the difficulties of the interpreters. There evidently is a serious ambiguity in Aristotle's initial formulation of the view that 'it is necessary for every affirmation or negation to be true or false'. Some of this ambiguity may persist through his discussion. Nevertheless, I fail to perceive any trace of the problem of future truth in Aristotle's *solution*. Aristotle probably thought that a solution of the problem of omnitemporal truth is *a fortiori* a solution of the problem of future truth.

(*vi*) An objection has occasionally been made to the line of thought represented here. According to this criticism, Aristotle's principle that omnitemporal *being* implies necessary *being* and that possible *being* implies sometime *being* are not applicable to *De Int.* 9 because Aristotle is here discussing omnitemporal *truth* rather than omnitemporal being, and possible *truth* rather than possible being.

It is hard to think of a suggestion that is more blatantly beside the point, however. Aristotle's general characterization of truth in *Met. Γ* 7. 1011ᵇ26–7 shows that for him it is *true* to say that *p*, if and only if it *is* the case that *p*. Hence everything that has been said in terms of truth in the course of this chapter could have been said in terms of being while keeping within the purview of genuinely Aristotelian ideas. Nor is this a consequence of some abstract principles the Stagirite did not consistently adhere to. The same general idea is introduced by means of an example in the very chapter under discussion : 'For if it is true to say that it is white or is not white, it is necessary for it to be white or not white, and if it is white or not white, it is true to say or deny this'

(18^a39-^b2). (The same point is applied in so many words to statements about the future in *De Gen. et Corr.* II 11. 337^b4-5.) Moreover, Aristotle practises what he preaches: the comparison above between the different stages I–III of Aristotle's solution shows that he is moving back and forth without any compunctions between a future *event* (or a pair of contradictory future *events*) and the *truth or falsity* of a statement about such an event. He reminds his readers of the justifiability of this procedure in passing from stage II to stage III. Thus any criticism that turns on the contrast between being and truth (as, e.g., that put forward by Dorothea Frede, pp. 90–1) is without a shadow of substance.

9. *Further evidence*

Aristotle's fundamental point in *De Int.* 9 concerns, we have argued, the relation of temporally qualified to temporally unqualified sentences. Is this suggestion borne out by Aristotle's way of handling temporal terms in *De Int.* 9?

Although Aristotle is not quite as clear as one might wish, it seems to me that the answer is affirmative. In any case, it is patent that Aristotle sometimes thinks and talks of what happens or is supposed to happen at some particular moment of time and that he at other times speaks of what happens at a great number of different moments of time. For instance, when he speaks of predicting an event 'ten thousand years beforehand' (18^b34), and says that it does not matter how old the predictions are, he is clearly thinking of predictions pertaining to one and the same moment or period of time. Likewise, when Aristotle discusses the possibility or necessity of a sea fight tomorrow, he clearly has in mind a sea fight on a specific day. He is not thinking of the predictions which on different days might be made by uttering the same form of words 'there will be a sea fight tomorrow'. Perhaps more importantly, in his fullest formulation of the problem he is discussing, Aristotle starts from something which is *now* true and goes on to consider potential predictions concerning it (see 18^b9-14, quoted above in section 8, part (*v*)).

On the other hand, it is plain that several expressions used by Aristotle presuppose a whole range of different times or different cases. Our outline of Aristotle's solution contains several instances of this. For instance, in (O.o) (19^a9-11) Aristotle speaks of 'things that are not always (μὴ ἀεί) actual'. In (O.4) (that is, 19ᵃ19–22) he discusses what happens 'as a rule' or maybe rather 'in most cases' (ὡς ἐπὶ τὸ πολύ). This expression is discussed at length at *An. Pr.* I 13. Aristotle's examples there make it obvious that he has in mind a variety of similar cases. A given individual man either becomes grey-haired or fails to do so. If we say that a man becomes grey-haired 'as a rule', we are really speaking of a variety of different men.

The statement that sometimes one member of a pair of contradictories is 'truer' (μᾶλλον ἀληθής) than the other appears to be a reformulation of the statement that it is true 'as a rule'; and a closer look at the situation bears this out. The well-known Aristotelian definition of truth leaves no room for different degrees of truth; things are either said to be as they are (and truly so) or else as they are not (and falsely so). The sense of the expression 'truer than' in Aristotle is brought out by his use of the closely related expression 'more in one way than the other' (μᾶλλον οὕτως ἢ ἐκείνως) at *An. Pr.* I 13. 32ᵇ17–18 (compare also *De Int.* 9. 18ᵇ8–9). The context there shows clearly that what is meant is simply 'happens *more often* in one way than the other'. And the company kept in *De Int.* 9 by the locution which Ackrill translated 'as chance has it' (ὁπότερ᾽ ἔτυχε) commits it to the same group of expressions as 'in most cases' and 'truer than'.

Again, this is confirmed by what we find elsewhere in Aristotle's writings. The locution ὁπότερ᾽ ἔτυχε is closely related to the locution ἀπὸ τύχης in Aristotle's discussion. The former is used when Aristotle is dealing with pairs of contradictories, the latter when he deals with individual events. Now ἀπὸ τύχης is used by Aristotle—for example, at *An. Pr.* I 13. 32ᵇ12—in a context that shows that it presupposes relative frequencies of events. The same point is attested by *Phys.* II 5, as is also our point concerning ὡς ἐπὶ τὸ πολύ (compare also *Met. E* 2, especially 1026ᵇ27–1027ᵃ28).

Once all this is perceived, it is also seen that Aristotle's solution of his problem turns on the use of temporally unqualified expressions which enable him to discuss a whole range of similar cases in one formulation. A comparison between stages O and III of our outline is especially instructive here. The phrase 'as chance has it' occurs both in (O.2) and in (III.2), and the paradoxical phrase 'truer than' is found both in (O.4) and in (III.4).

An examination of Aristotle's usage thus serves to corroborate the analysis that was offered of Aristotle's solution. Aristotle is sometimes thinking of individual events and sometimes of a number of similar events. He has to distinguish the two points of view from each other. What is more natural than to assume that he does so in (I.3) (that is, at 19ª25–6)? It may also be observed that Aristotle's putative arguments for determinism seem to be preponderantly in terms of statements about what happens at a particular moment of time, whereas his professedly libertarian conclusions (stage III) are, as we just saw, mainly in terms of expressions that are *not* tied to a particular moment of time. All this is just what is to be expected on our interpretation.

We can also understand the puzzling juxtaposition that occurs at 19ª36–9—that is, in the three clauses (III.1–2) and (III.4). How can Aristotle first say that one member of each pair of contradictories is necessarily true and the other member false, and then go on to remark—in (III.4)—that one of them often is merely 'truer' than the other, thereby unmistakably implying that sometimes neither of them is 'truer' than the other? If one member is in each case true and the other false, surely the former is 'truer' than the latter! This implication is further borne out by a comparison with (O.4).

An answer is implicit in what has been said. At each moment either *p* or not-*p* is for Aristotle true and the other false, no matter what *p* is. Hence (1) is always true and (2) therefore true. But it does not follow that if the two disjuncts are considered separately one of them is 'truer' than the other in the sense of being true *more often* than the latter. This presupposes that *p* is a sentence with a changing truth value; but we have seen that Aristotle was wont to operate with just such sentences.

10. *Generalization with respect to individuals or with respect to time?*

Thus there seems to be strong evidence for our interpretation. This interpretation, however, gives rise to a problem which I am not able to solve here.

I have asserted that for Aristotle, possibility tended to be identified with sometime truth, and necessity with omnitemporal truth. This formulation is not unproblematic. We have not made clear what exactly are the cases that have to be true in order for something to qualify as being true omnitemporally; and Aristotle never seems to make it unequivocally clear. Take, for instance, Aristotle's statement that 'this coat' may wear out but that it also may be cut before it wears out ($19^{a}12-18$). Now it is clear that in a sense, one of these two possibilities will never be realized. If the coat is cut, it will not wear out, and vice versa. Hence Aristotle can equate possibility with sometime truth only if he thinks that he is dealing with statements of the form 'a coat will wear out' and 'a coat will be cut' or perhaps 'such and such a coat will wear out' and 'such and such a coat will be cut', not with the statements '*this* coat will wear out' and '*this* coat will be cut'—or so it seems. In other words, a statement as to what is possible in a given moment to a given individual must be taken as an elliptical statement which really says something about all the similar individuals at all the different times. A mere generalization with respect to time is not enough; Aristotle apparently has to generalize also with respect to individuals. That this is what he does is strongly suggested by *An. Pr.* I 13. $32^{b}4$ ff.

Somewhat similar remarks pertain to the interpretation we have offered of Aristotle's solution of the problem of the sea fight tomorrow. I have suggested that Aristotle considers the occurrence of a sea fight tomorrow contingent because in similar circumstances in the past and in the future it sometimes is true and sometimes false to say 'a sea fight will take place tomorrow'. In other words, if one asserts the contingency of tomorrow's sea fight, one is not any more speaking of *this* individual naval engagement; one is speaking, however elliptically, of similar sea fights in the past and in the future.

Of this part of our solution I am not at all sure. It is obvious enough, on the evidence we have found, that Aristotle thinks he can escape his difficulties by making the assertion of the contingency of the sea fight an elliptical assertion of the truth of at least one case among several. But what these cases are is not obvious. There are indications that perhaps suggest that Aristotle may have thought that a mere generalization with respect to time is enough, without having to go beyond considerations pertaining to one individual sea fight.

By this I mean the following: Aristotle may have thought that the truth and falsity of a statement (made at a given moment of time) is determined by its agreement or disagreement with the facts *as they are at that particular moment*. It is possible that Aristotle's version of the correspondence theory of truth was a theory of *momentary* correspondence.[27] And if so, Aristotle might have thought that the reason the statement 'a sea fight will take place tomorrow' is contingent is that its truth value (momentary truth value in the sense mentioned) will still change. At this moment, the admirals are confident and in a fighting mood, and their intelligence underestimates the power of the enemy; in short, the situation is one which naturally leads to a fight. If so, it may be suggested, it will be true to say that there will be a sea fight. But after a couple of hours, the intelligence estimates may have become pessimistic and the admirals timid. The situation presumably will lead to a failure of the sea fight to materialize. If so, then it is perhaps false to say that a sea fight will take place. Now if a situation of the first kind never occurs between this moment and tomorrow, then (Aristotle may have thought) there is no chance that the sea fight would come about. By the same token, if a situation of the second kind will never come about, there is no opening for the sea fight to fail to take place. Then it presumably will take place necessarily.

Thus it is not impossible that Aristotle should have thought that a generalization with respect to time was enough to deal with his problem.

There is not much evidence one way or the other. The view just sketched is made implausible by the fact that it does not seem to leave Aristotle any reason to suppose that, of each pair of contradictories referring to a future event, one is at each given moment true and the other false, as he seems to assert in (III.1). For the situation might be such that it does not give rise to a sea fight any more naturally than to the absence of one. Hence I suspect that this view is mistaken.

There are, however, mild indications favouring it. At 19ᵃ1–6 Aristotle argues that if the nature of things has always been such that something is true, it will be *necessarily* true. This seems to refer to the state of affairs at different moments of time. One might also try to read something similar into 19ᵃ32–5—not very convincingly, because this sentence primarily serves to mark the

---

[27] Cf. Ackrill, op. cit., pp. 140–1. There is, however, a fairly clear counter-example at *De Gen. et Corr.* II 11. 337ᵇ4–6.

transition from stage II to stage III. The third piece of evidence is somewhat more conclusive. It is the word that Ackrill translates in (III.4) 'already'. This word is ἤδη, which can naturally mean something slightly more than 'already', namely 'from now on'. If it means this in (III.4), we really seem to have a statement that definitely supports the view I just sketched. For how can Aristotle first say that an affirmation or the corresponding negation concerning a particular future event must be true and the other false (III.1) and then add that neither of them is *already* true unless he means that neither of them is going to be true *from now on*?

It must be admitted, nevertheless, that the sense of the word ἤδη here is highly controversial. In any case, I have not been convinced by the attempts to understand it in some other way— for example, by Miss G. E. M. Anscombe's arguments to the effect that it has here a non-temporal sense, that 'not already' here means something like 'not thereby shown to be'.[28] The meaning of ἤδη is explained by Aristotle in temporal terms in *Phys.* IV 13. 222ᵇ7 ff. In a discussion of closely related matters in *Met.* Γ 3 it has a temporal meaning, as it indeed often has in comparable contexts; compare, for example, *De Int.* 13. 23ᵃ14. It would have been uncharacteristically careless of Aristotle to use it in a non-temporal sense in the midst of a discussion charged with temporal notions. Most importantly, I find Miss Anscombe's reading very difficult to reconcile with (III.1).

Thus I find it impossible to make up my mind here, finding some solace in the suspicion that Aristotle perhaps did not make up his mind, either. If so, it may be asked whether he tried other ways out of a dilemma which looks less an interpreter's problem than a difficulty intrinsic to his attempted solution.

11. *An alternative solution to the sea-fight problem*

The problem discussed in the preceding section—and indeed the whole ninth chapter of the *De Interpretatione*—is put to a new perspective by *Met. E* 3 where the problem of determinism is again discussed by Aristotle. At first sight, this other discussion might seem to support the 'momentary correspondence' view mentioned in the preceding section. In *Met. E* 3 Aristotle is

[28] 'Aristotle and the Sea-Battle', *Mind*, 65 (1956), 1–15.

concerned with following causal chains back and forth in time, and claims that their earliest starting-point must, on pain of determinism, be 'able to come to be . . . [without being in the process of] coming to be and being destroyed . . .' (tr. Kirwan). What Aristotle is worried about here is clearly whether there obtain at earlier moments of time objective conditions or states of affairs (for instance, someone's being thirsty) that will predeterminate later events (in Aristotle's example, a man's going out to drink and being ambushed as a consequence). In the framework of *De Int.* 9, this seems to prejudge the issue strongly in favour of the interpretation that takes Aristotle to be generalizing with respect to time only.

A much more radical conclusion than this is closer at hand, however. The kind of solution Aristotle briefly sketches in *Met. E* 3 relies on a conceptual framework altogether different from that of *De Int.* 9. The origins and causes that come to be without being in the process of coming to be are clearly *energeiai* in contrast to *kineseis* in the sense of the distinction which Aristotle explains on a number of occasions, especially in *Met.* Θ. Thus in *Met. E* 3 Aristotle utilizes this interesting and, in several respects, highly sophisticated distinction in order to disentangle himself from determinism. This type of solution, which will not be discussed here, is far beyond the natural but in the last analysis rather simple-minded manœuvre we caught Aristotle executing in *De Int.* 9, viz. the manœuvre of (in effect) denying the genuineness of the problem of future contingents by insisting that an attribution of a modal status to a future event is but to compare it with other similar events. It is not surprising it such a pseudo-solution did not fully satisfy Aristotle. It would not be surprising, either, if the direction of the generalization that is presupposed in the comparison should have been the source of irritation that prompted Aristotle to import sharper tools into the discussion of future contingents. However, there is scarcely enough textual material to assert this conjecture concerning the relation of *De Int.* 9 and *Met. E* 3, and in any case an adequate examination of the latter discussion is beyond the scope of this chapter. It is important to be aware of the other conceptual tools, however, which are illustrated by *Met. E* 3, and which Aristotle could have also applied (but did not) in *De Int.* 9.

SOME MODERN PUBLICATIONS CONCERNED WITH FUTURE CONTINGENTS

ABELARD, PETER, *Dialectica*, edited by L. M. de Rijk (Assen, Van Gorcum, 1956).

ACKRILL, J. L., *Aristotle's 'Categories' and 'De Interpretatione'* (trans. in Clarendon Aristotle Series, Clarendon Press, Oxford, 1963).

ALBRITTON, ROGERS, 'Present Truth and Future Contingency', *Philosophical Review*, 66 (1957), 29–46.

AMAND, DAVID, *Fatalisme et Liberté dans l'antiquité grecque* (Bibliothèque de l'Université, Louvain, 1945).

ANSCOMBE, G. E. M., 'Aristotle and the Sea-battle', *Mind*, 65 (1956), 1–15.

AYER, A. J., 'Fatalism', in *The Concept of a Person and other Essays* (Macmillan, London, 1963).

BAUDRY, L., *La Querelle des futurs contingents, Louvain 1465–1475: Textes inédits* (J. Vrin, Paris, 1950).

BAYLIS, CHARLES A., 'Are Some Propositions neither True nor False?', *Philosophy of Science*, 3 (1936), 156–66.

BECKER, A., 'Bestreitet Aristoteles die Gültigkeit des "Tertium non datur" für Zukunftaussagen?', *Actes du Congrès international de Philosophie scientifique*, 6. (Paris, 1936) 69–74.

—— *Die aristotelische Theorie der Möglichkeitsschlüsse* (Junker and Dünnhaupt, Berlin, 1933).

BOCHEŃSKI, I. M., *A History of Formal Logic* (trans., Indiana University Press, Notre Dame, 1961).

BOEHNER, PHILOTHEUS, *The 'Tractatus de praedestinatione et de praescientia Dei et de futuris contingentibus' of William Ockham. With a Study on the Mediaeval Problem of a Three-valued Logic* (Franciscan Institute Publications, vol. 2, The Franciscan Institute, St. Bonaventure College, St. Bonaventure, New York, 1945).

BRADLEY, R. D., 'Must the Future Be What It is Going to Be?', *Mind*, 68 (1959), 193–208.

BROGAN, A. P., 'Aristotle's Logic of Statements about Contingency', *Mind*, 76 (1967), 49–61.

BURRELL, D., 'Aristotle and "Future Contingencies"', *Philosophical Studies*, 13 (1964), 37–52.

BUTLER, RONALD J., 'Aristotle's Sea Fight and Three-valued Logic', *Philosophical Review*, 64 (1955), 264–74.

—— A review of papers by Saunders, Bradley, and Wolff, *Journal of Symbolic Logic*, 25 (1960), 343–5.

CAHN, STEVEN M., *Fate, Logic and Time* (Yale University Press, New Haven and London, 1967), Ch. III.

FREDE, DOROTHEA, *Aristoteles und die 'Seeschlacht'* (Hypomnemata, vol. 27, Vandenhoeck and Ruprecht, Göttingen, 1970).

GRANT, C. K., 'Certainty, Necessity, and Aristotle's Sea Battle', *Mind*, 66 (1957), 522–31.

HINTIKKA, JAAKKO, 'Necessity, Universality, and Time in Aristotle', *Ajatus*, 20 (1957), 65–90.

JOJA, ATH., 'Despre tertium non datur', *Studii de logica*, 1 (Editura Academiei Republicii Populare Romîne, Bucharest, 1960).

—— 'About tertium non datur', *Analele Universitaţii 'C. J. Parhon'*, Bucharest, seria Acta Logica, 1 (1958), 111–48.

JORDAN, Z., 'Logical Determinism', *Notre Dame Journal of Formal Logic*, 5 (1964), 1–38.

KING-FARLOW, JOHN, 'Sea-fights without Tears', *Analysis*, 19 (1958–9), 36–42.

KNEALE, WILLIAM, and KNEALE, MARTHA, *The Development of Logic* (Clarendon Press, Oxford, 1962).

LEMMON, E. J., a review of G. E. M. Anscombe, 'Aristotle and the Sea-battle', *Journal of Symbolic Logic*, 21 (1956), 388–9.

LINSKY, L., 'Professor Donald Williams on Aristotle', *Philosophical Review*, 63 (1954), 250–2.

ŁUKASIEWICZ, JAN, *Aristotle's Syllogistic from the Standpoint of Modern Formal Logic*, Clarendon Press, Oxford, (2nd ed. 1957).

—— 'Philosophische Bemerkungen zu mehrwertigen Systemen des Aussagenkalküls', *Comptes Rendus des Séances de la Société des Sciences et des Lettres de Varsovie*, Classe III, 23 (1930), 51–77.

McKIM, V. R., 'Fatalism and Future: Aristotle's Way Out', *The Review of Metaphysics*, 25 (1972), 80–111.

MONTAGUE, R., 'Mr. Bradley on the Future', *Mind*, 69 (1960), 550–4.

OESTERLE, JEAN T., *Aristotle: On Interpretation. Commentary by St. Thomas and Cajetan* (Mediaeval Philosophical Texts in Translation, vol. 11, Marquette University Press, Milwaukee, 1962).

PATZIG, GÜNTHER, *Die aristotelische Syllogistik* (Abhandlungen der Akademie der Wissenschaften in Göttingen, Philologisch-historische Klasse, Dritte Folge, Nr. 42, Vandenhoeck und Ruprecht, Göttingen, 1959). English trans. by Jonathan Barnes under the title *Aristotle's Theory of the Syllogism* (D. Reidel Publishing Company, Dordrecht, 1968).

PEARS, DAVID, 'Time, Truth, and Inference', *Proceedings of the Aristotelian Society*, 51 (1950–1). Reprinted in Anthony Flew (editor), *Essays in Conceptual Analysis* (Macmillan, London, 1956).

PRIOR, A. N., 'Three-valued Logic and Future Contingents', *Philosophical Quarterly*, 3 (1953), 317–26.

—— *Time and Modality* (Clarendon Press, Oxford, 1957).

—— *Past, Present, and Future* (Clarendon Press, Oxford, 1967).

—— *Papers on Time and Tense* (Clarendon Press, Oxford, 1968).

RESCHER, NICHOLAS, 'An Interpretation of Aristotle's Doctrine of

Future Contingency and Excluded Middle', in *Studies in the History of Arabic Logic* (University of Pittsburgh Press, Pittsburgh, 1963).

RYLE, GILBERT, *Dilemmas* (Cambridge University Press, Cambridge, 1954), Ch. 2.

SAUNDERS, JOHN TURK, 'A Sea Fight Tomorrow?', *Philosophical Review*, 67 (1958), 367–78.

SCHUHL, PIERRE-MAXIME, *Le Dominateur et les possibles* (Presses Universitaires de France, Paris, 1960) especially Appendices I and IV.

STRANG, COLIN, 'Aristotle and the Sea Battle', *Mind*, 69 (1960), 447–65.

TAYLOR, RICHARD, 'The Problem of Future Contingencies', *Philosophical Review*, 66 (1957), 1–28.

—— 'Fatalism', *Philosophical Review*, 71 (1962), 56–66.

—— 'A Note on Fatalism', *Philosophical Review*, 72 (1963), 497–9.

WILLIAMS, DONALD C., 'The Sea Fight Tomorrow' in *Structure, Method and Meaning*, edited by P. Henle *et al.* (Liberal Arts Press, New York, 1951, pp. 282–306).

—— 'Professor Linsky on Aristotle', *Philosophical Review*, 63 (1954), 253–5.

WOLFF, P., 'Truth, Futurity, and Contingency', *Mind*, 69 (1960), 398–402.

IX

ARISTOTLE AND THE 'MASTER ARGUMENT' OF DIODORUS

1. The problem

THE κυριεύων or 'Master Argument' of Diodorus Cronus was famous in antiquity; 'the great fame of Diodorus as a logician rested primarily upon it.'[1] For us, however, it presents a tantalizing problem. We know almost everything about it. We know what type of argument Diodorus used (it was a reductive proof); we know what the premisses of this proof were (see section 2 below); we know what purpose the argument was to serve; and we have some amount of information concerning the views Diodorus held on closely related subjects.[2] Almost the only thing we do not know is the argument itself. It has not been preserved to us, and no entirely convincing reconstruction has been offered. (Attempts at such a reconstruction have not been missing, but none of them seems quite satisfactory.)[3] This absence of reliable

[1] Benson Mates, *Stoic Logic* (University of California Publications in Philosophy, vol. 26 (Berkeley and Los Angeles, 1953); reprinted (University of California Press, Berkeley and Los Angeles, 1961), p. 38.

[2] General historical discussions of the argument and related matters are found in Mates, op. cit. especially pp. 38–40; in William Kneale and Martha Kneale, *The Development of Logic* (Clarendon Press, Oxford, 1962), pp. 117–28; Oskar Becker, 'Über den "Kyrieuon Logos" des Diodoros Kronos', *Rheinisches Museum für Philologie*, 99 (1956), 289–304, and in Pierre-Maxime Schuhl, *Le Dominateur et les possibles* (Presses Universitaires de France, Paris, 1960). Cf. also I. M. Bocheński, *A History of Formal Logic* (Notre Dame, Indiana, 1961). Further bibliographical information is supplied by these authors, especially by Bocheński.

[3] Eduard Zeller's interpretation, sketched in 'Über den κυριεύων des Megarikers Diodorus', *Sitzungsberichte der Königlichen Akademie der Wissenschaften zu Berlin* (Berlin, 1882) (reprinted in *Kleine Schriften*, vol. i, ed. by O. Lenze (Berlin, 1910), pp. 252–62), will be discussed in the sequel. A. N. Prior's interpretation is developed in 'Diodoran Modalities', *Philosophical Quarterly*, 5 (1955), 205–13 (cf. also 'Diodorus and Modal Logic', ibid. 8 (1958), 226–30). It would take me too far to explain why this ingenious and in many ways attractive reconstruction fails to convince me, in spite of Oskar Becker's interesting and learned defence of it in his article 'Zur Rekonstruktion des "Kyrieuon Logos" des Diodoros Kronos', *Erkenntnis und*

information concerning the argument is especially tantalizing in view of the fact that the argument was considered a very powerful one in antiquity.[4] Some of the most severe critics of Diodorus within the Stoic tradition (including Chrysippus and Cleanthes) in effect rejected one or the other of his premisses rather than challenged the argument itself.[5] Nevertheless, we do not seem to be able to perceive any particularly plausible chain of reasoning that would serve the purpose the Master Argument was apparently calculated to serve.

2. *The facts of the case*

The only extensive account we have of the Master Argument is given by Epictetus (*Dissertationes*, ed. Schenkl, II 19. 1):

The Master Argument seems to have been formulated with some such starting points as these. There is an incompatibility between the following three propositions:

(1) Everything that is past and true is necessary;
(2) The impossible does not follow from the possible;
(3) What neither is nor will be is possible.

Seeing this incompatibility, Diodorus used the plausibility of the first

---

Verantwortung: Festschrift für Theodor Litt, edited by Josef Derbolav and Friedhelm Nicolin (Verlag Schwann, Düsseldorf, 1960), pp. 250–63. Suffice it to say that Prior's interpretation is entirely based on the assumption that Diodorus would have taken a statement concerning the truth of past predictions as being a statement concerning the past in the sense of Diodorus' first premiss (1) (see below). I find this assumption rather strange, and I fail to perceive anything in the texts that unambiguously supports it. Other difficulties are pointed out by Prior himself in a later article 'Tense-logic and the Continuity of Time', *Studia Logica*, 13 (1962), 133–51. For other recent attempts at reconstructing the Master Argument, see especially Nicholas Rescher, 'A Version of the "Master Argument" of Diodorus', *Journal of Philosophy*, 63 (1966), 438–45; Herbert Guerry, 'Rescher's Master Argument', *Journal of Philosophy*, 64 (1967), 310–12; Nicholas Rescher, 'Truth and Necessity in Temporal Perspective', in Richard M. Gale, ed., *The Philosophy of Time: a Collection of Essays* (Doubleday, Garden City, N.J., 1967), pp. 183–220; Robert Blanché, 'Sur l'interprétation du κυριεύων λόγος', *Revue philosophique de la France et de l'étranger*, 155 (1965), 133–49.

[4] 'Our sources indicate that this argument . . . was very famous in antiquity, and that the logicians of that time did not challenge its validity', Mates in *The Journal of Symbolic Logic*, 21 (1956), 200.

[5] Mates, *Stoic Logic*, p. 38; cf. Max Pohlenz, *Die Stoa* (Vandenhoeck und Ruprecht, Göttingen, 1948), vol. 1, p. 102, and Max Pohlenz, *Stoa und Stoiker* (Artemis Verlag, Zürich, 1950), p. 92.

two propositions to establish the thesis that nothing is possible which neither is nor will be true.[6]

According to Alexander, the Master Argument was designed to establish Diodorus' definition of possibility as 'that which either is or will be'.[7] As pointed out by Mates, however, the full form of this famous definition seems to have been:

(4) The possible is that which is or will be true.

This is virtually all the direct information we have concerning the Master Argument. On the basis of this information alone, it seems rather difficult to say very much concerning the argument.

3. *Aristotle and the Master Argument*

There are important indirect sources of information, however, concerning the argument. Diodorus was a younger contemporary of Aristotle's.[8] Although we do not know very much of Diodorus, we of course know a great deal of Aristotle. Can this knowledge be used to extract information concerning the Master Argument? In this chapter I shall argue that it can. I shall argue that we can have a fairly clear idea of how Aristotle would have gone about it if he had wanted to carry out the kind of argument the Master Argument is known to have been. If it can be assumed, moreover, that the modes of reasoning that Diodorus used are likely to have been similar to those of Aristotle, we can fairly confidently say that we know at least a rough outline of how Diodorus argued. It is the initial working hypothesis of my discussion that we can do this. In general, it seems to me, scholars have tended to over-emphasize the differences between the modes of reasoning used by the different schools of thought in the ancient world at the expense of the important similarities that obtain between them. The professed doctrines of the several schools differed greatly, but some of the tacit presuppositions of the logical and philosophical enterprise were shared by most or all of them; and these are in many cases as important as the explicit doctrines.

---

[6] Trans. by M. Kneale, slightly modified; the numbering of the displayed sentences is of course mine, designed to facilitate reference to them.

[7] Op. cit., p. 37.

[8] If Diogenes Laertius is to be trusted concerning the year of Diodorus' death, he died about fifteen years after Aristotle (i.e. in 307 B.C.).

Be this as it may in general, in the special case of the Master Argument there is plenty of evidence to back up my working hypothesis. The unanimity of the later logicians of Antiquity is already indicative of widespread assumptions. Some of the results we obtain by starting from our hypothesis will turn out to fit other facts that are known concerning Diodorus or the Megarian school in general. And, what is more important, as far as the topics connected with the Master Argument are concerned, there was in any case a great deal of agreement between Diodorus and Aristotle.

4. *The materials of the argument are all in Aristotle*

In fact, both the premisses (1) and (2) of the Master Argument and its professed conclusion (4) were among the doctrines explicitly held by Aristotle. That Aristotle assumed (4) in some form or other has been shown in an earlier paper of mine.[9] I shall not recount the evidence here,[10] I shall merely point out that there are passages in which Aristotle seems to consider (4) not only as a truth about the concept of possibility but also as an explanation of the meaning of 'possible'. A case in point is found in *Met. Θ* 3. 1047ᵃ10–14:

Again, if what is deprived of potency is incapable, that which is not happening will be incapable of happening [viz. according to the doctrines Aristotle is criticizing]; but he who says of that which is incapable of happening that it is or will be will say what is untrue; for this is what incapacity meant.[11]

Another is found a little later:

Now if, as we have said, that is possible which does not involve any impossibility, evidently it cannot be true to say 'this is capable of being but will not be' which would imply that the things *in*capable of being

---

[9] 'Necessity, Universality, and Time in Aristotle', *Ajatus*, 20 (1957), 65–90. The same point is argued in Chapter V above. Meanwhile, it has also been made by Josef Stallmach in *Dynamis und Energeia* (Monographien zur philosophischen Forschung, vol. xxi, Verlag Anton Hain, Meisenheim am Glan, 1959), pp. 60–1, and by Schuhl, op. cit., p. 33. The similarity between Aristotle and Diodorus is brought out very aptly by S. Sambursky in *Physics of the Stoics* (Routledge and Kegan Paul, London, 1959), pp. 73–4.

[10] Much of it is given above in Chapter V which may be considered a revised version of 'Necessity, Universality, and Time in Aristotle'.

[11] For the evidential value of this passage, see Chapter V, sections 11–13 above.

would on this showing vanish. (*Met. Θ* 4. 1047ᵇ3–6, accepting Zeller's emendation.)

Hence (4) seems to have been almost as close to Aristotle's heart as to Diodorus'. Assumption (1) occurs in *Rhet.* III 17. 1418ª3–5: 'Forensic oratory deals with what is or is not *now* true, which can better be demonstrated, because not contingent—there is no contingency in what has now already happened.' This somewhat confusing passage suggests several interesting inferences. It suggests that the necessity that according to Aristotle attaches to the past is the same kind of necessity with which a scientific demonstration (*apodeixis*) deals. It also seems to suggest that for Aristotle everything that is *present* is necessary in the same way as is everything *past*. This in turn suggests that a highly important passage in the *De Interpretatione* makes the same point: 'What is necessarily is, when it is; and what is not necessarily is not, when it is not' (19ª23–5).[12] In any case, assumption (1) is also affirmed in *Eth. Nic.* VI 2. 1139ᵇ7–9 and in *De Caelo* I 12. 283ᵇ13 ff. The latter contains the following statement: 'There is no potency of having been, but only of being or going to be.'

It is interesting to observe that similar views are occasionally aired in Plato's dialogues; see, e.g., *Protagoras* 324 b. Apparently the doctrine was fairly common among the contemporaries of Aristotle.

The most important and the most difficult to understand of the premisses of the Master Argument is assumption (2). In Aristotle it is very closely connected with his notion of possibility. It occurs, in effect, in a passage which is referred to by him frequently as his definition of possibility: 'I use the terms "possibly" and "the possible" of that which is not necessary but which, being assumed, results in nothing impossible' (*An. Pr.* I 13. 32ª18–20).

Similar statements occur frequently in the Aristotelian corpus; see, e.g., *An. Pr.* I 9. 30ᵇ4–5; *Phys.* VIII 5. 256ᵇ10–12; *Met. Θ* 3. 1047ª24 ff.; *Met. Θ* 4. 1047ᵇ3 ff. (read in the way we read it above). In the terminology of Chapter II above we are of course dealing with the definition of contingency rather than of

---

[12] Notice also that in *De Int.* 9 present and past are grouped together and contrasted to the future. It is in the future alone that Aristotle tries to find room for contingency and chance. (See *De Int.* 9. 18ª28–37.) My interpretation of *Rhet.* 1418ª3–5 is based on the contrast between τὰ γεγονότα, τὰ ὄντα, and τὰ μέλλοντα; cf. e.g. Plato, *Rep.* 392 d.

possibility proper. However, the difference between these two varieties of the Aristotelian idea of possibility is here immaterial.

5. *Aristotle's definition of possibility*

The observation that theses (1), (2), and (4) of Diodorus are all to be found in Aristotle is by no means new.[13] It has not been pointed out, however, that there is more in Aristotle than this. It seems to me that the way Aristotle uses his assumptions throws a great deal of light on their meaning.

This is especially true of (2), which is the assumption hardest to understand. What did Diodorus mean by saying that 'the impossible does not follow from the possible'? We may reasonably assume that what he meant was not essentially different from what Aristotle meant by his similar statements. Now what did Aristotle mean? Some commentators have been greatly puzzled by the fact that Aristotle refers to the statement we quoted from *An. Pr.* I 13. 32ᵃ18–21 as a *definition* of possibility.[14] The puzzle is deepened by the fact that this passage is for him a genuine definition, a ὁρισμός—cf. 33ᵃ25—and not merely an explanatory formula or a λόγος. Since the notion of possibility in it is characterized by reference to what is impossible, it seems to be circular; and for this reason it has been dismissed as being unsatisfactory.

Whether we want to call Aristotle's statement a definition of possibility or not, it is a very clear observation of what is the basic logical characteristic of the notion of possibility. One of the most important principles of modal logic is the following: If a sentence of the form

(5) it is possible that *p* but it is impossible that *q*

is consistent, then the following sentence:

(6) *p* but not *q*

is also consistent.

Assuming the usual interrelations between the notions of possibility and necessity, this principle is tantamount to the case $k = 1$ of the condition (C.M&N⁺) mentioned in my article, 'The Modes of Modality', *Acta Philosophica Fennica*, vol. 16 (Helsinki,

---

[13] Cf. e.g., Schuhl, op. cit., pp. 33–4.
[14] See, e.g., Jan Łukasiewicz, *Aristotle's Syllogistic from the Standpoint of Modern Formal Logic* (Clarendon Press, Oxford, second edition, 1957), p. 141.

1963), pp. 65–81.[15] The whole force of the condition is obtained from this special case if the distributivity of necessity with respect to conjunction is assumed in a suitable form. In fact, it suffices to assume one half of the usual distributivity laws, viz., the one corresponding to $(Np \ \& \ Nq) \supset N(p \ \& \ q)$. (Here '$N$' is a short-hand for 'necessarily'. We shall likewise use 'M' for 'possibly'.) As briefly indicated in 'The Modes of Modality', the condition (C.M&N⁺) gives almost everything we want in modal logic. If the case $k = 0$ is admitted, the only obvious principle of modal logic that is not a consequence of (C.M&N⁺) is the trivial one that necessity implies actuality. Hence, the principle Aristotle is trying to formulate is in fact a central and powerful one in modal logic.

In an axiomatic and deductive approach Aristotle's principle amounts to a rule which from the provability of $p \supset q$ gives us the provability of $Mp \supset Mq$. This is a strong and important rule of proof. In von Wright's formulation of his basic system M (see *An Essay in Modal Logic* (North-Holland Publishing Co., Amsterdam, 1951), Appendix) this rule would replace the extensionality rule (inference from the provability of $p \leftrightarrow q$ to the provability of $Mp \leftrightarrow Mq$). Moreover, it would replace one half of the distributivity axiom, and it would replace the rule leading from the provability of p to that of Np if we add as an extra axiom $N(p \ \vee \sim p)$. Hence it could serve as the central principle of the basic system of modal logic.

It is in fact easy to see that this principle is related very closely indeed to Aristotle's 'definition'. Proposition (6) is consistent if and only if q is not logically implied by p; hence what our principle says is just that the proposition p, which was asserted to be possible, must not logically imply the proposition q which was asserted to be impossible (not possible). Hence the principle can be used in a way anticipated in Aristotle's definition. In order to examine whether a premiss of the form 'it is possible that p' is compatible with a number of other premisses, we may assume p. If we can deduce from p a consequence (say r) such that 'it is impossible that r' follows from the other premisses, then our set of premisses is inconsistent. If this never happens then 'it is possible that p' cannot cause an inconsistency in our set of premisses. The possible thus is, in a sense, exactly 'that which, being assumed,

---

[15] Reprinted in Jaakko Hintikka, *Models for Modalities* (D. Reidel Publishing Co., Dordrecht, 1969), pp. 71–86.

results in nothing impossible'; and Aristotle's 'definition' therefore touches the very core of the logic of possibility.

Notice that the procedure just described is of some logical
subtlety. It is not enough, having assumed p, to deduce from it
some consequence r which contradicts other consequences of our
premisses. It is not enough, we may say, to deduce from p something false. We must deduce from it some consequence r which is
impossible in the stronger sense that 'it is impossible that r' can
also be deduced. If we do not require this, we are in effect
replacing the valid (and important) rule of inference

$$\frac{p \supset q}{Mp \supset Mq}$$

by the unacceptable rule

$$\frac{p \supset q}{Mp \supset q}.$$

It may very well be the case that some of this subtlety escaped
Aristotle. There are indications that he did not always fully
understand the sense in which the consequences of p are or are not
impossible in the procedure we have described.[16] Apart from this
minor blemish, Aristotle follows the procedure very closely. (The
fact that we can say this is, to my mind, a remarkable tribute to
his logical acumen.) And it can be shown that his formulations of
(2) are intended to characterize this procedure.

There is plenty of evidence to prove this. A clear statement of
Aristotle's procedure is found in *An. Pr.* I 15. 34ᵃ25–33, followed
by interesting applications in 34ᵃ34–ᵇ2. They bear out our
interpretation. Similarly our view is strongly supported by the
parallelism Aristotle draws between proofs of impossibility in
mathematics and his procedure in logic. The following quotation
follows immediately the passage which we quoted earlier from
Met. Θ 4. 1047ᵇ3–6:

Suppose, for instance, that a man—one who did not take account of

---

[16] Sometimes Aristotle terminates the chain of inferences from p (assumed to be
true because he wants to test whether 'possibly p' can be true) when he reaches a
conclusion that merely contradicts something that is *in fact* true, rather than necessarily true. Cases in point are discussed later in this chapter in section 7 (*An. Pr.* I 15.
34ᵃ34–ᵇ6) and in section 17. Cf. also *An. Pr.* I 23. 41ᵃ30 where we would expect
'impossible' instead of 'false' (ψεῦδος). The assumptions mentioned in section 7
seem to have been apt to confuse him on this point.

that which is incapable of being—were to say that the diagonal of the square is capable of being measured but will not be measured, because a thing may well be capable of being or coming to be, and yet not be or be about to be. But from the premisses this necessarily follows, that if we actually supposed that which is not, but is capable of being, to be or to have come to be, there will be nothing impossible in this; but the result will be impossible, for the measuring of the diagonal is impossible.

Aristotle is here contemplating a proof of the incommensurability of the diagonal of a square with its side. This proof is obviously supposed to start from the assumption that there is a common measure of both and to go on to deduce a contradiction from this assumption.[17] For Aristotle, this is just the kind of proof that shows that the existence of common measure is not only false but also impossible.

Statements tantamount to (2) were already seen not to be uncommon in Aristotle. One may go so far as to say that they represent one of his most important assumptions concerning modal notions. Now we have seen what Aristotle means by these statements. What is involved is essentially the important principle that if p logically implies q, the possibility of p implies that of q. No wonder this consequence of his own basic assumption (it is in fact equivalent with it) was picked out for special emphasis by Aristotle in *An. Pr.* I 15. 34^{a}5–7 and *Met.* Θ 4. 1047^{b}14–16.

Steven M. Cahn has objected to my interpretation of Diodorus' premiss (2) in his book *Fate, Logic, and Time* (Yale University Press, New Haven, 1967), pp. 51–4. He says that 'it is not clear why anyone should be committed to [this] interpretation of premiss (2)'. In replying to this, it is useful to separate the question of historical evidence for attributing my interpretation of (2) to Aristotle or to Diodorus from the question as to what precisely the premiss amounts to on this interpretation. As far as the latter point is concerned, we have seen that what is involved is one of the most familiar and most fundamental principles of modal logic—a principle so fundamental that it is hard to see what sense modal notions can make if it is given up. In this respect, Cahn

---

[17] This is the kind of proof Aristotle also mentions in *An. Pr.* I 23. 41^{a}23 ff.: 'e.g. one proves that the diagonal of a square is incommensurable with the sides by showing that if it is assumed to be commensurable, odd become equal to even numbers.' Cf. *Rhet.* II 19. 1392^{a}16–17.

simply fails completely to understand what my interpretation of (2) means, which already renders his criticism worthless.

As far as historical evidence is concerned, it is clear that formulations reminiscent of (2) were interpreted by Aristotle exactly in the way I have done. Although no direct evidence exists that this is how Diodorus understood his premiss, the temporal proximity of Aristotle and Diodorus strongly suggests that this is the right interpretation in the case of the latter, too. In any case, there is no alternative interpretation that could make claims to comparable collateral evidence from antiquity. Hence Cahn's doubts concerning the construction I am putting on (2) cannot be based on historical evidence.

All told, we can thus see what must have been the first step of the reductive proof that we know the Master Argument was. It was the assumption that the possibility which by assumption (3) is never realized, nevertheless is in fact realized. Somehow or other, Diodorus deduced (or thought that he had deduced) an impossibility from this assumption.

6. *The terminology of Diodorus and the terminology of Aristotle*

But can we be sure that we can transfer results concerning Aristotle's procedure so as to apply to Diodorus? Doubts may arise on terminological grounds. The verb used by Diodorus (or at least by Epictetus in his report) to express assumption (2) is ἀκολουθεῖν. Zeller emphasized that the interpretation of this verb is far from obvious.[18] In fact, he tried to give it a sense entirely different from logical consequence.

Further doubts may result from Chapter III above. I argued there[19] that in certain writings of Aristotle's—primarily in *De Int.* 12–13—the verb ἀκολουθεῖν does not express logical consequence at all. It is ambiguous (or elliptical), but none of its senses in *De Int.* expresses logical consequence.

These doubts can easily be dispelled, however. The difference between Aristotle and Diodorus (or Epictetus) in this respect is simply one of terminology. The word used most frequently by Aristotle in his formulations of the principle 'the impossible does

---

[18] Zeller, op. cit., and *Die Philosophie der Griechen*, 5th edn., ed. Wellmann (O. R. Reisland, Leipzig, 1923), vol. ii, part I, pp. 269–70.

[19] See above, pp. 43–7.

not follow from the possible' and in the consequences he draws from it is συμβαίνειν (or one of its variants); it occurs in *An. Pr.* I 15. 34ᵃ26; 34ᵇ2; 17. 37ᵃ29; and 23. 41ᵃ25, 30; in *Phys.* VIII 5. 256ᵇ11; in *De Caelo* I 12. 281ᵇ23–5; and in *Met.* Θ 4. 1047ᵇ11. (The same word is typically employed by Aristotle when he draws consequences from assumptions he wants to prove untenable; see references in Bonitz, p. 713*b*.) This word is, as I have pointed out,[20] Aristotle's standard word for logical consequence; it occurs in his definition of logical inference in *An. Pr.* I 1. 24ᵇ19.

If συμβαίνειν is the normal term in Aristotle for logical consequence, ἀκολουθεῖν serves exactly the same purpose in Stoic (and Megarian) logic.[21] It was used by Diodorus in discussing the nature of implication (logical consequence). As Mates points out,[22] this makes it highly unlikely that Diodorus should have been a prey to an ambiguity concerning its meaning (as Zeller suggested) or have used it in other senses. Hence the difference between Aristotle and Diodorus in their respective formulations of assumption (2) is exactly the general difference between their terminology. Each logician uses his typical term for logical consequence.[23] Furthermore, it may be observed that the verb ἀκολουθεῖν was occasionally used by Aristotle, too, to express logical consequence.[24] If Zeller's emendation in *Met.* Θ 4. 1047ᵇ3 is correct, the word is once used by Aristotle in formulating the very assumption (2).

Hence there seems to be no reason to doubt that Diodorus had in mind exactly the same principle as Aristotle.

7. *Possibilities realized in time*

Aristotle allows us to make a further guess concerning the nature of the first few steps of Diodorus' argument. In *Met.* Θ 5. 1047ᵇ 35–1048ᵃ1 he writes: '. . . that which is "capable" is capable of something and *at some time* and in some way . . .' (my italics). In other words, it was not only required that whatever is possible

---

[20] See Ch. III, section 2, above.   [21] Mates, op. cit., pp. 43, 132.

[22] Mates, op. cit., p. 39.

[23] My point is neatly confirmed by Alexander, who was familiar both with the Aristotelian and the Stoic terminology. In commenting on *An. Pr.* I 15. 34ᵃ6–8 he reformulates Aristotle's assumption (2) in terms of ἀκολουθεῖν instead of συμβαίνειν. (I owe this piece of information to Professor Becker's papers.)

[24] Several cases in point are found in *An. Pr.* I 46, and in *Top.* II 8.

can be assumed to be true without getting involved in any impossibilities; it is further required that the possibility in question can be assumed to be realized *at some particular moment of time*. The implications of this further requirement will soon be apparent. (See section 16 below.)

There is further evidence that this is what Aristotle assumed. Perhaps the strongest piece of evidence can be obtained from *An. Pr.* I 15. $34^b 2-6$. This passage has been commented on in an earlier paper of mine.[25] What Aristotle does there is to assume that it is possible for B to apply to all C and that at some moment of time it is therefore true to say 'B applies to all C'. If it then is also the case that, at all moments of time, it is true to say 'A applies to all B', then at the moment in question we can truly say 'A applies to all C', and hence at any moment say 'it is possible for A to apply to all C'. Hence from the two premisses

(7) it is possible for B to apply to all C

(8) A applies to all B

Aristotle can deduce

(9) it is possible for A to apply to all C,

since he accepts the following two assumptions: (i) Every possibility must be thought of as being realized at some moment of time; and (ii) the premiss (8) can be understood omnitemporally. He argues to buttress (ii) in $34^b 7-18$. The other crucial assumption, viz. (i), is obviously made by him tacitly.

We may also observe that even the first step of mathematical proofs of impossibility was apparently conceived of by Aristotle as an assumption that a certain possibility is actualized *at some moment of time*. This is suggested by the strongly temporal terminology of passages such as we quoted from *Met.* Θ 4. $1047^b 3-6$ (cf. 'the diagonal of the square is capable of being measured but *will not be measured* . . .').[26]

---

[25] 'Necessity, Universality, and Time in Aristotle', pp. 81–2.

[26] It is not difficult to find further evidence for the connection between the Aristotelian concept of possibility and the notion of time which we have just pointed out. See *An. Pr.* I 15. $34^a 8-9$ ('. . . the possible, *when it is possible for it to be*, may come to be . . .'); and *Met.* Θ 4. $1047^b 27-30$. ('For to say that B must be possible if A is possible, means this, that if A is real *at the time when* and in the way in which it was supposed capable of being real, B also must then and in that way be real.')

8. *The argument*

Having come this far, we are beginning to see how Diodorus must have proceeded. The details of this part of his argument may be impossible to reconstruct, but the main trend is obvious enough. Diodorus had the following two premisses:

(10) it is possible that p;

(11) it is not the case that p nor will it be the case at any later moment of time.

He also had two principles of argument which are more explicit forms of (1) and (2):

(1)* any true statement concerning the past is necessary;

(2)* if a possibility is assumed to be realized, no impossible conclusions follow.

Because of (2)*, Diodorus could replace assumption (10) by the assumption that the possibility in question is or will be realized. (Cf. section 5 above.) If the original premiss (10) leads to no impossibilities, the new one will not do so either.

More accurately, because of the assumptions discussed in section 7, Diodorus thought he could assume that the possibility in question is realized at some particular moment of (future) time. In other words, he thought he could ·move from (10) to

(10)* at time t_0 it will be true that p,

where t_0 is some particular moment of future time. (Some further justification for this step will be given in section 11 below.) If some consequence of (10)* is made impossible by (11) and (1)*, it will show that the original set of premisses is inconsistent.

The way in which Diodorus probably thought he could obtain such an impossibility is as follows: Consider any moment of time t_1 later than t_0, say the day after t_0. From (10)* it follows that

(12) at time t_1 it will be true that p was the case yesterday.

From (11) it follows that

(11)* at time t_0 it will be false that p

and hence that

(13) at time t_1 it will be false that p was the case yesterday.

Now by virtue of (1)* it follows from (13) that

> (13)* at time t_1 it will be true that it is impossible for p to have been the case yesterday.

This is now the impossibility Diodorus was looking for. The conclusion (12) which we obtained from the assumption that the possibility (10) is realized is shown by (13)* to be not only false but also impossible. Hence Diodorus was ready to conclude that the original set of premisses was inconsistent.

Some comments on this argument are in order. The reader may have wondered why (11)* does not contradict (10)* strongly enough to show that the assumption (10)* involves an impossibility. The answer is that (10)* is not yet shown by (11)* to be impossible in the sense explained in section 5. What we must do to show the inconsistency of the original premisses is to obtain a consequence of (10)* that can be proved to be not only false but impossible by means of the other premisses. And this is not yet accomplished by (10)* and (11)*, but only by (12) and (13)*.

The most important question concerning the reconstructed argument is, of course, whether it is logically valid or not. This question will be postponed to sections 15–16 below, where it turns out to rely on important additional assumptions.

Our reconstruction of the Master Argument suggests that it may have been based on more assumptions than Epictetus mentions. In three steps, viz. in steps from (10) to (10)*, from (10)* to (12), and from (11)* to (13), we move from a statement pertaining to some given moment of time to a statement pertaining to a later moment of time. For us, these transitions may be perfectly unproblematic. For the Greeks, however, they perhaps were not quite as obvious. As I have pointed out elsewhere,[27] the ancients very rarely dealt with sentences whose content was tied to some objective chronology. The sentences they typically considered contain explicitly or implicitly the self-referential word 'now'. Hence the relation of a present prediction concerning a future moment of time to the corresponding present-tense statement made at that future moment of time was perhaps not quite as obvious for them as it is for us. For them, the truth of one perhaps did not imply the truth of the other without some additional assumption. And if it did not, then the fact that (12)

---

[27] See Chapter IV above.

and (13)* contradict each other in the desired way may not follow at all. Hence it would not be surprising if we found in some of the ancient sources an additional premiss to the effect that a true prediction concerning a future moment of time implies the truth of the corresponding present-tense statement made at that moment of time—to the effect that, in Cicero's words, 'a true future event cannot be changed into a false one' (*De Fato* IX 20). There are indications that this expectation is justified (cf. section 14 below).

9. *Zeller vindicated*

Although the details of our reconstruction are conjectural, various further comments on the general trend of the argument can be made.

First of all, not very much novelty can be claimed for the general trend of this reconstruction. In so far as I can understand the old reconstruction suggested by Eduard Zeller, it amounts to the same in its rough outline at least.[28] Now Zeller's reconstruction has been criticized because he defended it by rather implausible arguments.[29] He thought that assumption (2) served to justify the step from (10)* (which says something about time t_0), to (12) (which says something about the later time t_1); more generally he seems to have understood (2) as providing the basis for the assumption that 'a true future event cannot be changed into a false one'. In order to read (2) in this way, he naturally had to take the verb ἀκολουθεῖν in a temporal sense (in the sense of following *later*). But this is, as we saw in section 6 above, highly unlikely. In fact, there are further items of evidence to show that this cannot have been Diodorus' meaning. For one thing, the other uses of the verb ἀκολουθεῖν that I have found in Aristotle's logical writings do not fit Zeller's suggestion any better.[30]

Furthermore, the switch from time t_0 to time t_1 may be unnecessary. I surmised in section 4 above that Aristotle accepted the principle that whatever is true of the past *or of the present* is true necessarily. If Diodorus accepted this principle, we could simplify the reconstruction of his argument by identifying the

---

[28] See notes 3 and 18 above.
[30] Chapter III above, sections 3, 4, and 6.
[29] Mates, op. cit., p. 39.

moments t_1 and t_0 of time. And if so, there will be no question of *temporal* following at all.

Although the criticism Zeller's reconstruction has thus met seems to me justified, it also seems to me that it stems from Zeller's failure to see to what assumption (2) really pertains. If we follow Aristotle's indications, we can see that it serves to justify not the step from (10)* to (12), but rather the step from (10) to (10)*. And if it is so understood, the key term ἀκολουθεῖν may be taken (and has to be taken) in the exact sense it would ordinarily have in Stoic and Megarian writings. Hence the main objection to Zeller's reconstruction is eliminated.

The version of our reconstruction of the Master Argument in which the moments of time t_0 and t_1 are identified merits some further interest. In this version we obtain (11) and (11)* as before. Instead of proceeding to (12) and (13), we can obtain the desired impossibility more easily. If whatever is false of the present moment is impossible, then it follows from (11)* that

(11)** at time t_0 it will be impossible that p.

This contradicts (10)* in the same way (13)* contradicts (12).

10. *The Master Argument and determinism*

It is not only the case that the objections to a reconstruction along the lines suggested by Zeller are eliminable. It seems to me that there is indirect further evidence for our reconstruction beyond what Zeller gives and beyond what we have given so far. To see what this evidence may be, let us first try to see what prima facie objections there are to our reconstruction. The main objection has undoubtedly occurred to you already. Does not the argument we suggested prove far too much? So far, we have taken p to be a temporally unspecified sentence; that is, one that implicitly or explicitly contains the word 'now', i.e. contains a reference to the moment at which it is uttered or thought of as being uttered. What happens if we consider the corresponding temporally specified sentence? We may represent such a temporally specified sentence at 'p at t'; if 'p' is 'Socrates is awake', 'p at t' might be 'Socrates is awake at daybreak two days after the victory of Agathon's first tragedy'. What if we consider 'p at t_0' instead of 'p' *simpliciter*? Suppose that 'p at t_0' is possible but false. If assumption (2) holds in the form we argued Aristotle and

Diodorus understood this assumption, then we must be able to assume that it is in fact true without running into any impossible conclusions. But making this assumption is (under the most natural way of understanding the sentence 'possibly p at t_0') tantamount to assuming (10)*. On the other hand, the assumption that the sentence 'p at t_0' is false is tantamount to assuming (11)*. Now in the same way as (10)* and (11)* gave rise to an impossibility, in the same way we therefore have an impossibility here.

The conclusion is, therefore, that sentences

(14) it is possible that (p at t_0)

and

(15) not (p at t_0)

are incompatible. What does not happen cannot happen; and by the same token, whatever does happen happens necessarily. There is no difference between possibility and actuality.

This argument may very well be unhistorical, for as I already mentioned (see Chapter IV above), the ancient philosophers very rarely dealt with temporally specified sentences of the form 'p at t_0'. Nevertheless, a closely related argument can be put up in terms of temporally unspecified sentences. There is, in fact, an ambiguity in the premiss (10) of our reconstruction of the Master Argument. If someone now asserts 'it is possible that p', does he mean that it is possible that p should be the case *now* or that it should be the case *now or sometime in the future*? In our reconstruction, we assumed that the latter is what is meant. What happens if the former is what is meant? The answer is simple: Our reconstruction of the Master Argument can then be modified so as to show the logical incompatibility of

(16) it is possible that p

and

(17) p is not (now) the case.

For by the same token we argued that Diodorus thought he could assume (10)*, he could now assume

(10)** p is (now) the case

and go on to obtain an absurdity from (10)** and (17) in the same way as we obtained an absurdity from (10)* and (11). In fact, the argument will be exactly the one that is obtained by assuming in our reconstruction that t_0 is the moment of time at which (10) and (11) or (17) have been asserted. The conclusion is now stronger than the conclusion of the Master Argument: it will be false to assert that something is possible unless it is the case at the moment of time the assertion is made. In this sense, possibility and actuality again coalesce.

It may be suggested that these observations show that our reconstruction of the Master Argument is incorrect; for by the modes of reasoning that were employed in it a result can be obtained which is (it may be alleged) obviously unacceptable.

This suggestion would be entirely false. I am not claiming that the argument outlined above is logically valid. It will be seen later that it rests on important further premisses which are unacceptable. I do claim historical plausibility for my reconstruction, however. And in this respect there is nothing to worry about in the deterministic conclusion it yields. On the contrary, it shows that our reconstruction squares very nicely with certain other things we know of the views of the Megarians in general and of Diodorus in particular.

First of all, the conclusion we have just drawn using the modes of argument employed in our reconstruction may appear unacceptable to some people, but it may not have been equally unacceptable to the Megarians. The doctrine in question is a form of determinism; and some of the Megarians, including Diodorus, certainly held deterministic views. (See, e.g., Cicero *De Fato* VII 13 and IX 17.) In fact, the conclusion we have just reached is exactly the doctrine Aristotle imputes to the Megarians in *Metaphysics* Θ 3, which he takes some pains to refute. Hence, far from discrediting our reconstruction, the incompatibility of (14) and (15) rather suggests that we are on the right track.

11. *Aristotle's concept of possibility*

Our conclusion is not exactly what we would like to find. It may have been the case that some of the earlier Megarians held that possibility and actuality coincide, as Aristotle reports. Nevertheless we know for certain that Diodorus did not. Hence we cannot be satisfied with the present state of our reconstruction after all.

We can make further observations, however, which serve to

set matters right. In order to see what they are, we may have a look at Aristotle again. There is a striking peculiarity about his criticism of the Megarians to which scholars have not paid much attention. It is the fact that he does not criticize at all the *arguments* of the Megarians. Aristotle does not say much more than that the *conclusions* of those arguments (whatever they were) are absurd.

Now an inference from silence does not usually carry much weight. In the case of Aristotle, however, it carries much more weight than in the case of almost any other writer, for it was almost a speciality of Aristotle's to criticize the logic of his opponents' arguments. Hence we may reasonably surmise that Aristotle did not find any major flaw in the reasoning of his adversaries.

How, then, could Aristotle nevertheless deny the conclusion of these arguments? He does not make the situation quite clear. Yet his remarks give us a clue to his meaning. His clinching argument against the Megarians runs as follows:

Therefore these views do away with both movement and becoming. For that which stands will always stand, and that which sits will always sit, since if it is sitting it will not get up; for that which, as we are told, cannot get up will be incapable of getting up. But we cannot say this, so that evidently potency and actuality are different (but these views make potency and actuality the same, and so it is no small thing they are seeking to annihilate), so that it is possible that a thing may be capable of being and not *be*, capable of not being and yet *be*, and similarly with the other kinds of predicate. (*Met.* Θ 3. 1047ª14–22)

This argument may seem quite wrong-headed. The doctrine of the Megarians amounted to a form of determinism. Now determinism certainly does not imply that nothing in the world 'moves or changes'. The arguments we sketched in section 10 above show (if they are correct) that a sentence of the form 'not (p at t_0)' implies 'it is impossible that (p at t_0)'; alternatively, that whenever p is not the case, it is false to say 'it is possible now that p'. From these conclusions nothing follows, however, concerning moments of time other than t_0 or other than the particular moment at which p was assumed not the case.

It is therefore clear that Aristotle's criticism of the Megarians turns on a rather peculiar concept of possibility. It presupposes a concept of possibility on which 'impossible that (p at t_0)' implies 'not (p at t_1)' even when $t_1 \neq t_0$. Or, what is more likely, Aristotle presupposed a concept of possibility on which a statement of the form 'it is impossible that p' (with a temporally unspecified sentence p) implied that it is false to say that p at the time the statement is made and that it will remain false to say so at all later times. On the latter interpretation, a statement of the form 'it is possible that p' is true as soon as it will be true to say that p at some future moment of time. Furthermore, it is on this view true to say that 'it is necessary that p' only if it is at all future times true to say that p is the case. When in our reconstruction of the Master Argument we made the step from (10) to (10)*, we in effect assumed that something like this notion of possibility is used in (10). The fact that we have now found this notion in Aristotle serves to justify our step *ex post facto*.[31]

It is easily seen that the notion of possibility Aristotle is presupposing in his criticism of the Megarians is in fact of just this kind. The passage we quoted above as his clinching argument is immediately preceded by the first passage we quoted in section 4, which shows that for Aristotle 'it is possible that p' is implied by, and is indeed equivalent to, 'p is or will be the case'. And if this passage is not explicit enough, Aristotle puts the same point even more bluntly a little later in the second passage quoted in the same section above.

These observations show us how Aristotle was able to bypass the conclusions of the (early) Megarians even though he did not criticize their arguments. Whether or not he fully realized what he was doing, he in effect defined or, more likely, reinterpreted his concepts of possibility and of necessity in such a way that they could not be limited to a single moment. Saying that it is now possible that p, means simply that at some moment of time it will be true to say that p; saying that it is (now) necessary that p, means simply that it will always be true to say that p.

This interpretation of Aristotle's criticism of the Megarians in *Met.* Θ 3 is strongly supported, it seems to me, by what we have found in earlier chapters. In Chapter V, sections 11–13, it was

---

[31] The fact that statements concerning possibility and impossibility which apparently pertain exclusively to the present moment can, on Aristotle's view, really pertain to the future is borne out by his remarks in *Top.* VI 6. 145^{b}27 ff.: 'When, then, we say that a living thing is now indestructible, we mean that it is at present a living thing of such a kind as never to be destroyed.'

argued that what Aristotle does in *Met.* Θ 4 is to defend the principle of plenitude, i.e. to defend the assumption that every possibility is realized sooner or later. This is an assumption—the most important assumption—that has to go into the notion of possibility he was found to presuppose in criticizing the Megarians in *Met.* Θ 3. Thus *Met.* Θ 4 turns out to serve the natural purpose of buttressing Aristotle's immediately preceding discussion in Θ 3.

Even more importantly, the main strategy of Aristotle's discussion of future contingents in *De Int.* 9, analysed in detail in Chapter VIII above, is the same as that of his criticism of the Megarians. In both cases, Aristotle bases his line of thought essentially on the idea that the relevant sense of possibility is the Diodorean one, i.e. one in which 'it is possible that *p*' is equivalent to 'it is or will be the case that *p*', and in effect dismisses other senses of possibility as irrelevant or at best unimportant. From our point of view, this is unsatisfactory in several respects, and indicates a failure on Aristotle's part to handle satisfactorily the problem of determinism. (If something is possible to happen at *this very moment*, will it have to happen?) In view of what we have found in Chapters IV and VIII we can nevertheless see why the way out Aristotle attempted on the two occasions must have appeared to him as an especially tempting one.

12. *Diodorus' defence of his concept of possibility*

The concept of possibility which we have just found in Aristotle was not employed quite consistently by him. However, it was employed consciously by Diodorus; it was exactly the way we know he defined the notion (his notion) of possibility.

That he should have adopted this notion of possibility is natural enough. Adopting it was undoubtedly one of the most natural reactions of the Megarian school to Aristotle's criticisms. From Aristotle we know that the early Megarians had denied the applicability of any notion of possibility different from actuality. Against them, Aristotle had stressed the fact that we in fact constantly use such a notion, and that absurd consequences seem to follow from the equation of possibility with actuality. Undoubtedly his criticism carried a great deal of weight. And even

independently of Aristotle's criticism the need for some concept
of possibility different from actuality is obvious enough. How
could the Megarians defend themselves? How could they reconcile their arguments for determinism with the actual use of the
concept of possibility? The simplest way of doing so was to
develop further the reinterpretation of the notion of possibility to
which Aristotle had already resorted. And the result of this reinterpretation is just Diodorus' notion of possibility, which in this
way obtains a very natural place in the development of the discussion concerning possibility.

If Diodorus' notion of possibility was thus anticipated by
Aristotle, where did his claim to fame lie? Again we have an
answer to hand. What did Aristotle's reinterpretation of the
notion of possibility consist in? We have already seen (in section
11) that the essential step of the reinterpretation is to understand
'it is possible that p' (where p is temporally unspecified) to mean
'it is possible that p is true or will be true'. As we pointed out, on
this interpretation 'it is possible that p' is true as soon as p will be
true at some future moment of time. (Likewise, 'necessarily p'
will be true only if p will always be true in the future.) But the
converse implication does not follow at once. It does not follow
immediately that 'it is possible that p' implies 'it is or will be the
case that p'. (Likewise, it does not follow that 'necessarily p' is
true as soon as it is and always will be true that p.) We saw that
Aristotle assumed these converse implications, too; but he never
offered more than half-hearted arguments for them.

Now we can see one more piece of our jigsaw puzzle falling into
its place: we can see exactly in what sense Diodorus' Master
Argument served to establish his notion of possibility (as we know
from Alexander that it served). It served to establish the converse
implications Diodorus needed to equate 'possibly p' with 'it is or
will be the case that p'. And the fact that it did (on Diodorus' own
assumptions) serve to establish this is seen directly from our
reconstruction. For there we in fact implicitly interpreted 'it is
possible that p' to mean that it is possible that p is or will be true.
And this interpretation does not yet directly presuppose that the
converse implication holds, as we would have to presuppose if we
merely interpreted 'it is possible that p' as 'it is or will be the case
that p'. In the terminology of Chapter V above, Diodorus strove
to *prove* the principle of plenitude instead of just *assuming* it.

13. *Master Argument as Based on Determinism*

Thus interpreted, the Master Argument is not only compatible with the arguments I sketched for determinism. It is itself only a variant of such arguments. In fact, we pointed out that if we take, instead of a temporally unspecified sentence p, a temporally specified sentence of the form 'p at t_0' or if we understand 'it is possible that p' to mean 'it is possible that p should be now the case', then we transform the Master Argument into an argument of determinism pure and simple. The historical relation of the different arguments is of course likely to have been the converse: it is likely that Diodorus' Master Argument is basically just a more sophisticated version of the earlier Megarians' arguments for determinism.

We can also see that Diodorus' vindication of the concept of possibility as distinguished from actuality is largely an illusion. There are no genuine possibilities concerning what happens at any given particular moment; when we say that something is 'now possible', we merely say that it is true or will be true; we are not really speaking of what happens now, but of similar things happening in the future. In a way, using the Diodorean concept of possibility amounts to paying lip-service to libertarianism; in reality, it is based on a form of determinism. Of course, this is no objection to our interpretation of Diodorus, for we know that the Megarians were determinists, and that the Stoics also were determinists to the extent of believing in an inexorable fate. It is perhaps somewhat more surprising to find Aristotle adopting, albeit by implication, anything like a deterministic doctrine; but for a careful reader of his works this may not be so very surprising, either.[32]

In fact, there occur in Aristotle's writings passages that suggest a view not very unlike the one we have ascribed to Diodorus. A possibility has a tendency to realize itself; and does so as soon as it is not prevented from being actualized.[33] If it does not, then there

[32] Without wanting to claim that Cicero was a particularly careful reader of Aristotle, we may nevertheless register the fact that Cicero classified the Stagirite as believing that 'fate exercises the force of necessity' (*De Fato* XVII 39).

[33] Cf. 'When the agent and the patient meet in accordance with the potency in question, the one must act and the other be acted upon' (*Met.* Θ 5. 1048ᵃ6–7); 'The definition of what as a result of thought comes, from existing potentially to exist actually, is that, when it has been willed, if no external influence hinders it, it comes to pass' (*Met.* Θ 7. 1049ᵃ5–9); 'And in all cases where the generative principle

must be some external factors preventing it from being realized or, as we might equally well say, making it impossible for it to be realized.[34] It is true that there are contrary strains of thought in Aristotle's writings; but in one of his moods at least, he thus comes fairly close to Diodorean determinism.

This view of possibilities as 'tendencies' or 'powers' suggests an argument of which the Master Argument is a slightly more sophisticated version. One may be tempted to argue as follows: if a possibility is not realized at some moment of time, then it must be prevented by circumstances from being realized at that moment of time. But what about a possibility that is never realized? By the same token it must always be prevented from being realized. But a possibility whose realization is always made impossible by circumstances is clearly no genuine possibility at all. Hence every genuine possibility must be realized at some moment of time.

Some argument of this sort seems to be hinted at in certain passages in Aristotle.[35] In the reconstruction of the Master Argument offered above the rather simple-minded idea of unrealized possibilities as frustrated possibilities is replaced by assumption (1) as to the necessity of true statements about the past and the argument based on it. What is common to this primitive argument for (4) and to our reconstruction of the Master Argument is that both are essentially arguments designed to prove (4) on the basis of the earlier result that at any given moment nothing could have happened except what actually happened. In short, they are arguments designed to prove (4) on the basis of a form of determinism. They are essentially arguments that from the premiss 'it is possible that p is the case or will be the case' derive the conclusion 'p is the case or will be the case'; and they turn essentially on an additional premiss (or lemma) which says that whenever it is not the case that p at some

is contained in the thing itself, one thing is potentially another when, if nothing external hinders it, it will of itself become the other' (ibid. 13–15). The second of these quotations shows that in the cases of rational potentialities the desire to actualize the potentiality must also be present. See also *Phys.* VIII 4. 255[b]3–12; *De Motu Animalium* 7, *passim*; *Eth. Nic.* VII 3. 1147[a]30; *Rhet.* II 19. 1392[b]20 ff. and 1393[a]1 ff.

34 Cf. *Phys.* VIII 1. 251[a]23–8; 251[b]5–10; *Parva Naturalia* (*De Longitudine Vitae* 3) 465[b]15 ff.; *De Motu An.* 4. 699[b]29.

35 See the passages from the *Physics* mentioned in the preceding note, and compare them with the argument Aristotle gives in *De Caelo* I 12 (to be discussed in section 17 below).

particular moment of time t_0 then it is impossible that p should have been the case at t_0 (except of course in the sense in which 'possibly p' when asserted at t_0 simply means that p happens at *some*—future or present—moment of time). All these arguments are, in brief, attempts to find the concept of possibility a place in a universe governed by determinism or by fate.

There is important evidence to the effect that this was in any case true of the Master Argument. There are several statements by ancient writers that show that they regarded Diodorus' definition of possibility to be the only way of reconciling the use of the concept of possibility with determinism. For instance we read in Plutarch:

Is it not clear that Chrysippus' doctrine of the possible contradicts his doctrine of fate? For if the possible is not what either is or will be true, as Diodorus states, but if everything is possible that admits of happening even if it will not happen, then many of these things will be possible which according to insuperable and unviolable and victorious Fate will not happen. Thus either fate's power will dwindle or, if fate is what Chrysippus believes it to be, that which admits of happening will often become impossible. For all that happens is necessary, since it is part of the supreme necessity; and all that does not happen is impossible, since the most powerful cause prevents it from coming to happen (Plutarch, *De Stoic. Repugn.* 46, p. 1055 d).[36]

The denial of Diodorus' definition—that is, the simultaneous assumption of (10) and (11)—is here taken to contradict the doctrine of fate. The way this contradiction comes about seems to be just the one our reconstruction presupposes: the doctrine of fate is taken to imply that 'all that does not exist is impossible', and this is taken to be incompatible with the denial of Diodorus' definition.

A similar point is made in a briefer form by Alexander:

Their theory is that the possible and contingent does not exclude that everything shall happen according to fate, and they define the possible event as something that is not prevented by anything from happening even if it does not happen. 'There is nothing to prevent the occurrence even of the opposite of what happens through fate, for even though it does not occur it is still possible'. . . . Is not this view ridiculous? (Alex. Aphr., *De Fato* 176. 14; in von Arnim vol. ii, fr. 959.)

---

[36] The translation is mainly taken from S. Sambursky, *The Physics of the Stoics* (Routledge and Kegan Paul, London, 1959), pp. 136–7.

If you combine the ideas expressed by Plutarch and by Alexander here with Aristotle's assumptions, you are bound to obtain something very close to our reconstruction of the Master Argument.

14. *Cicero's testimony*

Further evidence of an intimate connection between the Master Argument and determinism is found in Cicero. In *De Fato* IX 17 we read:

Well, Diodorus holds that only what either is true or will be true is possible. This position is connected with the argument that nothing happens which was not necessary, and that whatever is possible either is now or will be, and that it is no more possible for things that will be to alter than it is for things that have happened . . . (Trans. by H. Rackham in the Loeb Classical Library)

This passage deserves some further remarks. Since we know that the Master Argument served to establish the view mentioned in the first sentence of our quotation, we may surmise that the argument briefly sketched in the rest of the quotation reproduces some of the main features of the Master Argument. If so, Cicero's statement brings out explicitly the connection between the Master Argument and determinism. The deterministic assumption here replaces assumption (1), as we have seen that it can do.

But what about the rest of the quotation? Does it throw any light on the Master Argument? Is it even connected with what we know about the argument? There are unmistakable connections. For one thing, we observed above in section 8 (last paragraph) that the argument is apparently based on the assumption that 'it is not possible for things that will be to alter'. Now we have found a clear statement of this assumption in ancient writers.

Cicero's report that Diodorus' notion of possibility was connected with the idea that 'whatever is possible either is now or will be' may seem circular, for this is exactly what the notion amounts to. However, we may perhaps understand what Cicero is saying here. The first step of our reconstruction of the Master Argument was from (10) to (10)*, i.e. was to assume on the basis of (2) that a certain possibility is or will be realized. Perhaps Cicero is really saying, in a somewhat misleading form, that whatever is possible may *be assumed* either to be realized or to be going to be realized without any impossibilities resulting from this assumption. If so, there is a perfect fit between the assumptions mentioned by Cicero and those mentioned by Epictetus (section 2), for then his second assumption will merely be another form of (2), on the interpretation of (2) given earlier.

Hence we have found room for both the main assumptions (1) and (2) in Cicero's report. Why, then, was the additional assumption that 'it is not possible for things that will be to alter' omitted by Epictetus although it is mentioned by Cicero? Probably because it was not a premiss proper but a consequence of the definitions of the notions in question. As Cicero says, 'those who say that things that are going to be are immutable and that a true future event cannot be changed into a false one, are not asserting the necessity of fate but explaining the meaning of terms' (*De Fato* IX 20).

15. *The logic of the Master Argument*

How are the Diodorean and Aristotelian arguments we sketched above to be evaluated? Here I shall disregard certain aspects of the argument, viz. those that take us from premiss (1) (the necessity of what is past) to Diodorus' (and perhaps also Aristotle's) deterministic ideas as to what can happen at any one moment of time. These aspects of the argument include the step from the moment of time t_0 at which a possibility was assumed to have been realized to a later moment of time t_1 (cf. section 8 above). I shall concentrate here on the question whether Diodorus' determinism was enough to yield a valid proof of the principle of plenitude.

Let us see how the problem can be sharpened. In a rather un-Aristotelian and unhistorical notation, 'p is true at time t' could be represented by '$p(t)$', and 'it is possible that p should be true at moment t' could be represented by '$Mp(t)$'. For simplicity, we restrict the range of t to moments of present or future time. Then the first premiss becomes

(18) $M(\exists t)p(t)$

and the alleged conclusion becomes

(19) $(\exists t)p(t)$

The deterministic assumption that we registered becomes in effect

(20) $(t) (\sim p(t) \supset \sim Mp(t))$

The negation of (19) is of course equivalent to

(21) $(t) \sim p(t)$

Here (18) is clearly very closely related to assumption (10) of our reconstruction of the Master Argument, and (21) is essentially assumption (11). The use of the original premiss (1)* was to give us (20). Hence the question we want to ask here concerning the validity of the Master Argument is essentially the question whether (18), (20), and (21) together entail a contradiction.

The answer is negative.[37] On the most natural assumptions concerning modal notions that we can make, it can be shown that the set of formulas (18), (20), (21) is consistent. Intuitively, the way in which the three can be compatible may be explained by saying that although under the actual course of (future) events p is never true and although it therefore follows that at each moment of time during the actual course of events it is true to say that it is impossible that p should be the case, some alternative course of (future) events may still be possible under which p would have happened.

How, then, could Diodorus think he was able to derive a contradiction from assumptions essentially tantamount to (18), (20), and (21)? The answer is not very difficult to find. He could have derived a contradiction if he had instead of (18) the closely related premiss

(18)* $(\exists t) Mp(t)$

For then he could have argued as follows: Let t_0 be some moment of time such as is asserted to exist in (18)*. Thus we have (by existential instantiation)

$Mp(t_0)$

If we now assume that this possibility is realized, we have

(22) $p(t_0)$

Can we now show that this assumption leads to an impossibility,

---

[37] This is easily verified by means of the techniques expounded in my article 'Modality and Quantification', *Theoria*, 27 (1961), 119–28, reprinted (in an expanded form) in *Models for Modalities* (p. 185 above), pp. 57–70. More accurately, the answer is negative as long as the condition (C.U**) or the condition (C.U$_*$) is not assumed to be satisfied. But if the view taken in 'Modality and Quantification' is sound, there is obviously no general reason for adopting these conditions.

i.e. can we prove $\sim Mp(t_0)$ from the other assumptions (20) and (21)? Such a proof is in fact forthcoming. From (21) we have

(23) $\sim p(t_0)$

by universal instantiation, and from (20) we have similarly

$\sim p(t_0) \sim Mp(t_0)$

By *modus ponens* these two together yield the desired contradiction.

An even simpler argument would have been possible. However, I have wanted to give the argument a form in which it parallels fairly closely our reconstruction of the Master Argument. In fact, (22) is obviously tantamount to (10)*. And if our reconstruction is formulated in the simpler form obtained by identifying t_0 and t_1 (as mentioned in section 9), (11)* will be tantamount to (23), and the modified form of (13)* or

(13)** at time t_0 it will be true to say that it is impossible for p to be the case

will be tantamount to $\sim Mp(t_0)$. Hence the argument I have just given in fact parallels our informal reconstruction rather closely.

16. *The presuppositions of the Master Argument*

Hence if we grant Diodorus his deterministic assumptions and also grant him (18)* instead of (18), he can argue in the way he wants. Historically it is obvious enough that he had his peculiar deterministic doctrines, however alien they may be to us. Hence the evaluation of his argument from the point of view of logic boils down to the question to what extent he was justified in making the transition from (18) to (18)*.[38] In a way, this is also an interpretational problem. Unless we can show that he was likely to make such a transition, our interpretation will be unlikely.

Now there are good reasons for saying that the transition from (18) to (18)* was a natural step for Diodorus to make. For one thing, the distinction between (18) and (18)* is not easy to make without logical symbolism such as the ancients did not use. Formulated in natural language, the difference is one between

it is possible that p should be the case now or in the future

[38] The question of the justifiability of the transition from (18) to (18)* is the same as the question of the justifiability of the familiar 'Barcan formula' mentioned in 'Modality and Quantification'.

and

> it is possible now or in the future that p should be the case;

and the difference between these may seem slight indeed.

Remember also what we found in section 7. We found that Aristotle did not only hold that every possibility may be assumed to be actualized without any impossible consequences resulting from this assumption; he also held that every possibility may be assumed to be actualized *at some particular moment of time* in this way. Now we can see what this doctrine amounts to. We cannot assume that the possibility that is asserted by (18) to obtain is realized at some particular moment of time without making (18) equivalent to (18)*. In fact, the general assumption that sentences of these two forms are always equivalent (no matter what sentence $p(t)$ is) is closely related to the kind of assumption we discussed in section 7. Intuitively, assuming that the equivalence holds generally may be said to amount to assuming that every moment of time during any course of events that we consider possible must be equated with some moment of time during the actual course of events.[39] This must have seemed a very natural assumption, for how could there be moments of time not identical with some moment of time in the actual history of the universe? It may even be taken to be a consequence of Aristotle's theory of time. For Aristotle the 'now' is what holds the time together.[40] Hence for him there does not seem to be any room for possible moments of time that the actual 'now' never reaches. Be this as it may, it is for other reasons obvious that the equivalence of (18) and (18)* is what Aristotle's idea of the realization of each

[39] In 'Modality and Quantification' it is shown that the general assumptions underlying an implication of the same form as the implication from (18) to (18)* may be expressed intuitively by saying that whatever individuals exist in alternative possible worlds (possible courses of events) must also exist in the actual world (the actual course of events). If these individuals are moments of time, as they are in (18) and (18)*, the assumption will be exactly the one mentioned in the text: every possible moment of time must be identical with some moment of time within the actual course of events.

[40] See *Phys.* IV 11. 219^{b}9–220^{a}4 and 13. 222^{a}10 ff. Notice also that when Aristotle speaks of entities that are or are not in time, he is not assuming that something could exist that is not contemporary with any moment of time. This interpretation of the phrase 'in time' is in fact ruled out in *Phys.* IV 12. 221^{a}19 ff. What Aristotle means is simply that the existence of some entities is bounded by earlier and later moments of time whereas the existence of others is not. The latter are 'not in time' in Aristotle's sense. (See *Phys.* IV 12. 221^{a}26–^{b}7, 221^{b}23–222^{a}9.) Nothing is for Aristotle really *outside* our time.

possibility *at some particular moment of time* will amount to. It is clear enough that by 'some moment of time' Aristotle means some particular moment *in the actual history of our universe*; and the observations just made show that this is all that is required for the equivalence.[41]

Aristotle was therefore committed to accepting the equivalence of (18) and (18)*. Whatever differences there may have been between him and Diodorus, this fact at least suggests that Diodorus might have made some similar assumptions.

Nevertheless, the equivalence is unacceptable. It is true that it has been accepted by certain modal logicians;[42] it is even true that it is provable in some formal systems logicians have devised;[43] but a closer analysis of the assumptions that underlie systems of modal logic shows that there is no general justification for it.[44] You may perhaps have a glimpse of the reasons for rejecting the equivalence if you recall the primitive form of our argument sketched above in section 13. If a possibility is always (*at each given moment*) prevented from being realized, the argument went, then it is not true to say that it is a genuine possibility at all. You may already have had your doubts about this argument. Why cannot we conceive of a different course of events under which some of the obstacles would not have materialized so that the relevant possibility could have proved its mettle? The conclusion that there is no possibility present at all was merely a result of trying to squeeze the moments of time in the alternative courses of events into one and the same chronology. A logician's reasons

[41] Thus the assumption that underlies the validity of the Barcan formula in the special case in which we quantify over moments of time is a form of the doctrine of the unity (necessary unity) of time. Since this assumption serves to justify the doctrine that all (genuine) possibilities are realized some time or other, it is perhaps not surprising to find the same doctrine in other thinkers (Kant is perhaps a case in point) who also assumed the 'necessary unity of time'.

[42] See, e.g., Rudolf Carnap, *Meaning and Necessity* (University of Chicago Press, Chicago, second edition, 1956); Saul A. Kripke, 'A Completeness Theorem in Modal Logic', *Journal of Symbolic Logic*, 24 (1959), 1–14.

[43] See A. N. Prior, 'Modality and Quantification in S5', *Journal of Symbolic Logic*, 21 (1956), 60–2, and my analysis of the reasons for Prior's apparent success in 'Modality and Quantification', p. 127. Essentially the same analysis is made (independently) by Saul A. Kripke in 'Semantical Considerations on Modal Logic', *Acta Philosophica Fennica*, 16 (1963), 83–94, especially 87–9.

[44] In terms of the approach outlined in my 'Modality and Quantification', this is fairly obvious. The import of the remarks that will be made in the text is also clear enough within the framework of 'Modality and Quantification'.

for rejecting the equivalence of (18) and (18)* are in fact abstractions from these intuitive ideas.

17. *Aristotle's own 'Master Argument'*

The observations we have made concerning the interrelation of (18) and (18)* in Aristotle and probably also in Diodorus derive some further support from the explicit (albeit rather brief) argument Aristotle himself gives for essentially the same conclusion as that of the Master Argument, i.e. for the principle of plenitude. This argument is given in *De Caelo* I 12. 281^{b}3–25. It has been discussed carefully and lucidly by C. J. F. Williams in his article, 'Aristotle and Corruptibility', *Religious Studies*, vol. 1 (1966), pp. 95–107, 203–15, especially pp. 98–9. The crucial passage is the following:

A man has . . . the capacity at once of sitting and of standing, because when he possesses the one he also posseses the other; but it does not follow that he can at once sit and stand, only that at another time he can do the other also. But if a thing has for infinite time more than one capacity, another time is impossible and the times must coincide.

This general point is then applied by Aristotle to the particular subject matter he is considering:

Thus if anything which exists for infinite time is destructible, it will have the capacity of not being. Now if it exists for an infinite time let this capacity be actualized; and it will be in actuality at once existent and non-existent.

This is treated by Aristotle as the kind of impossibility which suffices to show that anything that exists for an infinite time cannot be destructible.

The contrast Aristotle operates with here is called by Williams (though admittedly not by Aristotle) a distinction between *sensus compositus* and *sensus divisus*. Socrates cannot sit (at a given time) and not sit (at the same time), but he can sit (sc. at one time) and not sit (sc. at another). Williams argues that Aristotle's argument turns on neglecting the analogous modal distinction: Socrates may have an ability to stand while he is sitting, although he cannot stand and sit at the same time. Formally this would be a distinction between

(24) Mp & q

and

    (25) $M(p \mathbin{\&} q)$

where p and q are incompatible. In contrast, the earlier distinction is between

    (26) $p(t_1) \mathbin{\&} q(t_2)$

and

    (27) $p(t_1) \mathbin{\&} q(t_1)$.

The former may be called a modal *compositus–divisus* distinction, the latter a temporal one. According to Williams (p. 99), 'What Aristotle does not see is that the . . . purely modal variety of the *compositus / divisus* distinction is still available. . . . The temporal variety of the . . . distinction . . . is a red herring.' Aristotle's argument for the principle of plenitude, and presumably also his belief in it, are thus largely due to a logical confusion, not to say a fallacy. The temporal distinction collapses, Aristotle rightly points out, when the time reference covers all times : p(always) & $\sim p(t_1)$ is as impossible as $p(t_1)$ & $\sim p(t_1)$. But this leaves Aristotle, Williams suggests, the modal distinction between

    (28) $M \sim p(t_1) \mathbin{\&} p$(always)

and

    (29) $M(\sim p(t_1) \mathbin{\&} p$(always))

which seems to offer an alternative to Aristotle's argument. (Instead of $p(t_1)$ we can here have something else, e.g. p(sometime in the future), p(now), or even p *simpliciter* with a temporally indefinite p.)

All this is correct and illuminating. It seems to me, however, that we have to go deeper. I do not think that just pointing out the difference between the two distinctions sufficiently explains why Aristotle argues so as to apparently confuse the two.

What Aristotle's arguments amount to is shown by the references to his own definition of possibility. Immediately before the passage we quoted he writes: 'Thus it is not the same thing to make a false and to make an impossible hypothesis; and from the impossible hypothesis impossible results follow.' Thus he is clearly asking which possibilities we can assume to be realized without giving rise to impossibilities, and his point is that this cannot be done with the possibility in (28). This is wrong, but it is clear why Aristotle thinks that assuming the realization of the possibility in (28) leads to a contradiction. He thinks of the possibility as being realized at some time t_1 of the actual course of events, which would lead to the contradiction

(30) $\sim p(t_1)$ & p(always).

That this is the crucial idea underlying Aristotle's argument is acknowledged by Williams, but he does not go into the reasons why Aristotle should have argued in this way.

At first sight, the step from (28) to (30) may seem to illustrate merely the confusion I suspected (above in section 2) Aristotle to be guilty of. The consistency of (30) is a necessary condition of the truth of

(31) $M\sim p(t_1)$ & $N p$(always)

but not a necessary condition of the truth of (28). Confusing the two would amount to committing the mistake pointed out in section 2 above.

This is not all that can be said here, however. If we say that (28) can be true while (30) is inconsistent, we must think of the possibility expressed by $M\sim p(t_1)$ as capable of being realized under some course of events different from the one that will be actualized, for its realization under the latter would lead to (30). But we have already found reasons to suspect that such a realization was disregarded by Aristotle. Hence the reason why he took the crucial step from (28) to (30) was not just confusion concerning the precise import of his own principle (2), but the very same idea that only one sequence of moments of time is possible which we already found him harbouring. This makes much better sense of Aristotle's deeper reasons for his admittedly fallacious argument than merely accusing him of confusion.

Thus the conjecture made in Chapter V, section 12, turns out to be verified by Aristotle's argument in *De Caelo* I 12. If Aristotle's definition of possibility is combined with the assumption that possibilities can be assumed to be realized only within this gradually unfolding progression of actual nows, it leads straight to the principle of plenitude. Here we can therefore see a major reason why Aristotle held that each possibility is realized sooner or later.

Aristotle's argument is reminiscent of the early stages of our reconstruction of the Master Argument. The latter goes beyond the former, however, in circumventing the obvious objection which had already been made to Aristotle's argument. What the inconsistency of (30) shows is merely that assuming the actualization of the possibility mentioned in (28) leads to a *false* conclusion, not that it leads to an impossible one. In this respect, the Master Argument of Diodorus goes beyond Aristotle's less masterly one. But on a closer examination it, too, turns out to presuppose the same sort of 'necessary unity of time' on which Aristotle's argument falters. Hence Aristotle's blunter argument in some ways brings out the gist of the matter more directly.

18. *Conclusion*

To sum up very briefly: Diodorus tried to reconcile the actual use of the notion of possibility with determinism by his 'extensional' notion of possibility. The Master Argument was designed to show that Diodorus' notion was the only feasible one. The argument fails even if we grant the deterministic assumption, for it involves too narrow a view of the relation of possibility to time.

INDEX OF TEXTS

ARISTOTLE'S WRITINGS

Categories

1. 1^{a}2	14
1. 1^{a}12	23
5. 4^{a}10 ff.	67
5. 4^{a}23–30	66, 90, 150
5. 4^{a}34–^{b}2	67, 90, 150
7. 7^{b}27–30	75
10. 12^{b}38–13^{a}3	164
10. 13^{a}9–13	164
12. 14^{a}39	127

De Anima

II 1. 412^{b}22	14
II 10. 422^{a}26–9	130
III 3. 428^{b}8–9	76
III 5. 430^{a}22 ff.	1
III 6. 430^{a}30 ff.	70, 81
III 6. 430^{b}7	25
III 6. 431^{a}1–2	125
III 7. 431^{a}3–4	126
III 10. 433^{b}9	159

De Caelo

I 5. 271^{b}28–272^{a}7	121
I 11. 280^{b}1 ff.	21
I 11. 280^{b}13	26
I 11. 281^{a}5–7	109
I 12. 281^{a}28 ff.	104, 106
I 12. 281^{b}3–25	210
I 12. 281^{b}23–5	189
I 12. 281^{b}25	104
I 12. 282^{a}27 ff.	102, 151, 152, 161
I 12. 283^{b}12 ff.	94, 152, 164, 183

De Generatione Animalium

I 19. 726^{b}24	14
II 1. 734^{b}25	14
III 1. 735^{a}8	14

De Generatione et Corruptione

I 6. 322^{b}29 ff.	7, 9
I 7. 324^{a}26 ff.	25
I 10. 328^{b}21	8
II 9. 335^{a}32–^{b}7	105

II 11. 337^{b}4–6	169, 173
II 11. 338^{a}1–3	104

De Interpretatione

1. 16^{a}3–6	85, 89
1. 16^{a}18	159
3. 16^{b}6–18	70, 81
7. 17^{b}26–7	166
9. 18^{a}28–37	166, 183
9. 18^{a}34–^{b}16	154, 168, 169
9. 18^{b}9 ff.	105, 167, 168, 169, 170
9. 18^{b}17–25	154, 167
9. 18^{b}26	42
9. 18^{b}26–19^{a}6	154
9. 18^{b}34	169
9. 18^{b}36	91
9. 19^{a}1–6	167, 173
9. 19^{a}7–22	154
9. 19^{a}9–11	160, 169
9. 19^{a}12–18	100, 172
9. 19^{a}20–2	170
9. 19^{a}23 ff.	154, 155, 183
9. 19^{a}25–6	171
9. 19^{a}27–32	148, 154, 155
9. 19^{a}32–5	155, 173
9. 19^{a}32–^{b}4	154
9. 19^{a}35	42
9. 19^{a}36–9	171
9. 19^{a}39–^{b}4	165
9. 19^{b}1	149
10. 19^{b}11–18	81
10. 19^{b}20	17
10. 19^{b}21	26
10. 19^{b}36	52
10. 20^{a}16–18	69
10. 20^{a}20 ff.	47
11. 21^{a}22	55
12. 21^{a}37	41
12. 21^{b}12 ff.	44
12. 21^{b}14	50
12. 21^{b}31	50
12. 21^{b}35	43, 53
12. 22^{a}3 ff.	27
12. 22^{a}7 ff.	27

De Interpretatione (*cont.*):

12. 22^{a}11–13	41
13. 22^{a}14 ff.	28, 41, 43, 45
13. 22^{a}16 ff.	28, 34
13. 22^{a}24–7	46
13. 22^{a}29–31	55
13. 22^{a}32–8	28
13. 22^{a}33	43, 45
13. 22^{a}38 ff.	53, 54
13. 22^{b}1 ff.	27, 43
13. 22^{b}5	27
13. 22^{b}11 ff.	29, 41, 44, 48, 55
13. 22^{b}12	43
13. 22^{b}14–16	34, 43, 47
13. 22^{b}16	42
13. 22^{b}17–22	45
13. 22^{b}18	43
13. 22^{b}19	42
13. 22^{b}20	28
13. 22^{b}22–4	43, 49
13. 22^{b}25	43
13. 22^{b}26	43
13. 22^{b}28	42
13. 22^{b}29 ff.	29, 43, 53
13. 22^{b}36 ff.	44, 165
13. 23^{a}5–6	58
13. 23^{a}6 ff.	41, 55, 56, 57, 59
13. 23^{a}7–27	29
13. 23^{a}8–11	56
13. 23^{a}12–13	166
13. 23^{a}14	174
13. 23^{a}16	159
13. 23^{a}17	53
13. 23^{a}18–21	50
13. 23^{a}19	50
13. 23^{a}20	43
13. 23^{a}23–6	114

De Motu Animalium

4. 699^{b}17–22	130
4. 699^{b}29	202

De Partibus Animalium

I 1. 639^{b}25	130, 159
I 1. 640^{b}36	14
I 1. 642^{a}8	130
I 3. 643^{a}1 ff.	15
I 3. 643^{b}7	8
I 5. 644^{b}21–3	105
II 2. 647^{b}18	8
II 2. 648^{a}36	12
II 2. 648^{b}11	12
II 2. 649^{b}6	12

Eudemian Ethics

I 5. 1216^{b}6 ff.	125
VII 2. 1236^{a}16 ff.	8, 15
VII 2. 1236^{b}24 ff.	8, 15

Metaphysics

A 6. 987^{b}4–7	77
A 6. 987^{b}10	9
A 8. 989^{b}6–7	69
A 9. 990^{b}6	8, 9
A 9. 990^{b}29–1^{a}7	99
A 9. 991^{a}5–8	9, 14
a 2. 994^{b}20–7	129
B 6. 1003^{a}2	97, 98
Γ 2. 1003^{a}33 ff.	56, 22
Γ 2. 1003^{b}12–13	22
Γ 2. 1003^{b}13–14	22
Γ 2. 1004^{a}22 ff.	11
Γ 2. 1005^{a}7	12
Γ 3. 1005^{b}19–20	69
Γ 3. 1005^{b}23–32	69
Γ 4. 1006^{b}18	10
Γ 5. 1009^{a}32	25
Γ 6. 1011^{b}15–18	69
Γ 7. 1011^{b}26	168
Γ 7. 1012^{a}27–8	69
Γ 8. 1012^{b}24–8	77
Δ 3. 1014^{a}16–17	26
Δ 3. 1014^{a}36	127
Δ 5. 1015^{b}11–14	159
Δ 8. 1017^{b}23	26
Δ 11. 1019^{a}5	12
Δ 12. 1019^{b}32–3	58, 59
Δ 12. 1019^{b}33	13
Δ 14. 1020^{a}29	26
Δ 23. 1023^{a}27	25
Δ 30. 1025^{a}14–15	69
E 1. 1025^{b}10	13
E 1. 1025^{b}27	132
E 2. 1026^{a}33–4	12, 13
E 2. 1026^{b}27 ff.	103, 105, 170
E 3. 1027^{a}29–31	175
E 3. 1027^{b}25–7	125
Z 1. 1028^{a}10	12
Z 1. 1028^{a}31	12
Z 4. 1029^{b}30	26
Z 4. 1030^{a}29	7, 11
Z 4. 1030^{a}32–3	23
Z 7. 1032^{b}1–15	126
Z 9. 1034^{a}22–4	126
Z 9. 1034^{b}1	8
Z 10. 1035^{b}25	14
Z 15. 1039^{b}27–40^{a}5	76

H 1. 1042^{a}29   26

Θ 1. 1046^{a}4–6   6
Θ 1. 1046^{a}6   13
Θ 1. 1046^{a}9   57
Θ 1. 1046^{a}11–12   57
Θ 3. 1047^{a}10–14   104, 111, 151, 182
Θ 3. 1047^{a}14–22   197
Θ 3. 1047^{a}24 ff.   109, 183
Θ 4. 1047^{b}3 ff.   107, 108, 109,
         183, 186, 189, 190
Θ 4. 1047^{b}6–9   108
Θ 4. 1047^{b}9–13   110
Θ 4. 1047^{b}11   189
Θ 4. 1047^{b}14–16   187
Θ 4. 1047^{b}27–30   190
Θ 5. 1047^{b}35–1048^{a}1   189
Θ 5. 1048^{a}6–7   201
Θ 6. 1048^{a}35 ff.   13
Θ 6. 1048^{b}1–8   124
Θ 6. 1048^{b}9 ff.   114, 132
Θ 6. 1048^{b}14–17   131–4
Θ 7. 1049^{a}5–9   201
Θ 7. 1049^{a}13–15   202
Θ 8. 1049^{b}18–29   126
Θ 8. 1050^{b}6 ff.   97, 104
Θ 8. 1050^{b}20   104
Θ 8. 1050^{b}31–4   58
Θ 9. 1051^{a}21–33   127
Θ 10. 1051^{b}13 ff.   57, 150
I 10. 1059^{a}10 ff.   18
I 10. 1059^{a}13   9
K 1. 1059^{b}13   132
K 3. 1060^{b}31 ff.   7, 12, 26
K 3. 1061^{b}11–12   12
K 8. 1064^{b}32 ff.   105
K 9. 1065^{b}5   101
Λ 4. 1070^{b}33–4   126
Λ 6. 1071^{b}13   97
Λ 6. 1071^{b}18–20   98
Λ 8. 1074^{a}38–^{b}14   112
M 3. 1078^{a}21–31   132
M 3. 1078^{a}30–1   127
M 4. 1079^{a}2   8
M 6. 1080^{b}17   132
M 9. 1086^{a}33   132
M 10. 1086^{b}27   8
N 2. 1088^{b}23–5   104
N 2. 1089^{a}7   12
N 2. 1089^{a}16   12

Meteorology

I 3. 339^{b}27 ff.   112
IV 12. 390^{a}13   14

Nicomachean Ethics

I 6. 1096^{b}26 ff.   7, 8, 11, 13
V 1. 1129^{a}26 ff.   15
V 4. 1130^{a}32 ff.   15
V 9. 1136^{b}29   12
VI. 2. 1139^{b}7–9   93, 164, 183
VI 3. 1139^{b}18–23   76
VII 3. 1146^{b}32   25
VII 3. 1147^{a}30   202
VII 11. 1152^{b}27   25

Parva Naturalia

De Longitudine Vitae
3. 465^{b}14 ff.   202
De Memoria
1. 449^{b}24–30   85
1. 449^{b}30–450^{a}7   122
2. 452^{b}7 ff.   70
2. 452^{b}13–17   129
2. 452^{b}30 ff.   70

Physics

I 2. 185^{a}21   12
I 2. 185^{b}6   12
I 3. 186^{a}24   12
I 7. 190^{a}31   12
I 8. 191^{b}1 ff.   25
II 2. 193^{b}22–35   122
II 2. 194^{a}9–11   122
II 2. 194^{a}12   25
II 2. 194^{a}16   25
II 2. 194^{a}21 ff.   125
II 9. 199^{b}34–200^{b}42   130
II 9. 200^{a}16–18   120
III 1. 200^{b}26   101
III 1. 201^{a}10–11   106
III 2. 202^{a}9–11   106
III 3. 202^{a}27–8   15
III 4. 203^{b}17   120
III 4. 203^{b}18–20   133
III 4. 203^{b}22–5   118, 128, 133
III 4. 203^{b}30   105, 115
III 4. 204^{a}2–3 ff.   130, 131
III 5. 204^{a}34 ff.   122
III 6. 206^{a}12–14   115
III 6. 206^{a}14–18   115
III 6. 206^{a}18–21   122
III 6. 206^{a}21–3   115–16
III 6. 206^{a}23–5   116, 123
III 6. 206^{a}29–33   123
III 6. 206^{a}32–3   116
III 6. 206^{b}3–9   129
III 6. 206^{b}3–12   118

Physics (cont.):

III 6. 206^{b}12–15	116, 123
III 6. 206^{b}14–16	115, 124
III 6. 207^{a}21–32	124
III 7. 207^{b}10–13	128
III 7. 207^{b}17–18	117
III 7. 207^{b}19–21	117
III 7. 207^{b}27–34	118, 119
III 7. 207^{b}34–208^{a}4	124
III 8. 208^{a}8–11	133, 134
III 8. 208^{a}14–19	128, 129, 133
III 8. 208^{a}18	117, 118
III 8. 208^{a}20–1	128, 130
III 8. 208^{a}21–2	129
IV 11. 219^{b}9–220^{a}4	86, 208
IV 12. 220^{b}32 ff.	83
IV 12. 221^{a}19	208
IV 12. 221^{a}26–^{b}7	208
IV 12. 221^{b}3–5	84
IV 12. 221^{b}23–222^{a}9	105, 208
IV 13. 222^{a}10 ff.	86, 208
IV 13. 222^{a}24–8	70
IV 13. 222^{b}7 ff.	174
IV 14. 222^{b}30–223^{a}15	162
V 4. 227^{b}3	12
V 4. 228^{a}24 ff.	17
VI 2. 233^{a}24	25
VI 5. 236^{a}7–8	69
VI 8. 239^{a}23–^{b}4	162
VI 8. 239^{a}28–9	69
VII 3. 245^{b}16	8
VII 4. 248^{b}17	13
VII 4. 249^{a}3–8	17
VII 4. 249^{a}21–5	17
VII 4. 249^{a}23–5	14
VIII 1. 251^{a}23–8	202
VIII 1. 251^{b}5–10	202
VIII 4. 255^{b}3–12	202
VIII 5. 256^{b}10–12	183, 189

Poetics

15. 1454^{b}2–6	74
25. 1461^{a}26	24

Politics

I 1. 1253^{a}20–5	14
I 6. 1255^{a}4	25
II 5. 1264^{a}1–5	112
VII 10. 1329^{b}23–35	112

Posterior Analytics

I 2. 71^{b}33	25
I 2. 72^{a}20	50
I 4. 73^{a}21–4	93
I 4. 73^{a}28–9	68
I 4. 73^{b}22	55
I 6. 74^{b}33 ff.	76
I 6. 75^{a}12–14	93
I 6. 75^{a}31–5	101
I 8. 75^{b}21–36	68
I 8. 75^{b}31	125
I 10. 76^{b}35	50
I 33. 88^{b}31–4	76
II 3. 90^{b}23	125
II 17. 99^{a}22	125

Prior Analytics

I 1. 24^{b}18–22	42, 189
I 3. 25^{a}32–4	142
I 3. 25^{a}37 ff.	35, 37
I 3. 25^{a}39	38
I 3. 25^{b}7–14	36
I 3. 25^{b}14 ff.	36
I 3. 25^{b}18–19	35
I 4. 26^{a}2	45
I 4. 26^{b}6	45
I 8. 29^{b}29–35	137
I 9. 30^{a}21–3	139
I 9. 30^{a}27–8	142, 143
I 9. 30^{a}33–^{b}1	142
I 9. 30^{b}4–5	183
I 10. 30^{b}31 ff.	130, 159
I 10. 30^{b}33–40	144
I 10. 30^{b}37–8	69
I 10. 30^{b}38–40	130
I 11. 31^{a}31–3	142
I 11. 31^{b}8–10	69
I 13. 32^{a}18 ff.	30, 36, 51, 110, 183, 184
I 13. 32^{a}21–9	31, 33
I 13. 32^{a}29 ff.	31, 42
I 13. 32^{b}4 ff.	34, 36, 103, 105, 172
I 13. 32^{b}12	170
I 13. 32^{b}17–18	170
I 13. 32^{b}25–32	38, 40, 138, 145
I 14. 33^{a}24–5	39, 184
I 14. 33^{b}22	51
I 14. 33^{b}23	30
I 15. 33^{b}28	30
I 15. 33^{b}30–3	31
I 15. 33^{b}34–6	137
I 15. 34^{a}5–7	187
I 15. 34^{a}6 ff.	38, 189
I 15. 34^{a}8–9	190
I 15. 34^{a}12 ff.	58

I 15. 34ᵃ13	38
I 15. 34ᵃ25-33	186
I 15. 34ᵃ26	189
I 15. 34ᵃ34-ᵇ6	138, 186
I 15. 34ᵃ34-ᵇ31	144
I 15. 34ᵇ2-6	189, 190
I 15. 34ᵇ6 ff.	116, 166
I 15. 34ᵇ7-18	137, 138, 144, 159, 190
I 15. 34ᵇ17-18	68, 159
I 15. 34ᵇ27	30
I 15. 34ᵇ27-32	31
I 16. 35ᵇ32-4	31
I 17. 36ᵇ33-4	31
I 17. 37ᵃ16	16
I 17. 37ᵃ22 ff.	31
I 17. 37ᵃ27-8	30
I 17. 37ᵃ29	189
I 17. 37ᵃ36	42
I 20. 39ᵃ11-13	31
I 23. 41ᵃ23 ff.	187
I 23. 41ᵃ25	189
I 23. 41ᵃ30	186, 189
I 27. 43ᵇ11-13	55
I 29. 45ᵇ31-4	39

Rhetoric

II 19. 1392ᵃ16-17	187
II 19. 1392ᵇ20 ff.	202
II 19. 1393ᵃ1 ff.	202
II 23. 1402ᵃ9 ff.	35
III 2. 1404ᵇ37-1405ᵃ2	9
III 2. 1405ᵃ1 ff.	10

III 11. 1412ᵇ11 ff.	15
III 17. 1418ᵃ3-5	93, 164, 183

Sophistici Elenchi

1. 165ᵃ11 ff.	17
5. 166ᵇ38 ff.	158
5. 167ᵃ24	9, 10
6. 168ᵃ25	20
17. 176ᵃ4 ff.	21
18. 176ᵇ32	25
19. 177ᵃ11-25	20

Topics

I 5. 102ᵃ24-6	159
I 15. 107ᵃ3-12	18
I 15. 107ᵇ6 ff.	13, 24
I 18. 108ᵃ18 ff.	20
II 2. 109ᵇ4-6	10
II 3. 110ᵇ16 ff.	20, 21, 22, 24
II 3. 110ᵇ38-111ᵃ2	22
II 6. 112ᵇ1 ff.	28, 105
II 6. 112ᵇ5 ff.	47
II 7. 113ᵃ22-3	69
II 11. 115ᵇ11 ff.	158
II 11. 115ᵇ17-19	105
II 11. 115ᵇ29 ff.	12, 158
IV 5. 126ᵃ34	101
V 2. 129ᵇ30-2	9, 13
V 2. 129ᵇ35 ff.	20
V 3. 131ᵇ5-18	81
VI 2. 140ᵃ6-8	13
VI 6. 145ᵇ24 ff.	102
VI 6. 145ᵇ27 ff.	161, 198
VIII 13. 162ᵇ37	9, 10

PLATO'S WRITINGS

Cratylus

405 c	51
439 d-40 c	78

Gorgias

454 d	75

Laws

X 901 d	74

Meno

81 c	73
89 c	78

Parmenides

135 b-c	78

Phaedrus

275 d-276 a	89

Philebus

58 a-59 c	77

Protagoras

324 b	183

Republic

392 d	183
430 a	78
476 e	75

Sophistes

263 e	90

Theaetetus

152 c	75
152 d	77
183 a	77
190 a	90
201 a–c	79

Timaeus

34 a	83
37 d	83
37 e–38 a	83
51 d	78

OTHER WRITERS

Alexander of Aphrodisias
De Fato (Arnim, vol. ii, fr. 959) 203
In Ar. Met. Comm. (ed. M. Hayduck, Berlin, 1891), p. 241,
  line 24 8

Cicero
De Fato

VII 13	196
IX 17	196, 204
IX 19	70
IX 20	193, 205
XIII 30	70
XVI 37	163
XVI 38	167
XVII 39	201

Diogenes Laertius
Vitae

VII 63	71
VII 66	71

Empedokles
fr. 129 (*Diels–Kranz*) 74

Epictetus
Dissertationes

II 19. 1	180

Parmenides

fr. 2 (*Diels–Kranz*)	75
fr. 8 (*Diels–Kranz*)	82, 83

Plutarch
De Stoic. Rep.

46, 1055 d	203

Sextus Empiricus
Adversus Mathematicos

VIII 10–13	71
VIII 85	71
VIII 88–9	71
VIII 112 ff.	71

Simplicius
In Ar. Cat. Comm. (ed. Kalb-
  fleish, Berlin, 1907), p. 37,
  lines 3 ff. 10, 12

GENERAL INDEX

Abelard, 147
Accidents, 101
Ackrill, J. L., 43–4, 66, 91, 155, 162, 173
Actuality, 26
Actualization, in the soul v. outside the soul, 125–7
adynaton (ἀδύνατον), 34
aei (ἀεί), 166–7, 170
Aeschylus, 90
ageneton (ἀγένητον), 102
aidion (ἀΐδιον), 83
aion (αἰών), 83
aionion (αἰώνιον), 83
akolouthein (ἀκολουθεῖν), 33, 41, 43–53, 55, 111, 188–9, 193–4
alethes (ἀληθές), 57, 71, 155
Alexander, 8, 31, 45, 101, 117, 189, 203–4
Always, 167
Ambiguity, 3–26, 40
different kinds of, 5–6
amphibolia (ἀμφιβολία), 19
Amphiboly, 19, 21–5
Analogy, 11, 13–14
anangkaion (ἀναγκαῖον), 34, 36, 41, 46, 148
anangke (ἀνάγκη), 36–7, 60, 166
Anscombe, G. E. M., 147, 174
antikeimenos (ἀντικείμενος), 33
aphtharton (ἄφθαρτον), 102
apodeixis (ἀπόδειξις), 183
Apostle, H. G., 122, 127
Argumentation:
the structure of Aristotelian argumentation, 3–4, 115, 153–5, 156–7
Austin, J. L., 105
axioma (ἀξίωμα), 70–1, 91
Ayer, A. J., 65

Barcan formula, 207
Bar-Hillel, Y., 87
Barker, E., 112
Barr, J., 63
Becker, A., 34, 38, 135, 143
Becker, O., 179, 189

Being, 12–13, 18, 22–3, 50
atemporal, 82–4
in time, 83–4, 96
Being and truth, 168
Being as being, 4
Black, M., 63
Blanché, R., 180
Bluck, R. S., 73
Bocheński, I. M., 43, 45, 179
Boehner, P., 152

Cahn, S. M., 187, 188
Carnap, R., 209
Case, T., 5
Category, 12, 13, 18, 19
Change, 106, 175, 197
Cherniss, H., 117, 118
choriston (χωριστόν), 132
Chronology, 87, 88, 151
Chrysippus, 180, 203
Cicero, 70, 163, 167, 193, 196, 201, 204–5
Cleanthes, 180
Collingwood, R. G., 92
Compatibility, logical, 43–6, 51–2, 53–5
Conceivability:
implies realizability, 124–30
of the infinite, 114, 118
Conceptual presuppositions, 62, 63
Consequence, logical, 42, 43, 188, 189
Contingency, 29–38, 40, 49, 56–60, 96, 98, 99, 160, 183
definition of, 30–4
subdivision of, 34–5, 103
and the principle of plenitude, 96–7
Contradiction, the law of, 69
Contradictories, 44
Conversion of syllogistic premisses, 31, 35–8, 140
Cornford, F. M., 79, 91

Definition, 11, 13
partial and complete discrepancy of definitions, 10, 15
Determinism, 152, 154–5, 160–1, 196, 197, 203, 204, 213

diairesis (διαίρεσις), 120
Diodorus Cronus, 71–2, 100, 102, 160, 179–209
Diogenes Laertius, 71, 181
Disjunction:
  necessity of disjunction *v.* necessity of either disjunct, 148, 163
doxa (δόξα), 67, 151
  orthe (ὀρθή), 73
dynamis (δύναμις), 57
dynaton (δυνατόν), 37–8, 41, 46, 49, 54, 55, 56, 57

ede (ἤδη), 174
eidenai (εἰδέναι), 73
eidos (εἶδος), 30, 57
Einarson, B., 153
ekthesis (ἔκθεσις), 136
Empedocles, 74
endechesthai (ἐνδέχεσθαι), 31
endechomenon (ἐνδεχόμενον), 32, 33, 35, 37, 41, 46, 49, 57
endoxa (ἔνδοξα), 153
energeia (ἐνέργεια), 57–8, 175
epi to poly (ἐπὶ τὸ πολύ), 103, 170
Epictetus, 180, 192, 205
episteme (ἐπιστήμη), 73, 75
Equivalence, logical, 45–7, 51–2, 55
Eternal sentences, 64, 71
Eternity and the principle of plenitude, 104–5
Eternity *v.* omnitemporality, 83–4, 96
Euclid, 119–21
Evans, M. G., 115
Extension, realized in the soul only by way of analogy, 128–30

Fallacy, 19, 20
Fate, 201, 203
Focal meaning, 11, 21–4
Forms, Platonic, 18, 78, 98–9
Fränkel, H., 82, 88
Frede, D., 169
Frege, G., 86
Friedländer, P., 89
Function, 14
Future, 69, 112, 152, 165
Future contingents, 147–75, 199–205
  alternative solution to the problem of, 174
  Aristotle's solution of the problem of, 155, 158–9
  why a problem for Aristotle, 151–3

Future truth, problem of, 148–9, 152

Geach, P. T., 72, 134
Generation, 58, 59, 60
genos (γένος), 30
Geometrical constructions, 119–21, 127
Geometry, Euclidean and non-Euclidean, 119–21
Georgius, 31
gignosko (γιγνώσκω), 73
Goodman, N., 65
Greenberg, J., 63
Guerry, H., 180
Gulley, N., 77

haplos (ἁπλῶς), 50, 105, 158–9
Havelock, E., 88, 89
Heath, T., 115, 118, 119, 121, 127
Hegel, G. F. W., 62
hepesthai (ἕπεσθαι), 53–5
Heron, 121
Homer, 73, 74, 90
homonymia (ὁμωνυμία), 8, 19, 30
homonymon (ὁμώνυμον), 6, 7, 8, 13, 14, 19
  to apo tyches (τὸ ἀπὸ τύχης), 8
homonymos (ὁμωνύμως), 7, 31
homonymy, 3, 6–11, 13, 29, 40, 56
  accidental, 3, 7
  applied to words *v.* things, 9
  definition of, 9
  total, 8
horismos (ὁρισμός), 184
Hume, D., 1

Implication, 71–2
Impossibility, 27–30, 41, 46–9, 96
  and the principle of plenitude, 107–10
Incommensurables, 108, 187, 190
Indestructible, 102, 161
Infinite:
  only infinite divisibility needed in geometry according to Aristotle, 119–21
Infinite extension, not even potential for Aristotle, 117–22
Infinity, 100, 114–34
  allegedly only potential for Aristotle, 114–17
  conceivable in a sense, 127–30
  does not exist separately for Aristotle, 115–17, 123–4, 132
  exists in a sense actually for Aristotle, 115–17

mode of existence of, 115–17, 123–4,
132–4
and matter, 115, 124
in mathematics, 118–21

Jaeger, W., 5

kata chronon (κατὰ χρόνον), 159
kinesis (κίνησις), 57, 106, 175
Kirwan, C., 175
Kluckhohn, F. R., 63
Kneale, M., 71, 91, 107–8, 148, 149,
150, 163, 179
Kneale, W., 71, 91, 139, 179
Knowledge, always true, 75–6
and perception, 72–9
as acquaintance, 72–9
only of what is eternal, 72, 74–80
v. true belief, 78, 79
Kripke, S. A., 209
kyrieuon (κυριεύων), 178

Language, spoken *v.* written, 88–91
legesthai dichos (λέγεσθαι διχῶς), 16, 20,
25, 26, 30, 39
hosachos (ὁσαχῶς), 60
haplos (ἁπλῶς), 12, 13, 56
kata duo tropous (κατὰ δύο τρόπους),
26, 30, 34–5
kata to auto eidos (κατὰ τὸ αὐτὸ εἶδος),
57
kath' hena tropon (καθ' ἕνα τρόπον), 7,
11, 26
kyrios (κυρίως), 102
pleonachos (πλεοναχῶς), 130
pollachos (πολλαχῶς), 6, 7, 8, 10, 11,
12, 13, 14, 15, 16, 19, 20, 21, 22,
26, 30, 61
posachos (ποσαχῶς), 12, 61, 130
trichos (τριχῶς), 16
Leibniz, G. W., 84, 94
lekton (λεκτόν), 70–1, 91
Lenz, J. W., 70
Lewis, C. S., 158
logos (λόγος), 9, 11, 24, 65, 90, 151, 184
Lovejoy, A. O., 94–5, 97–100, 113
Łukasiewicz, J., 60, 135, 148, 184

Maier, A., 103
Master Argument (Diodorus), 100,
179–213
logic of, 205–7
presuppositions of, 207–10
and Aristotle, 181–96, 210

and determinism, 194–6, 201–5
Mates, B., 43, 70, 72, 179–80, 189
Maula, E., 95
McCall, S., 135, 136, 146
Megarians, 71, 101–2, 161, 182, 194,
196, 197, 198, 199, 200, 201
Metaphor, 13
Metaphysics, 4, 5
Minio-Paluello, L., 32
Modal logic, 184
Modal *v.* non-modal logic, 112–13
Modalities, *de dicto*, 139, 145
de re, 139, 145
Moore, G. E., 66
Movement, 162
Multiplicity of applications, 6–7, 11–15,
18–26, 29, 34–5, 56, 60–1

Nature, 25
Necessity, 27–30, 36–7, 41, 46–9, 93, 96,
151, 160
statistical concept of, 103
and fate, 201
and omnitemporality, 96, 105, 152–3,
166–8, 171
and the principle of plenitude, 96–7,
104–5
Niebel, E., 127
Now, 64, 86, 87, 110, 151, 192, 208, 212

Occasion sentences, 64
Oesterle, J. T., 155
Omnitemporality, 151, 153
v. eternity, 83–4
onoma (ὄνομα), 8
Opposites, 28, 32, 33, 52, 54, 58
ousia (οὐσία), 123
Owen, G. E. L., viii, 3, 5, 21–5, 82–4,
107–8, 153, 162

Parallels, postulate of, 119
Parmenides, 75, 82
Paronymy, 10, 11, 21–4
Past, 69, 112, 165, 193
necessary for Aristotle, 164, 183
necessary for Diodorus, 180
Patzig, G., 5, 42
Philo, 72
Philoponus, 101, 117
Plato, 72–9, 82, 83, 89–92, 95, 99, 183
Plutarch, 203, 204
Pohlenz, M., 180
Porphyry, 101

Possibility, 41, 42, 46–9, 93, 96, 98, 99, 160, 182 (*see also* Contingency)
 absolute, 130–1
 always realized in the long run, 52, 94–113, 151, 212
 definition of, 16, 30–5, 39, 102–3, 109–10, 181, 183, 184, 185
 different cases of, 29, 55–6
 different senses of, 27–40
 no distinction between logical and physical possibility in Aristotle, 107, 124–7, 130–1
 realization of, 97–9, 109–10
 realized in time, 109–10, 189–90, 208–10
 relative, 130–1
 statistical concept of, 103, 162, 175, 196–9, 200
 and the principle of plenitude, 96–7, 104–5
Possibility proper, 29–38, 39, 40, 49, 56–60, 184
Potentiality, 26, 98
 as source of change, 57
 and the principle of plenitude, 104–5
Predecessors, Aristotle on his, 3–4, 111–12
Present, 69, 112, 152, 164, 193
Present tense, conjunctive sense, 80–4
Principle of plenitude, 94–113, 114–17, 122, 136, 151, 181, 182, 198–9, 202, 212
 apparent counter-examples to, 97–102, 114–17
 Aristotle's reasons for, 105–7
 different forms of, 94
 evidence for, 103–5, 110–11
 formulations of, 95–7
 rejected by Plato, 95
 and infinity, 114–18, 134
 and the definition of possibility, 109–10
Prior, A. N., 65, 150, 179, 180, 209
Proclus, 121–2
Proposition, 66, 70, 91
pros hen (πρὸς ἕν), 7, 11, 21
pros to auto eidos (πρὸς τὸ αὐτὸ εἶδος), 57
pseudes (ψευδής), 155

Quine, W. V., 6, 64, 150, 163

Rackham, H., 204
Rescher, N., 135, 180

Robinson, R., 50
Ross, W. D., viii, 6, 32, 36, 38, 45, 59, 98, 101, 104, 110, 118, 123, 132–3
Runciman, W. G., 73, 77, 79
Russell, B., 65, 85
Ryle, G., 149

Sambursky, S., 182, 203
Schuhl, P.-M., 179, 182, 184
Science, 7, 22, 23
semainein (σημαίνειν), 104
 hen (ἕν), 9, 11
 pleio (πλείω), 9, 17
 polla (πολλά), 9
sensus compositus, 210
sensus divisus, 210
Sentences, temporally indefinite, 63–72, 85–92, 150–2, 160–2, 192–200
Sextus Empiricus, 71
Simplicius, 10, 12, 101
Snell, B., 72, 73
Socrates, 76
Solmsen, F., 83, 117, 120
Sorabji, R., 134
Species, difference in, 15, 17, 18
 the permanence of, 107
Spengler, O., 86
Stallmach, J., 182
Standing sentences, 64
Stoics, 3, 43, 70–2, 189, 194, 201
Strang, C., 148, 154, 163
Strodtbeck, F. L., 63
Syllogisms, 42
 apodeictic, 93, 113, 135
 assertoric, 93, 113, 135
 assertoric and apodeictic s's not sharply distinguished by Aristotle, 93, 136–8, 144
 modal, 135–46
 principles for rejecting apodeictic's s's, 141–4
 problematic, 31, 38–40, 134, 145
 through signs, 101
Syllogistic premisses, structure of apodeictic premisses, 138–40, 143–4
 structure of problematic premisses, 38–40
 their relation to time, 68–9, 138, 144
symbainein (συμβαίνειν), 42, 101, 189
synaletheuein (συναληθεύειν), 52
synonymon (συνώνυμον), 8
Synonymy, 8–9, 10

Tarán, L., 83
Taylor, A. E., 74
Term, covering different cases, 16, 18
tertium non datur, 149, 153, 168
Themistius, 144
Theophrastus, 144
Thought and language, 66, 90
Timeless present, 80–4
tode ti (τόδε τι), 123
Token-reflexive expressions, 64, 85, 150
Tredennick, H., 39, 58
True belief, 76
Truth, changing, 66–8, 80, 84–6
  as momentary correspondence, 173–4
  degrees of, 77, 170–1

Truth-values, changing, 66–8, 150

Unit idea (Lovejoy), 99
Universe, necessarily finite for Aristotle,
  117–18, 122

Velocity, 162

Wedberg, A., 127
Williams, D. C., 65, 103, 104, 106, 210
Words, *v.* things, 17
Wright, G. H. von, 60, 185

Zeller, E., 179, 183, 188, 189, 193–4
Zeno, 162